THE IDEA OF DECADENCE IN FRENCH LITERATURE

UNIVERSITY OF TORONTO ROMANCE SERIES

A. E. CARTER

THE IDEA OF

DECADENCE

IN FRENCH

LITERATURE

1830 - 1900

UNIVERSITY OF TORONTO PRESS – 1958

Copyright ©, Canada, 1958
University of Toronto Press
Printed in Canada
London: Oxford University Press

TO

A. F. B. CLARK

**PROFESSOR EMERITUS OF FRENCH
UNIVERSITY OF BRITISH COLUMBIA**

PREFACE

THE CULT of decadence is usually dismissed as an eccentricity of French literature, a final twitter of Romantic neurosis, convulsing the lunatic fringe of letters during the last third of the nineteenth century. Such was my own view of it when I set to work on the research for this book. I had chosen Louis Maigron and Mario Praz as my guides, and Gautier's preface to the *Fleurs du Mal* as my starting-point. Written in 1868, it seemed a useful introduction; and after discussing it, I intended to proceed to the "decadence" proper, the period of *Monsieur Vénus, Le Vice suprême,* and all the other disordered works whose obscenities now sleep quietly in the stacks of the Bibliothèque Nationale. But I soon found that there was a good deal more to the matter than this. I began looking into Gautier's earlier books, and I discovered that he said nothing in 1868 he had not said previously— and very little that many writers had not said before him. His essay on Baudelaire, in fact, is more a mid-point than a beginning; it merely sums up an idea very generally entertained from 1830 on—that contemporary civilization was somehow degenerate. This was not the pose of a few lurid hacks like Mendès and Péladan; it fascinated men of the calibre of Taine, Baudelaire, Flaubert, Zola, Aurevilly, Huysmans, Lemaître, Bourget—not to mention a whole school of psychopathologists.

A theory with such influence is no baroque curiosity; it must spring from the very spirit of its age. And I think that the nineteenth century's preoccupation with decadence provides us with a key to the secret places of its thought, to all the obscure passages and backstairs behind the triumphant façade. "Nous vivons dans un siècle orgueilleux," wrote Baudelaire in 1855, "qui se croit au-dessus des mésaventures de la Grèce et de Rome." The remark throws a flood of light on one aspect of those strange years between 1814 and 1914: they have no sense of disaster, no tragic sense. Civilization had become a habit, a side product of political constitutions and applied science. History was viewed pragmatically: of what use were such traditional symbols as throne and altar? Both are essentially propitiatory, evidence of man's uneasy knowledge that power is dangerous and destiny im-

placable. And both seemed anachronisms in a world where (it was
thought) human reason had solved or would solve all the old problems.
The theory of decadence is very largely a protest against this comfort-
able belief. Had the decadents not written, we should hardly suspect
that the nineteenth century suffered from the same doubts and hesi-
tations as all other ages, before and since.

The precise moment when decadence ceased to be a literary pose
and became a serious preoccupation lies somewhere between 1850 and
1870—during the Second Empire. The fact is significant. For those two
decades are the historic instant which determined the catastrophe of
nineteenth-century civilization. Until 1850, the age was fluid; it might
have turned any number of ways. But after Sedan it hardened,
like cooling lava. It was no longer "post-Revolutionary" or "post-
Napoleonic," but pre-1914, pre-1939, pre . . . ? Tacitus might have
written his "repente turbare fortuna coepit" with Napoleon III's
régime in mind. Beneath its raffish gloss, the Second Empire is profoundly sinister, a gilded hinge upon which the whole century turned
with irresistible violence. There is something both ludicrous and
appalling about the whole episode, as if the Eumenides had suddenly
emerged from a can-can by Offenbach.

It is only now, of course, across a perspective of a hundred years,
that we can understand all this; even after 1870, it was not immediately perceptible. The tremendous momentum of centuries of pros-
perity and progress was sufficient to hide the fact that a historic
watershed had been passed and a new era begun. But, though the
horizons remained clear, there was thunder below them; and we can
hear its echoes in the morbid writing of the decadents. They produced
the literature of a disaster—though it had not yet taken place. Since
they knew nothing of actual disaster, they had to use their imagination:
consult Suetonius, consult Lampridius, think themselves back to the
court of Heliogabalus or Arcadius. The results are not always con-
vincing, and most decadent work is now little more than a pretentious
mummy. But it has considerable value as a document. Before we dis-
miss it all as so much nonsense, we should reflect that there is not
one horror in Péladan, Rachilde, Mirbeau and the rest which has not
become commonplace since they wrote. We no longer need to hunt up
atrocities in an obscure Latin chronicler; they are in the newspapers.
The Barbarians have stormed the city not once, but a dozen times;
and the Garden of Punishments is no longer a bookish fancy, but a
recognized cog in the machine of power, a terror to whole nations.
"Nous autres, civilisations, nous savons maintenant que nous sommes

mortelles." Valéry wrote the phrase in 1919; it reads like a conclusion to Baudelaire's article of sixty-four years before.

The present volume is based on a Ph.D. thesis presented at King's College, University of London, under the direction of Professor J. M. Cocking, to whom thanks are due for his help and suggestions. I owe the chance to rewrite it and add new material, however, to the Royal Society of Canada, which supplied me with a Fellowship to that end. Acknowledgment must also be made to the Publications Fund of the University of Toronto Press, and to the *University of Toronto Quarterly* for permission to include material which appeared in its pages in slightly different form. I wish particularly to express my gratitude to Professors J. Darbelnet (Bowdoin College), H. Steinhauer (Antioch College), and G. Bonfante (Princeton and Genoa) for their protests and emendations. All three showed a remarkable patience with the recurrence of the word "decadence" in letters and conversation. I must also thank the editorial staff of the University of Toronto Press for their painstaking work in getting the manuscript ready for printing.

Enfin, il y a ce que doit tout archéologue de littératures mortes à ces guides sans prix : le personnel de la Bibliothèque Nationale. A Monsieur Seguin, donc, et à ses aides, grâce à qui je dois plus d'une trouvaille introuvable, j'exprime ici toute ma reconnaissance.

A. E. C.

CONTENTS

THE IDEA OF DECADENCE IN FRENCH LITERATURE

CHAPTER 1

THE PERVERTED LEGEND

Horum omnium fortissimi sunt Belgae, propterea quod a cultu atque humanitate provinciae longissime absunt, minimeque ad eos mercatores saepe commeant atque ea, quae ad effeminandos animos pertinent, important.

Caesar, *Comm.*, I, 1

Tout ce qui éloignait l'homme et surtout la femme de l'état de nature lui paraissait une invention heureuse. Ces goûts peu primitifs doivent se comprendre chez un poète de *décadence*, auteur des *Fleurs du mal*.

Théophile Gautier, preface to Baudelaire,
Les Fleurs du Mal, 1868

AMONGST OCCIDENTAL LEGENDS, there is one which crops up with peculiar insistence, filling pages in writers as dissimilar as Caesar and Tacitus, Montaigne, Montesquieu and Rousseau.[1] It is something more than a legend, indeed; it is a platitude and a generalization, one of those generalizations without which Western thought seems unable to function. It even has its hero, tilling his farm or hunting his meat in virgin forests: the Noble Savage, ignorant of wine, precious metals, commerce, the arts, philosophy and, in fact, everything which is usually called "civilization": a creature entirely primitive, whose virtues result from his very primitivism. Caesar's Belgians, Tacitus' Germans, Montaigne's cannibals—they are all of the same kind; and the idea is so ingrained and fundamental that it goes back to the very roots of our culture: both Greek and Hebrew theology presuppose a primitive state, Arcadia or Eden, the loss of which explains all human woe. Civilized man, though at times so proud of his civilization, has never been able to rid himself of the sneaking fear that it is all somehow

---

[1]Caesar, *Comm.*, I, 1; Tacitus, *Germania*, especially II, III, V, VII, XIII–XX; Michel de Montaigne, "Des Cannibales," *Essais*, I, xxx; Charles de Secondat, Baron de Montesquieu, *Grandeur et décadence des Romains*. For a full discussion of the Greek and Latin roots of the idea, see A. O. Lovejoy and A. Boas, *A Documentary History of Primitivism and Related Ideas* (Baltimore, Johns Hopkins, 1935), I.

unnatural, artificial and corrupt. Whether because of obscure atavistic forces which call him back to the seas and jungles from which he emerged, or a spirit of sheer contradiction, he dislikes what he builds. Or rather, what he builds makes him uneasy.

This uneasiness is nowhere more curiously demonstrated than in the idea of decadence as it flourished in nineteenth-century French literature. The more so since decadence (as the writers of the period understood it) looks at first glance like a revolt against primitivism. In one way it is. But in a much more important sense it is simply another manifestation of the old myth: it is primitivism—*à rebours*. The theory that nature is the norm and civilization a degeneracy had languished during the classical ages. Classicism is a highly civilized point of view. Boileau and Dr. Johnson were quite well aware of the vices of Paris and London, but they saw the virtues too, and they never thought of living anywhere else. "The man who is tired of London is tired of life, for London contains all that life has to offer." The "philosophes" like Voltaire and Diderot would have rapped their snuff-boxes and approved. The value of civilization, as represented by the town, was axiomatic in the middle years of the eighteenth century. Montesquieu, it is true, in his essay on the Romans, had suggested that too much culture might be enervating. But he discussed the point as an abstract principle, applied to a dead civilization. Not until 1750, in Rousseau's famous *Discours de Dijon*, were civilized values seriously challenged. The *Discours*, as Rousseau admits himself,[2] was based on Tacitus and Montaigne, and it contains little more than one idea— that the elaborate culture of the eighteenth century was not an achievement but a degeneracy. He repeated the argument in later books (*Emile*, the *Lettre à D'Alembert, La Nouvelle Héloïse*), and drove it home with an ardent dialectic which bears no resemblance to Montesquieu's cool generalizations. As a result, the badness of civilization and the virtues of nature became part of a new sensibility, which we usually call Romantic; so much a part of it, in fact, that any revolt against Romanticism—when it came—was bound to be a revolt against the primitive and the natural. The cult of decadence is just such a revolt. But here is the paradox: the decadents, even when they refused to live by Rousseau's gospel, never denied its truth. They were like unfrocked priests celebrating the Black Mass—perfectly aware that their cult was blasphemous. They accepted Nature as the norm, and primitivism as synonymous with virtue. They admitted, either tacitly or enthusiastically (depending on the individual writer's desire to

[2]*Discours sur les sciences et les arts, Œuvres* (Genève, 1782), XIII, 41, 61.

shock and astonish), that anything different, anything civilized or "artificial," was *a priori* unnatural and depraved. From the very beginning, decadent sensibility is thus self-consciously perverse; and its cult of the artificial distinguishes it sharply from Romanticism, whatever traces of depravity may be found in certain Romantics.

The reaction against Rousseau's ideas began even before 1800 in the works of a man whose thought, however subterranean and unavowed, was to set its mark on most literary productions of the next hundred years—the Marquis de Sade. Attacks on Rousseau's nature-cult occur several times in De Sade's novels; and each attack shows (such was the force of Rousseau's doctrine) how Nature had become so identified with the normal that a renunciation of it led to the abnormal—in De Sade's case, to sexual perversions. A character in *Justine*, Almani, declares that, far from being a benevolent force as a certain "modern philosopher" (Rousseau) maintains, Nature is really destructive and anti-human; and a little further on, a Mme d'Esterval says that, for the same reason, her dearest pleasure is to "outrage Nature" in every way possible. They both conclude that the best means to this end is the practice of sexual perversions. "C'est elle [la Nature] que je voudrais pouvoir outrager. Je voudrais déranger ses plans, contrecarrer sa marche, arrêter le cours des astres... l'insulter en un mot dans ses œuvres... Le mal seul m'émeut; je ne respire qu'en le commettant; mon organisme n'est délecté que par lui seul... J'aime à voir périr une créature dans quelques-unes de mes expériences... Je suis bestialitaire et meurtrier."[3] The conclusion of such arguments is quite logical: the abnormal becomes a proof of man's superiority to natural law, a demonstration of free will, an "artificiality" which, although more lurid than face-paint or dyed hair, is of the same order.

This is the main idea behind the cult of artificiality, and, for that matter, behind the whole theory of decadence. Most subsequent developments can be traced back to it. Succeeding writers did little more than paint De Sade's monstrous lily, sometimes with direct reference to the Marquis. One of the first of them was Théophile Gautier.

To call Gautier an initiator of the decadent movement seems at first a contradiction in terms. He survives in literary history as a critic, the writer of gay picaresque novels such as *Fracasse*, the neo-pagan founder of the Parnassian school, the Romantic who abandoned mediaevalism for the plastic beauty of Greek art. Yet his cult of form and his devotion to the Greek ideal (as he conceived it) are only one side of his work, more especially of his later work. There is another

[3]*Justine et Juliette* (1797), IV, 40, and III, 65–7.

Gautier—the poet of "bas-romantisme," the friend of Pétrus Borel and Philothée O'Neddy, the master to whom Baudelaire dedicated his "fleurs maladives." Above all there is the essayist who wrote the "Notice" on Baudelaire for the 1868 edition of *Les Fleurs du Mal.* Everyone has read this famous preface, and Havelock Ellis long ago recognized its importance as a definition of decadence.[4] Yet it is usually dismissed as a piece of bravura, a "hommage" from "le bon Théo" to a comrade of his youth, a sympathetic effort to understand the eccentricities of a poet with whom he had little in common. The truth is very different. The "Notice" is a final statement of ideas which had preoccupied Gautier for over thirty years; to write it, he scarcely needed to read Baudelaire at all; he had only to consult some of his own poems, novels and critical articles. One of its main ideas (the identification of the modern with the artificial) occurs in several of his previous works.

It is worth noting here that this fusion of the artificial and the modern which is one of the identifying marks of decadence united two fundamentally opposed ideas: a hatred of modern civilization and a love of the refinements modern civilization made possible. Since decadent sensibility never resolved this contradiction, the movement suffered throughout its lifetime from a sort of literary schizophrenia. The decadent writers were all dutiful aesthetes; they inherited Romanticism's contempt for the bourgeois doctrines of the nineteenth century —mercantilism, progress, utility, industrialism, etc.—and they had a quite legitimate horror of their own for the mediocrity of the century's official art. Yet, as practitioners of decadence, they were obliged to wax enthusiastic over certain results of industrialism, results which allowed man to live more and more divorced from his natural state. They revelled in artifice while detesting the applied science which was its source. This paradox was pointed out by Jules Lemaître in 1887, when it had become much more obvious than it was half a century earlier: "On maudit le 'Progrès,'" he says, in an attempt to define "baudelairisme"—and by 1887, "baudelairisme" had become nearly synonymous with decadence—"on déteste la civilisation industrielle de ce siècle... Et en même temps, on jouit du pittoresque spécial que cette civilisation a mis dans la vie humaine et des ressources qu'elle apporte à l'art de développer la sensibilité."[5]

This remark would apply just as well to Gautier. From the beginning of his career he professed a true Romantic dislike of the modern;

4In his essay on Huysmans in *The New Spirit.*
5"Baudelaire," *Journal des débats,* 4 juillet 1887.

his poems are full of the horror he felt for the physical results of industrialism, which he saw symbolized in the unglamorous squalor of
contemporary Paris. The city has a "soleil terne et mort," it is draped
in smog;[6] its streets are "boueuses et infectes," it smells of "l'atmosphère
de gaz hydrogène et de mélasse de la civilisation moderne,"[7] and the
theories behind it are as distasteful as its physical appearance: "Dès
qu'une chose devient utile, elle cesse d'être belle... Il n'y a de vraiment
beau que ce qui ne peut servir à rien; tout ce qui est utile est laid."[8]
Charles X was right to suppress the freedom of the press; the Paris
journals had attacked the two finest things in human life, royalty and
poetry.[9] Yet, even when he was denouncing the most characteristic
details of nineteenth-century civilization, Gautier was quite ready to
enjoy the artificial effects it made possible. Very early in his writing
he showed a preference for the work of art over the work of nature,
and from this to preferring the artificial to the natural was an easy
step. His life as a critic and boulevardier, eternally occupied with first
nights of plays and ballets, fostered the tendency: "Enclos dans un
mode de vivre relativement restreint, limité aux boulevards, aux
théâtres," writes Maxime du Camp, one of his friends, "Gautier n'était
jamais sorti de Paris... Emprisonné dans cette existence convention-
nelle où les décors de l'Opéra éclairés aux quinquets remplaçaient la
placidité des paysages lumineux, n'ayant jamais vu de véritables forêts,
de vraies montagnes, de vraies plages, de vraies mers, Gautier... s'était
créé une sorte de nature imaginaire."[10] We find ample justification for
this passage in some of Gautier's early works. In 1833 he formulated
his love of artificiality in phrases which were to echo throughout the
rest of the century: "Je n'ai vu la mer que dans les marines de Vernet;
je ne connais d'autres montagnes que Montmartre. Je n'ai jamais vu
se lever le soleil... Je suis un Parisien complet... Les arbres des Tuile-
ries et des boulevards sont mes forêts; la Seine, mon Océan... Je ne
trouve pas le soleil de beaucoup supérieur au gaz... Je déteste la campagne : toujours des arbres, de la terre, du gazon !... C'est ennuyeux à
crever."[11] The tone is deliberately irreverent; it suggests a conversation
in some café when, seated before a glass of absinthe, each man was
free to bring out his paradoxes and keep the company amused. *Bou-
tades* of the kind were doubtless relished in the circles Gautier fre-

[6]"Paris," a poem dated 1831, *Premières poésies* (Charpentier), I, 108–10.
[7]*Fortunio* (Garnier), 156–7.
[8]Preface to the *Poésies*, I, 4–5.
[9]Preface to *Mademoiselle de Maupin*, dated mai 1834 (Fasquelle), 22, 34–5.
[10]*Théophile Gautier* (Hachette), 98–100.
[11]Preface to *Les Jeunes-France* (Charpentier), vii–ix.

quented; some of his friends had very similar tastes—Nestor Roqueplan, for example, whom Gautier knew around 1830: "Il avait déjà commencé sa croisade contre le soleil, contre la campagne, contre les voyages, contre la nature, qu'il n'admettait que dans les tableaux."[12] The same eccentricities are reproduced in D'Albert, the hero of *Mademoiselle de Maupin* (1834), Gautier's best book. He is always proclaiming his preference of art to nature and sophisticated to unadorned beauty. His taste in women does not run to milk-maids, but to ladies of high-fashion, with silk gowns and pearls.[13] Fortunio, in the story of that name (1837), leads a completely artificial existence, shut up in a windowless house with a glass-roofed courtyard of tropical plants. A sprinkler system supplies rain whenever a change of climate is desired, and there are dioramas of the Swiss Alps, the Bay of Naples, etc., to spare Fortunio the boredom and exertion of travel: "Le valet de chambre entrait le matin dans sa chambre et lui demandait : 'Quel paysage voulez-vous qu'on vous serve aujourd'hui ?' — 'Qu'avez-vous de prêt ?' disait Fortunio, 'voyons votre carte.' "[14] Fortunio's artificiality is essentially modern: he owes his dioramas to nineteenth-century applied science. And when eleven years later Gautier advised young painters to seek inspiration in contemporary life rather than in the past, he represented modern civilization by man-made, artificial symbols: "Nous acceptons la civilisation telle qu'elle est, avec ses chemins de fer... ses machines, ses tuyaux de cheminée... Le monde antique peut être balancé par un monde nouveau tout resplendissant d'acier et de gaz, aussi beau dans son activité que l'autre dans sa rêverie sereine."[15]

However serious these passages are, there is a suggestion of irony about them all, a desire to shock and astonish. It is not easy to say just how far they represent Gautier's own convictions. And, while he did not hesitate to equate the modern with the artificial, he did not go to the point of calling the artificial decadent. The nearest he came was in "Paris," an early poem where he calls the nineteenth century

>Une société qui retombe en chaos,
>Du rouge sur la joue et la gangrène aux os.

But the idea is not developed. A fusion of the three terms did not

[12]"Nestor Roqueplan," essay dated 21 mai 1870, reprinted in *Notices romantiques* (Flammarion), 152.

[13]*Maupin*, 53–4.

[14]*Fortunio*, 154–5.

[15]"Plastique de la civilisation," dated 8 août 1848, reprinted in *Souvenirs de théâtre, d'art et de critique* (Charpentier), 202–3. This essay may owe something to Baudelaire's *Salons* of 1845 and 1846.

occur to him until he had read Baudelaire; and it was Baudelaire, in fact, who first combined them.

Baudelaire's contribution to the cult of artificiality is much richer than Gautier's. However much Gautier might praise the modern world, he was considerably more at home in the ancient: his Greek, Roman and Egyptian exoticism reveals his own preferences clearly enough. His dislike of the nineteenth century was, on the whole, aesthetic; he missed the monumental splendours of the ancient world, not to mention its unbridled lusts. Baudelaire, on the other hand, ignored antiquity as subject-matter. It has no place in his work. A poem like "Lesbos" is a hymn to sexual inversion, not a reconstruction of ancient life. His disapproval of the modern world is much less aesthetic than moral—a contempt for the nineteenth century's progressive and humanitarian beliefs. "De l'amour impie de la liberté est née une tyrannie nouvelle, la tyrannie des bêtes, ou zoöcratie." "Quoi de plus absurde que le Progrès, puisque l'homme... est toujours à l'état sauvage." "La vraie civilisation... n'est pas dans le gaz, ni dans la vapeur... Elle est dans la diminution des traces du péché originel."[16] Baudelaire attacked the popular beliefs of his time with all the grim purpose of a gardener scything down weeds. He had an almost Augustinian end in view; for, if he strips modern man of his pretensions, he gives him back all his awful grandeur as a descendant of fallen angels; the Darwinian ape recovers that tragic greatness which seems incompatible with the idea of progress. This is certainly one of the reasons for the present-day vogue of Les Fleurs du Mal. Amidst the disasters of our time, we like to have at least one poet who is in legitimate descent from Dante and Milton, even if he is a smaller man than they. Baudelaire's modernism—like his anti-modernism—is based on a metaphysical sub-structure unknown to Gautier, the neo-pagan; and it explains why there is no Romantic exoticism in his work, no Gothic gimcracks or Renaissance trunk-hose. He found all the tragic beauty he needed in modern settings and modern dress: "N'est-il pas l'habit nécessaire à notre époque," he says of the frock-coat, "souffrant et portant sur les épaules noires et maigres le symbole d'un deuil perpétuel ?"[17] His ideas on the question are summed up in his Salons (1845, 1846, 1859) in what he calls "l'héroïsme de la vie moderne." He declares that Balzac's heroes are more interesting than Homer's, and praises the engraver Méryon for etching the factory chimneys,

---

[16]"Edgar Poe, sa vie et ses œuvres" (1856), Œuvres complètes (Conard), IV, ix; "Fusées," Œuvres (Pléiade), II, 637; "Mon Cœur mis à nu," ibid., 649.
[17]"Le Salon de 1845," Œuvres (Pléiade), II, 134.

heavy skies and massed buildings of Paris: "J'ai rarement vu, repré-
sentée avec plus de poésie, la solennité naturelle d'une ville immense.
Les majestés de la pierre accumulée... les obélisques de l'industrie
vomissant contre le firmament leurs coalitions de fumée... le ciel
tumultueux, chargé de colère et de rancune, la profondeur des perspectives, augmentée par la pensée de tous les drames qui y sont con-
tenus, aucun des éléments complexes dont se compose le douloureux
et glorieux décor de la civilisation n'est oublié."[18] The passage is
magnificent, and we find many like it in *L'Art romantique*, *Le Spleen
de Paris* and *Les Fleurs du Mal*. The prose-poems of *Le Spleen de
Paris* were inspired by Aloysius Bertrand's *Gaspard de la Nuit*. But,
says Baudelaire, "ce qu'il avait fait pour la vie ancienne et pittoresque,
je voulais le faire pour la vie moderne et abstraite."[19] Amongst his
papers was found an unfinished "Epilogue à la ville de Paris," which
seems to have been intended as a conclusion and explanation of either
the prose-poems or *Les Fleurs du Mal*:

> Je t'aime [Paris], ô ma très-belle, ô ma charmante...
> Ton goût de l'infini
> Qui partout, dans le mal lui-même, se proclame...
> Tes monuments hautains où s'accrochent les brumes,
> Tes dômes de métal qu'enflamme le soleil...
> Tu m'as donné ta boue, et j'en ai fait de l'or.[20]

Without doubt this "heroic" side of Baudelaire is the most important as far as posterity is concerned. But it was the side which impressed his contemporaries least. Their near-sightedness had some
excuse, for Baudelaire's modernism is usually in rather doubtful taste.
Like Gautier, he constantly identified it with the artificial—the artificial in its most lurid sense. The best illustration occurs in his essay
on Constantin Guys (1860) whom he called "le peintre de la vie
moderne." Guys was fond of sketching the overdressed and over-
rouged courtezans who loitered away their afternoons in the Bois de
Boulogne, and this aspect of his work fascinated Baudelaire. He devotes a whole chapter to it, the "Eloge du maquillage." His remarks
resemble curiously the Marquis de Sade's attacks on Rousseau: Baudelaire understood how artificiality contradicted the nature-cult, and,
like De Sade preaching sexual perversions, he begins his praise of
cosmetics by criticizing Rousseau's theory that Nature is the "base,

[18]"Le Salon de 1859," *ibid.*, 271.
[19]Dedication of *Le Spleen de Paris* (the prose-poems) to Arsène Houssaye,
Œuvres, I, 637–8.
[20]*Ibid.*, 228–9.

source et type de tout bien et de tout beau possibles," concluding that everything natural in man is bad, and that whatever is good is artificial and acquired, from face-paint to virtue.[21] As Mario Praz points out,[22] this conclusion is quite logical for, if we take the badness of Nature as our premise, then we must end by deciding that the supreme artificiality, the supreme *outrage* is . . . the practice of virtue! The fact that De Sade did not end in this way shows how little real interest he took in the philosophical "justifications" scattered through his books. Baudelaire was a much better metaphysician. But unfortunately his arguments are vitiated from the beginning. For by no stretch of the imagination could the painted ladies he is talking about be called virtuous. To present Cora Pearl or Hortense Schneider to the readers of the Second Empire as examples of virtue through cosmetics was an enormous paradox—amusing, no doubt, but carrying little conviction. Indeed, Baudelaire's whole conception of modern heroism, however authentic in poems like "Le Cygne" and "La Mort des pauvres," was inclined to the disreputable: for if Rastignac is a good example of it, so, he adds, are the criminals and prostitutes whose doings fill the police-gazettes.[23] Heroism of this kind, like the virtue of Cora Pearl, can hardly be accepted without suspicion; and Baudelaire's real opinion of it comes out in his *Notes nouvelles sur Edgar Poe*, where he finally takes the step of calling artificiality decadent— or at least nearly does so. He begins by saying that whenever he hears a book called "decadent" he concludes that it must be something more interesting than the *Iliad*, and he sees two women before him: "l'une, matrone rustique, répugnante de santé et de vertu, sans allure et sans regard, bref, *ne devant rien qu'à la simple nature*; l'autre, une de ces beautés qui dominent et oppriment le souvenir, unissant à son charme ... toute l'éloquence de la toilette... Mon choix ne saurait être douteux."[24] He goes on to say that since the term "littérature de décadence" implies that literature has an infancy, maturity and senility, there is nothing to be ashamed of in obeying the laws of this evolution, and using a decadent style if one happens to live in a decadent age. What had begun as an attempt to clear Poe of the charge of decadence, thus ends very ambiguously.

Both the *Notes nouvelles* and the essay on Guys leave one with the

[21]"Le Peintre de la vie moderne" (the first title was "Le Peintre de la modernité"), *Œuvres*, II, 354–5.

[22]*La Carne, la morte e il diavolo nella letteratura romantica*, terza edizione, (Firenze, Sansoni, 1948), 109.

[23]"Le Salon de 1845," *Œuvres*, II, 135–6.

[24]"Notes nouvelles sur Edgar Poe," *Œuvres complètes* (Conard), V, v–vi.

impression that the poet of modern life and the painter of modern life
are the artists of a decadent period, and that modernism, artificiality
and decadence are one and the same thing. And, if we are to judge
from certain scraps of Baudelaire's conversations and letters that have
come down to us, this was precisely the impression he wished to give.
He never hesitated to advertise his love of artificiality. In replying to
a friend who asked him to write some nature-poetry, he said that he
disliked the sea, only swam in a bath-tub, and preferred a music-box
to a nightingale. He was fond of cultivating a reputation for this type
of anti-naturism amongst his friends: "Je raffole des dames qui se
maquillent," he told Adrien Marx. "Pour moi, la femme n'est belle
qu'avec du kohl aux yeux, du fard au visage et du rouge aux lèvres."[25]
And again: "Je voudrais les prairies teintes en rouge, les rivières jaune
d'or et les arbres peints en bleu. La Nature n'a pas d'imagination."[26]
One might be reading Gautier's preface to Les Jeunes-France, written
when Baudelaire was twelve.

Baudelaire reproduced the same tastes in Samuel Cramer, a half-
ironical self-portrait (La Fanfarlo, 1847). Samuel becomes the lover
of Mlle Fanfarlo, a dancer, but mere possession is not enough. She
must receive him dressed as Columbine, one of her roles, and (the
point is stressed) highly rouged. "N'oubliez-pas le rouge!" he shouts.
"Ce trait caractéristique," adds Baudelaire, "ne m'a nullement étonné...
[Cramer] aimera toujours le rouge et la céruse, le chrysocale et les
oripeaux de toute sorte. Il repeindrait volontiers les arbres et le ciel."[27]
His love of artificiality, furthermore, reveals his "imagination dépravée" and explains why "l'amour était chez lui moins une affaire des
sens que du raisonnement."

This calculated, intellectual side of the cult of artificiality is an
essential part of decadent sensibility. It fascinated Baudelaire, and he
wrote of it in his two treatises on drugs, Du vin et du haschisch
(1851) and Les Paradis artificiels (1860). Artificiality, by its very
essence—an effort to alter and improve Nature—is a manifestation of
will-power; and this point comes out several times in what Baudelaire
says of alcohol, hashish and opium. They pander to the human animal's passion for infinity—infinite joy, infinite ecstasy, infinite multiplication of the ego: a passion which is thus a further denial of the
"natural" emotions. Wines are the liquids by which man procures

[25]Adrien Marx, Indiscrétions parisiennes (Faure, 1866), 217.
[26]Jules Levallois, "Au pays de Bohème," La Revue Bleue, 5 janvier 1895.
[27]La Fanfarlo, Œuvres, I, 553–4. Marx (Indiscrétions, 217) represents Baudelaire as writing to a well-known lady of the town: "J'irai vous rendre visite ce soir,
peignez-vous bien."

courage and gaiety *à volonté*; and through hashish and opium he can turn himself into a sort of god. This development of the spiritual side of artificiality is extremely important. It assigns to will and intellect a prime role in transforming the natural; and the fact that it manifests itself in a passion for drugs—as artificiality had appeared in the guise of a painted strumpet, and modern heroism as a burglar or a prostitute—makes the identification of civilization with decadence as complete as any disciple of Rousseau could desire.

It is an identification which the nineteenth century was quick to make from 1857 on. Sainte-Beuve called *Les Fleurs du Mal* a marquetry gazebo where debauches of drugs took place. Other critics regretted that the volume had nothing of the space and time exoticism of Romantic poetry.[28] The very title, "Flowers of Evil," was a convenient excuse for purple passages; it also contributed to the craze for hot-houses and monstrous plants which characterizes so much writing during the next fifty years. Edouard Thierry called the book a conservatory of poisonous flowers, "une serre de vitrage," containing "toutes les écumes, toutes les lies, toutes les perles verdâtres de la corruption végétale."[29] Barbey d'Aurevilly defined Baudelaire's talent as "une fleur du mal venue dans les serres-chaudes d'une Décadence," the expression of a dying age, and later referred to the poet, with italics, as "un Héliogabale *artificiel*."[30] Gautier compared the poet's muse to the alchemist's daughter in Hawthorne's story, a fatal beauty impregnated with poison, living in a garden of venomous exotics, "plantes aux feuillages bizarrement découpés, d'un vert noir ou minéralement glauque, comme si le sulfate de cuivre les teignait."[31]

Gautier's interest in artificiality reached full expression in passages like these: it is impossible to escape the impression that he insisted on such aspects of Baudelaire because they flattered his own tastes. Perhaps he realized that they owed something to his influence. Baude-

---

[28]For example, Louis Veuillot, Amédée Pichot, E. Deschanel. Their articles are quoted by W. T. Bandy in *Baudelaire Judged by His Contemporaries* (New York, Columbia University Press, 1933), 40, 49, 71.

[29]Article of 1857, reprinted in the appendix to the Lévy edition of *Les Fleurs du Mal*, 294–5.

[30]*Les Fleurs du Mal*, Lévy ed., 310–11, and Bandy, *Baudelaire Judged*, 47–8.

[31]Gautier, *Les Poètes français* (Hachette, 1862), IV, 597. Compare with George Rodenbach's description of *Les Fleurs du Mal* as "fleurs de décadence, germées de bitume parisien... floraison satanique et cruelle," and of Mallarmé's poems as "sensitives de serre, la serre chaude d'un cerveau en fièvre, plantes à la croissance artificielle et violentée," *L'Elite* (Charpentier, 1899), 12. Much of the verse in Maeterlinck's *Les Serres chaudes* (Bruxelles, Lacomblez, 1890) is as characteristic as its title. It would be literally impossible to count all the characters in the poetry and fiction of the period who collect exotic flowers—usually orchids.

laire may even have told him so: they knew each other well. The "Notice" to the first posthumous edition of *Les Fleurs du Mal* is designed to show Baudelaire as a poet of artificiality, decadence and modernism: all three terms used nearly synonymously. The idea returns like a theme: "Il convient de citer comme note particulière du poète le sentiment de l'*artificiel*. Par ce mot, il faut entendre une création due tout entière à l'art, et d'où la nature est complètement absente." "Le poète aimait... le style de décadence... l'idiome nécessaire et fatal des peuples et des civilisations où la vie factice a remplacé la vie naturelle." "Il se plaisait dans cette espèce de beau composite et parfois un peu factice qu'élaborent les civilisations très avancées et très corrompues."[32] He quotes all the relevant passages from Baudelaire and elaborates them; the sketch of Poe's muse, for example, becomes a portrait of Woman as Baudelaire preferred her, plastered with cosmetics, drenched in scent, her hair dyed, seated before a toilet-table covered with tweezers, lotions, perfumes, etc. "Tout ce qui éloignait l'homme et surtout la femme de l'état de nature lui paraissait une invention heureuse. Ces goûts peu primitifs... doivent se comprendre chez un poète de *décadence* auteur des *Fleurs du mal*." He adds that Baudelaire liked Guys' drawings because they were entirely unclassical and profoundly imbued with modern corruption, and the work of Delacroix because of that painter's "savante pratique d'artiste de la décadence."[33] Just as Baudelaire's fusion of modernism, artificiality and decadence had been more definite than Gautier's, so Gautier's, after reading Baudelaire, is even more conclusive than *his*: "Ce goût excessif, baroque, anti-naturel, presque toujours contraire au beau classique, était pour lui un signe de la volonté humaine corrigeant à son gré les formes et les couleurs fournies par la matière," which leads him to a remark of great significance: "La *dépravation*, c'est-à-dire l'écart du type normal, est impossible à la bête, fatalement conduite par l'instinct immuable. C'est par la même raison que les poètes *inspirés*, n'ayant pas la conscience et la direction de leur œuvre, lui causaient une sorte d'aversion, et qu'il voulait introduire l'art et le travail même dans l'originalité."[34] This passage is the nerve-centre of decadence—as the nineteenth century understood the term. It sums up everything that had been said previously, and contains whatever was said later. The conclusions to which it leads are obvious: Baudelaire liked depravity,

[32]"Notice," in Baudelaire, *Les Fleurs du Mal* (Lévy, 1868), xxxvii, xvi, xxv.
[33]*Ibid.*, lii: "Baudelaire aimait dans ces dessins l'absence complète d'antiquité, c'est-à-dire de tradition classique, et le sentiment profond de ce que nous appellerons *décadence*." The reference to Delacroix is on page liv.
[34]*Ibid.*, xxvi.

which is an essential part of decadence, a last refinement of artificiality, since it is anti-natural. If Gautier was not writing with the Marquis de Sade in mind, at least his thought is the same. That taste for sexual perversions, so characteristic of decadent literature, receives theoretic justification in the "Notice." Even painstaking craftsmanship becomes a variety of perversion. To complete the picture, he notes that the setting of Baudelaire's verse is the degenerate capital, "ce dédale infect ... cet immonde fourmillement de misère, de laideur et de perversités."[35]

A sense of modern corruption becomes more and more wide-spread during the middle years of the century. Even a conscientious philosopher like Taine saw modern civilization in much the same way as Gautier and Baudelaire, and used nearly the same terms to describe it. In his essay on La Fontaine (1853), he compared Paris to the decadent cities of antiquity, Alexandria and Rome, "un terreau puissant, étrangement composé de substances brûlantes, capables de produire des fruits extraordinaires, maladifs souvent, enivrants parfois."[36] Five years later, writing about Balzac, he called the *Comédie humaine* a typical product of the corrupt city: "Le gaz s'allume, le boulevard s'emplit, les théâtres regorgent, la foule veut jouir, partout où la bouche, l'oreille, les yeux soupçonnent un plaisir, elle se rue; plaisir raffiné, artificiel, sorte de cuisine malsaine faite pour exciter, non pour nourrir, offerte par le calcul et la débauche à la satiété et à la corruption... Tout cela bout ensemble et... pénètre tous les nerfs d'un plaisir maladif et vénéneux." The passage reads like a prose version of Baudelaire's "Crépuscule du soir." Balzac's novels are flowers of evil produced by this hot-house: "Voilà ses alentours et sa vie : vous prévoyez quelles plantes ont dû pousser sur ce terreau artificiel et concentré de substances âcres. Il en fallait un pareil pour faire végéter cette forêt énorme, pour y empourprer les fleurs de ce sombre éclat métallique, pour y emplir les fruits de ce suc mordant et trop fort."[37] If "Balzac" were changed to "Baudelaire," the paragraph would fit into an article by Thierry, Gautier, or Barbey d'Aurevilly on *Les Fleurs du Mal*.

The artificiality which appears in the work of Baudelaire's first disciples, Verlaine and Mallarmé, is such a part of decadent sensibility that it must be discussed in our next chapters. Its main characteristics, however, may be referred to here. Verlaine's essay on Baudelaire (1865) presented him as the poet of modern man, a creature of artificial vices which were the results of an advanced civilization—drugs, tobacco, alcohol, etc.—a denizen of the great city. Paris is the

[35]*Ibid.*, xxxv.   [36]*Lafontaine et ses Fables* (Hachette), 60.
[37]*Essais de critique et d'histoire* (Hachette), 57–8.

setting of most of Verlaine's poetry, and where it is not (as in *Fêtes galantes*), the "natural" themes are carefully artificialized by Louis-Quinze details: patches, rouge, high-heels, fans. The eighteenth century, with the intensity of its social life, the mannerisms of its art, the legends of its corruption, and the bloody catastrophe that brought it to an end, provided excellent material for decadent writing. Verlaine always thought of Paris as the centre of vice, in which he took a morbid pleasure. Such is the theme of "Nocturne parisien" (in *Poèmes saturniens*), "La 'Grande Ville'" (*Sagesse*), etc. In the latter poem, dated 1877, the city is "un tas criard de pierres blanches" where "tous les vices ont leur tanière, les exquis et les hideux," where there is "toujours un remûement de la chose coupable." We might be reading a summing-up of dozens of poems and novels produced during the next twenty years. Mallarmé praised Emmanuel des Essarts' *Poèmes parisiens* for their artificiality: "La nature ici paraîtra dans son charme civilisé, comme dans les squares, et ne laissera passer dans les vers que les quelques bouffées humaines respirables à travers la vie qu'elles poétisent."[38] In "L'Azur" he compares his heart to a "pot de fard," and in "Tristesse d'été" tells his mistress that "je goûterai le fard pleuré par tes paupières." The characters of his *Hérodiade* and *Igitur* live in curtained boudoirs, carefully excluding the sunlight (which symbolizes Nature) behind heavy draperies; the Hérodiade, like La Fanfarlo, is seated at her toilet-table.

Writers began to be attracted by Paris as formerly they had been attracted by "maisons du berger," or by Spain and the Orient. Baudelaire and Taine spent long evenings in theatres, casinos and music-halls, and so did the Goncourt brothers. Descriptions of such haunts are frequent throughout the *Journal* of the latter. A sketch of prostitutes at the Casino Cadet, a night-spot which Baudelaire also visited, shows a perverse delight in vice and depravity which is characteristic of the period, and, for that matter, of the rest of the century: "Ces femmes enfarinées de poudre de riz... les lèvres peintes en rouge au pinceau, ces femmes maquillées d'un teint de morte... l'œil charbonné, avivé de fièvre, avec des cheveux pareils à un morceau d'astrakan... ces femmes avec leurs figures de folles et de malades, semblent des spectres et des bêtes de plaisir... se faisant tentantes... par un renversement de nature parlant à des appétits d'amour viciés."[39]

[38]Mallarmé, *Œuvres complètes* (Pléiade), 250.
[39]*Journal des Goncourt* (Flammarion), II, 202. Paul Bourget, writing on the Goncourts in 1885, called attention to the "tristesse épileptique et luxurieuse" of this passage (*Nouveaux Essais de psychologie contemporaine*, Lemerre, 188). By 1885 it was even more "in the period" than when it was written.

This passage is particularly interesting because it brings us in touch with the Naturalist school; and most of the Naturalists adopted the same identification: civilization-artificiality-corruption. The link between the Gautier-Baudelaire formula and Zola's novels is supplied, not only by the Goncourts, but by Huysmans in the preface he wrote for Théodore Hannon's *Rimes de joie* in 1879. Hannon's verse, of slight poetic value, is a hymn to cosmetics; it reads (as Huysmans points out) like a verse-rendering of Baudelaire's "Eloge du maquillage." One of the longest poems, "Maquillage,"[40] is typical of the rest. The poet's mistress is described painting her face:

> Sachant mon dégoût libertin
> Pour tout ce que le sang jeune éclaire
> De son hématine — un matin
> Tu te maquillas, pour me plaire.
>
> De l'inflexible azur de ciel
> Irrémédiablement ennemie,
> Mon âme, tu le sais, ma mie,
> N'aime que l'artificiel.

A list of lotions and paints follows. In his preface to the volume, Huysmans begins by comparing Hannon to Baudelaire and ends by comparing him to Zola. The *Rimes de joie*, he says, is the only book since *Les Fleurs du Mal* "qui se soit attaqué aux grâces maladives de la femme, aux névroses élégantes des grandes villes. Par là, les *Rimes de joie* se rattachent... au grand mouvement du naturalisme." Artificiality, in short, is not only urban and modern, but sickly . . . decadent. It is typical of the anti-classical nature of the cult (a point Gautier and Baudelaire had mentioned) that Huysmans should go on to declare Hannon's neurotic, overdressed women superior to the "bovine" goddesses of Greek art. It is also typical of the tendency to confound artificiality, modernism and decadence that he should find in the work of Baudelaire and Hannon the beginnings of Zola's interest in neurosis and disease. Hannon, he declares, has "un goût de terroir flamand, compliqué d'un arôme très fin de nervosine. Là est la note spéciale de ce coloriste, et elle est complétée par une sollicitude inquiète pour ces raffinements mondains... qui ont fourni à Emile Zola de si belles, de si admirables pages."

The admirable pages referred to are *La Curée* (1872), a novel (one of the first of the *Rougon-Macquart*) in which Zola depicted what he

[40]Théodore Hannon, *Rimes de joie* (Bruxelles, Gay et Doucé, 1881). Huysmans was a practising Naturalist in 1879; three years before, in 1876, he had proclaimed himself a disciple of Zola in an enthusiastic article.

calls "the Parisians of the Decadence," that is, of the Second Empire. The book is full of descriptions of the clothes and the boudoir of the heroine, Renée Saccard; they doubtless fit into the context, but they are a little too lush for mere background painting. Nor is this all. Zola had set out to write a study of manners, and he ended in a description of moral and aesthetic degeneracy. The plot turns on an incestuous adultery between Renée and her stepson Maxime. From first to last, this theme is symbolized by the exotic flora in Renée's conservatory, a hot-house in direct descent from the allegoric botany dear to the critics of Baudelaire, and pointing in no uncertain fashion to the orchids of *A Rebours* and the *Jardin des supplices*. The idea of incest first occurs to Renée in this conservatory, and whenever she craves what is described as "une ivresse plus âcre," she takes her stepson there. A catalogue of the plants is given; it is more scientific than similar lists in Thierry and Gautier (Zola had consulted a treatise on botany), but it fulfils the same function: the caladiums, begonias, stanhopeia, pandanus, etc., are all symbols of Evil. The identification of cosmetics with decadence appears again in *Nana* (1879), when Count Muffat's morbid passion for the actress begins as he watches her making up for the stage: "Elle ajouta, avec le doigt, deux larges traits de carmin sur les lèvres. Le comte Muffat se sentait plus troublé encore, séduit par la perversion des poudres et des fards, pris du désir déréglé de cette jeunesse peinte, la bouche trop rouge dans la face trop blanche, les yeux agrandis, cerclés de noir, brûlants, et comme meurtris d'amour."[41]

Zola's interest in artificiality was more or less incidental; but the whole matter was of supreme importance to Huysmans. In *Le Salon de 1879, Croquis parisiens* (1880) and *L'Exposition des indépendants en 1880*, he develops the sketches Gautier and Baudelaire had made of the industrialized landscapes of the Paris suburbs (factory chimneys, ravaged earth, sick vegetation, etc.) which he considers evidence of man's superiority to nature: "Créée incomplète dans la prévision du rôle que l'homme lui assignera, la nature attend de ce maître son parachèvement et son coup de fion."[42] Although in *L'Art moderne* he recommends something like Baudelaire's "modern heroism" and advises young painters to stop dealing in classical and mediaeval subjects, the modernism he admires is almost invariably artificial, and, because artificial, sickly. For example, he notes (as in the preface to Hannon) how much more beautiful dressmakers' dummies are than Greek

[41]Zola, *La Curée* (Charpentier), 231, and *Nana* (Charpentier), I, 162–3.
[42]"Vue des remparts du Nord-Paris," *Croquis parisiens* (Plon), 101.

statuary: "Combien supérieurs aux mornes statues de Vénus, ces mannequins si vivants des couturiers; combien plus insinuants ces bustes capitonnés dont la vue évoque de longues rêveries : — rêveries libertines, en face des tétons éphébiques et des pis talés — rêveries charitables, en face des mamelles vieillies, recroquevillées par la chlorose ou bouffies par la graisse."[43] All these variations on an artificial theme are carried out in full orchestration in A Rebours (1884). The hero, Des Esseintes, is described as having found in artificiality an equivalent of the Romantic ivory tower, a shelter against the unpleasantness of contemporary life—for of course he hates the nineteenth century even while delighting in its "corrupt" refinements. "Je me figurais," Huysmans wrote in a preface composed twenty years after the novel, "un monsieur... qui a découvert, dans l'artifice, un dérivatif au dégoût que lui inspirent les tracas de la vie et les mœurs américaines de son temps; je le profilais fuyant à tire d'aile dans le rêve, se réfugiant dans l'illusion d'extravagantes féeries, vivant, seul, loin de son siècle, dans le souvenir évoqué d'époques plus cordiales, de milieux moins vils."[44] Artificiality, the desire to violate nature, to live à rebours, is the guiding principle of Des Esseintes' life: "L'Artifice paraissait à Des Esseintes la marque distinctive du génie de l'homme... La nature a fait son temps; elle a définitivement lassé, par la dégoûtante uniformité de ses paysages et de ses ciels, l'attentive patience des raffinés... quel monotone magasin de prairies et d'arbres, quelle banale agence de montagnes et de mers!... Cette sempiternelle radoteuse a maintenant usé la débonnaire admiration des vrais artistes, et le moment est venu où il s'agit de la remplacer... par l'artifice."[45] All the embryonic suggestions of Mademoiselle de Maupin, Fortunio, La Fanfarlo, etc., are developed to their extreme limit. Des Esseintes' mistresses have to paint their faces and dress up; one of them, a ventriloquist, is even obliged to practise her art while he caresses her. He refuses to travel, contenting himself with various subterfuges— sitting in a bath of salt water, watching a school of mechanical fish, and so on. He prefers the locomotives of the French railroads to women in point of beauty;[46] has a set of cosmetics with every sort of

[43]"L'Etiage," ibid., 131.
[44]A Rebours (Charpentier-Fasquelle), vi.
[45]Ibid., 31.
[46]The exaltation of the machine was an inevitable side-product of the cult of artificiality. It was further developed a year after A Rebours by Villiers de l'Isle Adam in his Eve future. The story is little more than a "scientific" rewriting of Gautier's Roman de la momie (1858). Gautier told how a German Egyptologist, Dr. Rumphius, unearthed an "ideal woman" (the mummy of Princess Tahoser) for Lord Evendale, a bored young English dandy, in the Valley of Kings. In Villiers'

perfume, paint, lotion, brush and tweezer (the description occupies nearly two pages); buys a collection of monstrous orchids whose main virtue is that they all look artificial: "Il voulait des fleurs naturelles imitant des fleurs fausses." "Son but était atteint; aucune ne semblait réelle; l'étoffe, le papier, la porcelaine, le métal paraissaient avoir été prêtés par l'homme à la nature pour lui permettre de créer des monstres." "La nature est, à elle seule, incapable de procréer des espèces aussi malsaines et aussi perverses."[47] Man's intervention, as always, produces something which is of necessity perverse and corrupt. Like all the rest of the cult of artificiality, this is orthodox Rousseauism turned inside out. The last refinements occur at the end of the novel. Des Esseintes succumbs to attacks of neurosis, complicated by indigestion. He can only take nourishment by enemas and, far from finding this a nuisance, he thinks it a delightful violation of nature: "Son penchant vers l'artificiel avait maintenant atteint l'exaucement suprême; on n'irait pas plus loin; la nourriture ainsi absorbée était, à coup sûr, la dernière déviation qu'on pût commettre... Quelle décisive insulte jetée à la face de cette vieille nature dont les uniformes exigences seraient pour jamais éteintes!"[48] The last sentence might have been extracted from a page of *Justine*. The Marquis de Sade's characters outraged Nature by crime, Des Esseintes does it by artificiality. Finally, Huysmans links artificiality to the return to Catholicism which (in *En Route*) overtook Durtal. When the novel begins, Des Esseintes is an atheist, or at least an agnostic;[49] but his scepticism is beginning to weaken—largely because of his craving for the artificial: "Ses tendances vers l'artifice... n'étaient-elles pas, en somme, des résultats d'études spécieuses, de raffinements extraterrestres, de spéculations quasi-théologiques... des transports vers une béatitude lointaine, désirable comme celle que nous promettent les Ecritures ?"[50] The lines show clearly from what a contaminated source the *fin-de-siècle*'s religiosity flowed.

After such a display of artificiality as *A Rebours*, in which every aspect of the theory was expressed and amplified, there was little more to be said; and indeed during the rest of the century little more was said: writers confined themselves to repetition. From 1884 on there is no new contribution to the idea, nothing that cannot be found

story, Lord Evendale becomes Lord Ewald; Dr. Rumphius, Thomas Alva Edison; and Princess Tahoser, Miss Hadaly, a robot with golden lungs and electric joints, who eats pills of zinc, potassium and lead. Edison manufactured her in one of his laboratories.

[47]*A Rebours*, 119–25.   [48]*Ibid.*, 278.
[49]*Ibid.*, 105.   [50]*Ibid.*, 106.

already stated by Huysmans. Artificiality had become such a characteristic part of literature that it could be parodied. Gabriel Vicaire, in
his amusing travesty on the decadent style, *Les Déliquescences,
poèmes décadents d'Adoré Floupette* (1885), wrote a caricature of
passages we have already examined in Gautier, Baudelaire and Huysmans: "L'Amour est une fleur de maléfice... lourde, aux parfums
troublants... avec des striures verdâtres... son calice est gonflé de sucs
vénéneux... Ce n'est pas trop pour l'enfanter que l'artifice d'une civilisation profondément corrompue." The "ideal woman" is not a "gar-
deuse de vaches," but "une belle tête exsangue, avec de longs cheveux
pailletés d'or, des yeux avivés par le crayon noir, des lèvres de pourpre
ou de vermillion... Le charme alangui d'un corps morbide... douze fois
trempé dans les aromates : voilà l'éternelle Charmeuse."[51]

The "decadent" school was officially inaugurated a year later by
Anatole Baju's little periodical, *Le Décadent*. In the number of
October 1886, we find a rewriting of Musset's "Nuit de mai" in
decadent terms signed Albert Aurier:

La Muse

Regarde : le peignoir que tu veux m'enveloppe,
Celui de satin noir, aux froufrous enchanteurs,
Le peignoir aimé, doux fleurant l'héliotrope
Et le corylopsis, parfums incitateurs !
Oh ! vois, mon œil gris flambe et mon ventre frissonne !...
Je veux t'aimer ! Veux-tu ? Je serai bien mignonne...

Le Poète

Oh ! oui, je veux t'aimer ! Car, tu n'es pas la Muse
Bégueule d'autrefois ! Ton œil gris est fripon ;
Ton nez n'a rien de grec, ô ma chatte camuse ;
Tu ne détestes pas qu'on trousse ton jupon...
Tu n'as pas les grands airs des Muses romantiques ;
Ta robe est à la mode, et tu ne vas jamais,
Aux bords des lacs, vêtue en des péplums antiques...

The piece might have been written, and very possibly was, with
Hannon's *Rimes de joie* under the parodist's eyes.

These two caricatures are a good introduction to much of the prose
and poetry of the rest of the century. Like most parodies, they supply
a very good idea of the theories they exaggerate; and on the whole,
they exaggerate very little: they might have been signed in all serious-

[51]G. Vicaire, *Les Déliquescences, poèmes décadents d'Adoré Floupette, avec sa
vie par Marius Tapora* (Vanier, 1885), préface, xxxv–xxxvii.

ness by a number of contemporary writers. Artificiality is the dominant note of the period: it appears everywhere, in metaphors, similes and vocabulary; in the craze for setting plots and poems in boudoirs; in the constant references to rice-powder, painted eyelids and painted lips; in the obstinate *hantise* of Paris—not even the "Paris laborieux" of Baudelaire, but the Paris of midnight suppers, brothels, theatres, music-halls, gambling dens and dives—a sinister mixture of decayed realism and exacerbated Romanticism which looks nowadays like the cardboard settings of a theatre seen by daylight. The matter went so far that Paul Bourget diagnosed it as a profound spiritual crisis at the heart of European civilization: "Lentement, sûrement, s'élabore la croyance à la banqueroute de la nature, qui promet de devenir la foi sinistre du xxe siècle, si la science ou une invasion de barbares ne sauve pas l'humanité trop réfléchie de la lassitude de sa propre pensée."[52] For this artificiality took on a neurotic gloss. It became the chief characteristic of decadent sensibility and a source of perversion, degeneracy and psychosis. All the men and all the women of the period are heavily painted. Even when, as the century waned, a species of neo-Romanticism came into fashion—a return to the excessive and flaming characters of fifty or sixty years before—cosmetics still reigned. One of the things that makes the creatures of Mendès, Bourges, Rachilde, Péladan, Lorrain, etc., decadent instead of Romantic is their cosmetics. Julia Belcredi, the heroine of Bourges' *Crépuscule des dieux* (1883), could change places with Hugo's Lucrèce Borgia and the substitution pass unnoticed, but for her face-paint. She is described as "blanche et nue, frottée de parfums, terrible à la lueur des bougies, avec son fard et ses paupières peintes, dont l'artifice libertin attisait les désirs du jeune homme [her lover]": details which Hugo would never have added.[53] The characters of Joséphin Péladan's intolerable "éthopée," *La Décadence latine*, whose innumerable volumes began to appear in 1884, all divide their time between over-heated boudoirs and the Parisian slums, either painting their faces or seeking "l'ignominie des mœurs décadentes" in the dives of the capital. In Mendès' *Zo'har* (1886) the hero's neurasthenia, we are told, results directly from Parisian artificiality, as represented by rice-powder. Paris is "la ville femme, la femelle de l'Europe, et quelle femme! ni chair, ni sang, ni os ; du maquillage, rien dessous... Ce qui vous délabre... c'est la poudre de riz. Il en sort de partout... des théâtres, des cages, des magasins, des

---

[52]"Baudelaire" in *Essais de psychologie contemporaine* (Lemerre, 1883), 15.
[53]Bourges, *Le Crépuscule des dieux* (Stock, 1901), 249. The novel, published in 1883, was written between 1877 and 1882.

ateliers et des égoûts... La pluie sent la poudre de riz, comme si l'eau du ciel tombait d'une cuvette de fille. De là, les névroses, les détraquements."[54] Like Péladan's characters, Mendès' spend their lives in a boudoir-to-slum pursuit of "new sins," and the same applies to the extraordinary creatures of Rachilde's novels: they are seeking a "volupté factice." Paul de Fertzen, the hero of Les Hors Nature (1897), prefers silk to female skin. "Cela," he says of a bolt of satin, "c'est de la beauté artificielle, mais c'est réellement, suprêmement beau. Toute beauté naturelle a une tare. Il n'y a pas... d'épiderme de gorge ou d'épaule qui puisse me donner une pareille sensation au toucher."[55] When he goes to the country in an effort to cure his neurosis, the natural surroundings only accentuate his artificiality: "Venu à la nature après une existence d'artificiel, la nature le faisait paraître plus artificiel, outrant ses défauts au plein soleil de la réalité."[56] His penchants for the artificial end in a dabbling with sexual perversions—according to the formula supplied by Gautier in the "Notice." The same is true of most of the other heroes and heroines of the time. Varieties of homosexuality were especially popular. It is certain that this craving for the sexually abnormal arose from the belief that it was somehow artificial. Verlaine defined pederasty as "un affranchissement de la lourde nature."[57] Paul Adam made a remark which is characteristic of the period when he called the Wilde scandal "contre-nature: mais le propre de la moindre civilisation est de répudier la Bonne Mère."[58] In Lombard's novel L'Agonie (1888), dealing with Heliogabalus, the emperor (painted and jewelled in fin-de-siècle style) is represented as trying to impose homosexuality, "l'amour artificiel," on the Roman Empire, in contrast to "l'amour naturel."[59]

A typical author of this sort of writing was Jean Lorrain. Remy de Gourmont called him "un esprit de serre-chaude, une plante rare," which produced poisoned flowers.[60] His poems, short stories and novels are filled with pictures of Parisian corruption: strumpets and perverts, all in a setting of boudoirs, music-halls and theatres, and all plastered with cosmetics. For example, we read of an old whore, "les cheveux visiblement teints, les chairs travaillés par l'émailleuse ... les lèvres

---

[54]Mendès, Zo'har (Charpentier, 1886), 54–5.
[55]Rachilde, Les Hors Nature (Mercure de France), 79.
[56]Ibid., 195.
[57]Verlaine, "Ces Passions," in Parallèlement (1889).
[58]Quoted by Dr. Laupts in Perversions et perversité sexuelles (Carré, 1896), 161. Zola wrote a preface for this treatise.
[59]J. Lombard, L'Agonie (Ollendorff, 1901), 76–7.
[60]Gourmont, Le Deuxième Livre des masques (Mercure de France, 1898), 60.

carminées... une tête chancelante sous son fard";[61] of the Duchess of Althorneyshare, "ses épaules luisantes de fards, ses bras gras de céruse, ses pommettes allumées de rouge... Mauve de la racine de ses cheveux teints à l'orteil de ses pieds gantés de soie... mauve par la fanerie de ses chairs recrépies, repeintes et marinées dans trente ans de baumes, d'onguents et de benjoin";[62] of the Comtesse Borosini, "rien de plus artificiel... Sous la dorure des cheveux violemment teints et le rouge des lèvres brutalement soulignées de fards, c'étaient des yeux mouillés de kohl, des narines touchées de rose... Factice! était-elle assez adorablement factice!"[63] And, of course, the men are as bad as the women: Monsieur de Bougrelon, who "poudrait sa face de cadavre, avivait de rouge les narines pincées de son nez, ses lèvres sèches et minces... ravivait au crayon et ses sourcils et les poches de ses yeux sans cils, replâtrait son vieux visage en ruine";[64] Prince Noronsoff, who lives in an "atmosphère de parfums et de fards," has "les joues frottées de rouge," who, in an emotional scene, "sentait la sueur désagréger son fard," "se décomposait sous son fard," who is "un vrai cadavre vernissé, fardé et peint," a "poupée macabre et fardée."[65] Finally, there is the Duc de Freneuse, an imitation of Des Esseintes, a synthesis of decadence. Highly rouged, he frequents music-halls, brothels and theatres (which he compares with the pleasure-haunts of decadent Rome), and comes to the conclusion that all this artificiality is the source of the neurosis which is driving him insane: "Tous ces visages de femmes, fardés et peints, toutes ces bouches au minium et ces paupières soulignées de kohl, tout cela a créé autour de moi une atmosphère de transe et d'agonie... Le maquillage! c'est là d'où vient mon mal."[66] This passage doubtless contains an echo of Mendès' remarks on rice-powder. To escape this life he tries, like Paul de Fertzen, a country retreat: "Un bain de verdure, un bain de rosée... voilà ce qu'il faudrait à mon âme endolorie et faussée... J'échapperai ainsi à Paris, à son atmosphère délétère et néfaste... Paris qui me corrode, me déprave et m'épouvante!"[67] But—again like Paul—he has become so steeped in artificiality that the simplicity of Nature only accentuates his disease.

[61]"La Dame aux portraits," dedicated to Huysmans, in *Histoires de masques* (Ollendorff, 1900), 175–6.
[62]*Monsieur de Phocas* (Ollendorff, 1901), 158–9.
[63]*Fards et poisons* (Ollendorff, 1903), 99.
[64]*Monsieur de Bougrelon* (Ollendorff, 1903), 67, 82.
[65]*Le Vice errant; Coins de Byzance; Les Noronsoff* (Albin Michel), 160, 180, 282, 324, 359–60.
[66]*Monsieur de Phocas*, 74.
[67]*Ibid.*, 304–5.

The hero of Octave Mirbeau's *Jardin des supplices* (1899) begins his confessions with a familiar sentiment: "La nature est... toujours et partout, semblable à elle-même... elle manque d'improvisation. Elle se répète constamment... Moi... je ne tolère les fleurs que chez les modistes et sur les chapeaux."[68] It is true that he follows this with a general admission that he was wrong; but he was too much of his age to profit by such easy repentance. When he sets out to rediscover natural beauty, his search leads him to a nightmarish China, to an atrocious array of sexual perversions, all set in a "garden of punishments" which, although its plants flourish out of doors, is nothing more nor less than the old Conservatory of Evil. The impression left on the reader is that by 1900 most writers had become so depraved by sixty or seventy years of artificiality that they were incapable of seeing Nature except in artificial terms.

Artificiality, in fact, is the chief characteristic of decadence as the nineteenth century understood the word. By a voluntary contradiction of the nature-cult, writers were able to see all the traditional Romantic themes in a new light and a new perspective. Their whole approach, of course, was entirely deliberate: from Gautier to Mirbeau, everybody who took up a pen realized that he was going "against the grain." There is something provocative and irreverent, a delicious sense of schism, about them all. They accept civilization as corrupt, but take a perverse pleasure in that very corruption, preferring the civilized to the primitive and the artificial to the natural. They add nothing new to Rousseau's premise; they simply adopt a different attitude—eschewing inspiration in favour of cold calculation, whether in aesthetics, literary theory, or psychology. This insistence on will as opposed to emotion led to a new type of sensibility: the dandy, soon to become the decadent, with his self-mastery, intellectualism, ennui, satiety and his perverse obsessions.

[68]Mirbeau, *Le Jardin des supplices* (Charpentier, 1923), 71–2.

CHAPTER 2

DECLINE AND FALL

Nihil tam efficere concupiscebat, quam quod posse effici negaretur.

Suetonius, *Caligula*

Je ne suis pas de ma famille ; je ne suis pas un branche de ce noble tronc, mais un champignon vénéneux poussé par quelque lourde nuit d'orage... Je suis attaqué de cette maladie qui prend aux peuples et aux hommes puissants dans leur vieillesse : — l'impossible.

Théophile Gautier, *Mademoiselle de Maupin* (1834)

THERE IS a painting in the Louvre which, though its colours are anaemic and its moral lesson painfully obvious, has nevertheless a certain theatrical and didactic charm. It represents a marble triclinium, filled with a sprawl of drunken revellers. Stern ancestral busts line the walls, gazing in austere disapproval at the scene of licence before them; and in the background, through a line of Corinthian pillars, stretch the wide perspectives of the Eternal City, bathed in the voluptuous half-light of a setting sun. It is Thomas Couture's "Romans of the Decadence"; and, subtitled with a line from Juvenal ("Luxury has fallen upon us, more terrible than the sword, and the conquered East has revenged herself with the gift of her vices"), it was the sensation of the Salon of 1847.

After what we have been saying about artificiality and decadence, the impact of such a canvas is not hard to understand. For this scene of debauch, set amongst the appurtenances of a high civilization, is part of the same legend: the metropolis, at the zenith of its glory, seeking relief from boredom and satiety in all manner of excess. Every literary type must have his setting; and Couture's painted rhetoric does for decadent sensibility what Delacroix's "Marino Faliero" had done for the Romantic mood of ten or twenty years before. Decadent sensibility develops from the theory that civilization is artificial and corrupt; it dwells orchid-like in the hot-houses of an excessive and aging culture, in the boudoirs and brothels of the great city.

There are three phases to its evolution. All have characteristics in common while remaining more or less distinct. The first is the late Romantic phase (the subject of the present chapter) when the moody, introspective and fatal hero of 1830 adopts the cult of the artificial and the abnormal; then the Naturalist phase, marked by the influence of psychopathology, which leads to an interpretation of decadence in terms of nervous disease; finally the *fin de siècle* phase, when there is a return to the monstrous characters of late Romanticism. The first period goes from 1830 to the beginnings of Naturalism; the second from Naturalism to 1884 (the Goncourts and Zola to *A Rebours*); the last from 1884 to the first years of the new century—from the nerve-storms of Des Esseintes to the emotional garbage of *Monsieur de Phocas* and *Le Jardin des supplices*.

The cult of artificiality begins in the perversion of a Romantic legend, and decadent sensibility in the perversion of a Romantic type. Or rather, of two Romantic types, the languid, receptive character (Saint-Preux, René, Werther) and the dynamic "fatal man," who starts in the Don Juan tradition as the wicked Lord, borrows metaphysical lights from a variety of sources (including Milton's Satan), and runs lushly to seed in the melodramas of Byron, Hugo and Dumas.[1] Both produce in turn two decadent types—the languid neurotic and the stoic dandy. And, just as we often find a union of the fatal man and the effete sentimentalist during the Romantic period, so in decadents like Des Esseintes there is a combination of dandyism and neurosis.

Not that it was very difficult to pervert the Romantic type. From the beginning, there was something hectic about Romanticism, something unbalanced and neurotic. Its great founder, Rousseau, was a psychopath; and after 1789 began a period of political and social anarchy which certainly had an unsettling effect on the writers who lived through it. As H. Taine pointed out in 1865, the Romantic found himself living in a world without rules, where the old absolutes of throne and altar had been destroyed, where anything could be questioned and nothing answered. With the result that he fell back into a state of perpetual dissatisfaction. "Ni l'amour, ni la gloire, ni la science, ni le pouvoir, ne peuvent le satisfaire, et l'intempérance de ses désirs... le laisse abattu sur les ruines de lui-même, sans que son imagination surmentée, affaissée, impuissante, puisse lui représenter l'au-delà qu'il convoite et le *je ne sais quoi* qu'il n'a pas."[2] The

[1]See the analyses of Louis Maigron, *Le Romantisme et les mœurs* (Champion, 1910), 293–4, and of Paul van Tieghem, *Le Romantisme dans la littérature euro-péenne* (Albin Michel, 1948), 281 *et seq.*
[2]H. Taine, *Philosophie de l'art* (Hachette), 96–7.

definition would do almost as well for the decadents of 1880, but since the resemblances are so close, it is perhaps as well to note the differences at once.

Two things saved the Romantic from the worst consequences of his internal conflicts—the cult of Nature and the cult of ideal love. His anti-socialism has, as it were, excusable causes: he hates society because it has mistreated him, made him pay unjustly for some accident of birth, or balked his right to an ideal passion. The maladjustment of Hugo's Hernani, for example, is principally due to the fact that he has been deprived of his estates by the King of Spain. There is something more decadent about René, that first of all Romantics: his sexual abnormality and even more his confusion of libidinousness and religiosity—the brutal fact of incest cloaked in the white veils and holy waters of a nunnery. This sort of mysticism was later defined by the psychopathologists as a characteristic stigma of degeneracy. But amongst the vaporings we find such apostrophes as "O Dieu! Si tu m'avais donné une femme selon mes désirs!"[3] It is difficult to imagine anything less decadent than such a wish. The tragedy of Musset's Rolla, despite certain details, also fails to be really decadent. It begins with a lament for lost faith—Rolla lost his by reading Voltaire—and a good deal of his unrest is attributed to this loss. There is a hint of world-weariness: like Musset himself, "il est venu trop tard dans un monde trop vieux"; and he is a child of the great city, infected by its corruptions. But he is also "grand, loyal, intrépide et superbe... un noble cœur, naïf comme l'enfance, bon comme la pitié"; Paris has never really depraved him; his love-affairs are quite orthodox, and he commits suicide when his money runs out. George Sand's Bénédict is sketched in terms which at first sound decadent enough: "L'ennui, ce mal horrible qui s'est attaché à la génération présente plus qu'à toute autre époque de l'histoire sociale, avait envahi la destinée de Bénédict dans sa fleur... Il avait déjà flétri la plus précieuse faculté de son âge, l'espérance."[4] But all his anguish disappears when he meets Valentine, the *femme selon ses désirs*; the ensuing complications are due entirely to the social barriers between them, not to any fundamental corruption in Bénédict's soul.

The true decadent, on the other hand, is neurotic. He is not suffering from some mysterious fatality, but from nervous disorders, usually inherited from a line of tainted ancestors. Nor is he in revolt against society because it has frustrated him. Generally it has not. The writers

[3]*René* (Garnier), 88.
[4]*Valentine* (Calmann-Lévy), 13. The novel was written in 1832

of the decadence completely threw over all the conventional Romantic plots—the nobleman forced to live as a bandit, the great-souled convict, the virtuous whore. Amongst its dramatis personae we find dukes, princes, countesses, baronesses, all belonging to the best society and all well provided with cash. In such characters Romantic revolt has lost all justification, has soured, become spleen, boredom, *taedium vitae*, the result not of frustration but of surfeit. The decadent has passed beyond revolt. Whether he derives from the languid Romantic and lapses into sterility and impotence, or from the dynamic fatal man, and adopts the dandy's spiritual corsets, or (as often happens) unites the two, he is recognizably the same: resigned, indifferent, *blasé*; seeking, not a supreme emotion, but a new sensation; demanding not an ideal, but a fresh titillation for his jaded senses. Hence he is intellectual rather than sentimental, a creature almost logical in his manias. His sensuality is not the emotional orgy of Romanticism, but "la débauche sérieuse des siècles ennuyés," it is "moins une affaire des sens que du raisonnement."[5] From this comes his interest in perversions: they are artificial, voluntary. They held relatively little attraction for the Romantics because the cults of Nature and ideal love were so strongly implanted in Romantic sensibility. The two best analyses of the Romantic temperament we have, *Madame Bovary* and *L'Éducation sentimentale*, are studies in erotic idealism. When the cult of Nature was replaced by the cult of artificiality, the whole picture was altered. The search for love became a search for perversions—a conclusion Gautier was quick to draw from his discussion of Baudelaire's artificiality: "La *dépravation*, c'est-à-dire l'écart du type normal, est impossible à la bête, fatalement conduite par l'instinct immuable."[6]

This new sexual attitude is one of the great differences between Romantic and decadent; another is the character of their respective exoticisms. Romantic space-exoticism turned to the hot landscapes and passions of Italy, Spain and the Orient, and its time-exoticism sought similar qualities in the Middle Ages and the Renaissance—the mystery of Gothic architecture, the ecstasies of mediaeval faith, and the excessive and demonic characters of the Cinquecento as represented by Borgia popes, Valois kings, or the heroes of Elizabethan tragedy—all personalities who, whatever their vices, were intoxicated by splendour and agitated by strong passions. Decadent space-exoticism, on the other

[5]Baudelaire, "Le Salon de 1846" (*Œuvres*, Pléiade, II, 87) and *La Fanfarlo* (I, 554): the latter phrase describes Samuel Cramer.
[6]"Notice," in Baudelaire, *Fleurs du Mal* (1868), xxvi.

hand, scarcely exists; the decadents set their poems and novels in Paris, amongst the corruptions of the great city; and their time-exoticism, seeking similar corruptions, went back to antiquity. Not, however, to the antiquity of seventeenth-century classicism, the age of Graeco-Latin perfection represented by Sophocles and Virgil, but to the antiquity of the post-Augustan empire with its crimes and perversities, the world of Nero, Caligula, Messalina and Heliogabalus which had sinned madly and ended in appalling downfall. The world, in short, of Couture's painting. It is worth pausing for a moment to consider this type of exoticism, for it plays a huge role in the history of the decadent idea.

Imperial Rome (or rather, the legend of Imperial Rome, and in such matters the legend is more important than the reality) offered an alluring scene of corruption, carried out with unparalleled magnificence and, by a singular chance, immortalized by a galaxy of highly readable authors, many of whom shared the primitivist bias so that the picture they have left of their world is as lurid as a scandalized mind could make it. The content of some Latin writers (not to mention Greek) of even the pre-decadent period, such as Catullus, Tibullus, Horace and Virgil, is often sufficiently scabrous; and perversion becomes a standard ingredient of post-Augustan literature (Petronius, Juvenal, Apuleius). But the historians were the great painters of decadence, and it is in the characters of the Caesars and their ladies as they have come down to us in Tacitus, Suetonius and the Scriptores Historiae Augustae that the nineteenth century found its richest material. Tiberius' long retirement at Capri produced hair-raising legends of debauchery. Messalina survives as an almost clinical case of nymphomania: Juvenal sketches her spending nights in a brothel and returning to the Palatine at dawn, "lassata viris, sed non satiata," a verse which became more and more popular after the 1850's. Caligula was a typical "décadent de grande race," the victim of diseased heredity manifesting itself in neurosis of the most lurid sort—insomnia, nightmares, megalomania, ferocious sadism and sexual aberrations. He had a craving for the impossible: "Nihil tam efficere concupiscebat, quam quod posse effici negaretur,"[7] a craving which occurs again in nearly every nineteenth-century hero and heroine from D'Albert on down. All these characteristics exist in Nero, along with an aesthetic bent which was very seductive to the literary mind. Nero was the last scion of a great race; he showed a taste for low haunts and "encanaillement," sallying forth on nocturnal junkets in

[7]Suetonius, *Caligula*, XXXVII.

the slums like any character of Mendès or Péladan. His frantic extrava-
gance and wild building projects were symptoms of his desire for the
impossible, as was also his burning of Rome because he wanted to
rebuild it on a more splendid scale, and, as an artist, needed a model
for a poem on the destruction of Troy. In Heliogabalus we have a
sexual pervert elevated to the imperial throne, with all the eccentricities of Caligula and Nero heightened to their ultimate point.

The distinguishing mark of these emperors was an effort to violate
nature, to turn night into day, normal passion into abnormal; to live,
as Seneca put it, *retro*, a phrase which, as Irving Babbitt pointed out,
can only be translated as *à rebours*.[8] Add to all this the background
and the conclusion—the Barbarians on the frontiers and the catastrophes of the fifth and sixth centuries—and a highly charged atmosphere results: world-weariness, sense of doom, craving for "frissons
nouveaux"—an atmosphere in many ways analogous to the nineteenth
century, and made even more so by a little wishful thinking. Hence
Roman echoes persist throughout all decadent literature.

Since Latin reigned supreme in the nineteenth-century schoolroom
and many of the decadents were good Latinists, they would probably
have discovered all this ancient vice for themselves. Even if they had
not, the Marquis de Sade would have supplied the deficiency: he
presented the corruptions of antiquity in literary form. Pétrus Borel
doubtless had this fact in mind when, in 1830, he called him a Roman
Emperor.[9] References to Tiberius, Nero and Heliogabalus abound in
Justine et Juliette, as well as to Louis XI, Herod, Gilles de Rais and
the more depraved Byzantine Caesars[10]: they knew how to "allumer
la volupté au flambeau de leurs crimes." De Sade transformed this sort
of material into pure time-exoticism: something to be sought out and
imitated. He is always stopping his narrative to preach a sermon in
favour of corruption: "L'état le plus heureux sera toujours celui où
la dépravation des mœurs sera la plus universelle, parce que le bonheur étant bien visiblement dans le mal, celui qui s'y livrera le plus
ardemment sera nécessairement le plus heureux."—"Ce ne sera jamais
qu'au sein de la corruption la plus étendue... que les individus... trou-
veront la plus forte dose de félicité sur la terre."—"La dépravation des
mœurs est nécessaire dans un état."[11] The last sentence is illustrated
by a number of historical examples.

[8]*Rousseau and Romanticism*, quoted by Mario Praz, *La Carne, la morte e il diavolo
nella letteratura romantica*, terza edizione (Firenze, Sansoni, 1948), 414, note 39.
[9]Quoted in *ibid.*, 129.
[10]For example, I, 32, and VI, 128–9.
[11]*Ibid.*, III, 48; III, 51; V, 331.

La Philosophie dans le boudoir, Justine et Juliette and *Les 120 journées de Sodome* are enormous developments of the perversions hinted at or briefly described by the Latin historians, whom De Sade, of course, had read; and this is certainly the main reason for the influence such books exercised upon subsequent writers, and for whatever interest De Sade himself still has today. He was the first to catalogue perversions. Before the manuals of Krafft-Ebing, Jung, Stekel, etc., he produced a museum of erotology in which every species of algolagnia is represented by its appropriate wax-work, as doll-like and abstract as the engravings which adorn the ten volumes of *Justine* in the Enfer of the Bibliothèque Nationale.[12] Besides this, he developed to its extreme the Don Juan type of personality, thus pointing the way to the Romantic fatal man and the decadent dandy. He may have owed something to the example of Laclos' *Liaisons dangereuses* (1782): the two principal characters of which, Valmont and Mme de Merteuil, dominate themselves and their acquaintances by the exercise of an inhuman will-power. Baudelaire pointed out their significance, noting that Valmont was the ancestor of the Byronic hero and the dandy, an example of "recherche du pouvoir par le dandysme," while Mme de Merteuil was even his superior: "Chez elle tout ce qui est humain est calciné."[13] For while their search for power expresses itself in sexual terms, neither is looking for the conventional pleasures of love, either sentimental or sensuous. Both use love as an excuse for intellectual triumphs—particularly Mme de Merteuil, whose eroticism exists for no other purpose than as a test of the will. The vocabulary of her letters shows this clearly enough (words like *étude, volonté, pensée, méditation* occur throughout). Their love is dandyism at its purest, a sort of erotic geometry, in which sentiment is nothing, will and intellect everything. Yet, while it is certainly akin to the dandyism of the fatal man and the decadent, it is not quite the same thing: the world of *Les Liaisons dangereuses* was still the prismatic world of eighteenth-century classicism, undistorted by metaphysical or emotional shades. There is no Satanism in Valmont and Mme de Merteuil, no hint of neurosis. They are neither in revolt against society nor the victims of a psychotic condition; they pursue their "recherche du

[12]Such at least is the opinion of Dr. Sarfati in his medical doctorate on the Marquis: "Ses livres, ses écrits, sont des monuments illustres de la psycho-pathologie sexuelle; ils ont apporté à la science avant Krafft-Ebing toute la gamme des perversions, sous tous leurs aspects, avec toutes leurs gradations. Cet homme... a écrit à lui seul, les manifestations des plus ténébreuses diathèses psycho-sexuelles..." Quoted by Maurice Heine, *Le Marquis de Sade* (N.R.F.), 106. Sarfati's thesis was presented in 1930.

[13]Baudelaire, "Les Liaisons dangereuses," an unfinished article on Laclos, *Œuvres*, II, 438.

pouvoir" in a vacuum, ignoring rather than defying the rules of morality, whether human or divine. They are cleverer than their victims, but not superhuman. This is not the case with De Sade's creatures. Although the crapulous debauchery of a Juliette (for example) does not affect her heart, it does affect her imagination—which is the great difference between Laclos and Sade. Besides developing to its ultimate point the cruelty which lurks in the lust for domination, and describing its results with a detailed obscenity which Laclos, obeying the rules of classical taste, would never have ventured on, the Marquis dowered his characters with a sort of lubricious ecstasy which bursts the exquisite limits of eighteenth-century libertinage and has nothing in common with the gelid elegance of Mme de Merteuil. As one of them, Noirceuil, declares in a frantic harangue to Juliette: "Si j'étais souverain, Juliette, je n'aurais pas de plus grand plaisir que celui de me faire suivre par des bourreaux qui massacreraient dans l'instant tout ce qui choquerait mes regards... Je marcherais sur des cadavres, et je serais heureux; je déchargerais dans le sang dont les flots couleraient à mes pieds."[14] At first glance it seems absurd to charge the dandy as D'Aurevilly and Baudelaire have sketched him with vices such as these. His cold-blooded deliberation has no similarity, it would seem, with the frenzies of Noirceuil. Yet his lust for domination shows that he belongs to the same family: even when it assumes a stoic elegance, it never changes in fundamentals. And, with Des Esseintes or Prince Noronsoff or Freneuse, it is always ready to break out in words or acts which would not be misplaced in a page of *Justine* or *La Philosophie dans le boudoir*.

There is, however, one element in the dandy's character which does not exist in De Sade's personages: ennui. Noirceuil and Juliette and the others are not vicious because they have exhausted normal pleasures but because they really like perversions. Satiety is perhaps the only attendant of vice which one never finds in the fifteen or twenty volumes the Marquis has bequeathed us; he was, after all, a legitimate child of the eighteenth century, born in 1740, and his productions have the same tireless quality—quite free from introspection or regrets—which distinguishes other works of the time. The fact that it is a tireless obscenity instead of a tireless elegance is beside the point. But Romanticism, with its exacerbated emotions, added a new element, an "hypertrophie de l'imagination et de la sensibilité" as Louis Maigron defines it, of which the fruits were dissatisfaction and ennui.[15] Ennui

---

[14]*Justine et Juliette* (1797), V, 327–8.

[15]Maigron, *Le Romantisme et les mœurs*, Quatrième partie, ch. I, "La Neurasthénie romantique."

dogged it from the beginning like a malignant fate. The first generation of victims, René, Hernani, Bénédict, had their ideals for consolation; but others, and at a comparatively early date, began to look for
a very different panacea—in perverted sensation. The syndrome of
decadence, indeed, may be said to come into existence when the
Marquis de Sade's influence plays on the exhausted sensibility of
Romanticism. As early as 1830-7 the impact of his bloodthirsty erotomania was analysed by Auguste Barbier in his curious volumes,
Iambes, *Il Pianto* and *Lazare*. Considering their dates, they are remarkably complete, and show how soon Romanticism's emotional
debauch began to sour. Ennui, according to Barbier, is the main symptom of this degeneracy; it flourishes best in the great city, Paris, that
"précipice ouvert à la corruption" whose inhabitants are physical and
moral degenerates, seeking relief from boredom in "la moindre occasion de débauche qui passe." Ennui is

> Un mal sans nul remède, une langueur de plomb...
> Un vent qui séchera la vie en un instant...
> Qui la fera déserte, et qui poussera l'homme
> A toutes les fureurs des débauches de Rome.[16]

Taking the form of Spleen it declares that

> C'est moi qui mis l'Asie aux serres d'Alexandre,
> Qui plus tard changeai Rome en un grand tas de cendre,
> Et qui menant son peuple éventrer les lions,
> Sur la pourpre latine enfantai les Nérons.[17]

Its victims turn to drugs, drink, sadism:

> O corrompus! ô vous que mon haleine enivre...
> Je planerai sur vous, et vous aurez beau faire...
> Demeurer, vous enfuir : vous n'échapperez pas...
> Et nous irons ensemble...
> Heurter, tout haletants, le seuil ensanglanté
> De ton temple de bronze, ô froide cruauté![18]

> Du gin! du gin! — à plein verre, garcon!
>
> ....
>
> C'est le soleil, la volupté suprême,
> Le paradis emporté d'un seul coup.[19]

From a theoretical standpoint, this is decadent sensibility fully

[16]"Bianca," dated 1833, *Iambes et poèmes* (Dentu, 1862), 183.
[17]"Le Spleen," dated 1837, *ibid.*, 273.
[18]*Ibid.*, 275. Compare with "Le Campo santo" (1833), 115: "Vous, femmes, que
l'ennui mène à la cruauté."
[19]"Le Gin," *ibid.*, 204-5.

expressed: debauchery, consequent ennui, and consequent search for perversions to relieve the ennui, perversions which recall those of Imperial Rome. Succeeding writers added very little; and the frequent echoes of Barbier's verse in their work (*Les Fleurs du Mal* is the most illustrious example) show how thoroughly he had analysed the subject. Yet, though he describes decadence, he is not himself decadent, especially in intention. He was writing *iambes*, with a satiric and moral purpose. They contrast the purity of nature with the corruptions of the city in good Rousseau style; and they draw attention to the black misery of the industrialized proletariat:

> Puisse cet hymne sombre
> Susciter en tous lieux
> Des avocats sans nombre
> Au peuple noir des gueux![20]

The true decadent nearly emerges as a full-grown character in Sainte-Beuve's *Volupté* (1834). Like the *Iambes*, the book shows how the literary currents were hesitating and changing their course even during the triumph of Romanticism. *Volupté* enchanted such later connoisseurs of decadence as Baudelaire and Verlaine.[21] Its purpose, according to the author, was to analyse "une sorte de langueur rêveuse, attendrie, énervée,"[22] which he calls *volupté*—hence the title—but which is really *impuissance*, that powerless sterility which plays such a role in the history of decadent sensibility and which later, when the doctors had looked at the patient, was to be diagnosed as *aboulie*, a sort of spiritual paraplegia, an inability for any kind of action. Another theme is joined to this: a divorce between spiritual and physical love. The hero Amaury leads a double existence between his ideal passion for the angelic Mme de Couaën ("une vie monotone et subtile, des pages blanches... des amas de commentaires sur un distique gracieux comme dans les jours de décadence"[23]), and orgies with the prostitutes he picks up during his nocturnal promenades in Paris. He reaches a state of emotional exacerbation which produces "une science, la connaissance raffinée du bien et du mal, tantôt dans la mêlée des carrefours, tantôt sur les nuées éthérées."[24] The better to taste this contrast between purity and corruption, he even looks for strumpets whose

[20]"Epilogue," *ibid.*, 289.
[21]Baudelaire's poem to Sainte-Beuve, *Œuvres*, I, 225–7; Verlaine, "Chez soi à l'hôpital": "Ce livre [*Volupté*] est peut-être mieux compris de nos jours que de son temps." *Œuvres posthumes* (Messein), II, 170–6.
[22]*Volupté* (Fasquelle), 394.
[23]*Ibid.*, 59–60.
[24]*Ibid.*, 126–7.

charms have least in common with Mme de Couaën's. He has lost his faith through studying sceptical philosophy (Hobbes and Hume), but he still feels the need of it; and the need takes the form of reading Thomas à Kempis and Bourdaloue to spice up his debauchery![25] The result is an increase of moral impotence: "Ma jeunesse ne fait que commencer aux yeux du monde ... et pourtant le plus beau de sa course est achevé... Mon enfance m'a connu si pur! Que dirait-elle en me voyant si intrigué, si capable de ruse, si sali?... Trop de maivais germes sont chez moi en travail, trop de corruption a entamé mon cœur."[26] To escape from this blind alley, he takes Roman Catholic orders and emigrates to America.

There is certainly more than a hint of decadence about *Volupté*. It has an over-ripe quality, a flavour of the sleepy pear: Amaury's impotence and corruption, developing side by side with a longing for religious faith, were bound to interest writers like Verlaine and Baudelaire. On the other hand, his decadent potentialities are not really developed. His story derives from the sterile philanderings of Adolphe, and his true descendants are less the decadents of the fin-de-siècle than Flaubert's Frédéric Moreau.[27] He is too simple a character to interest Des Esseintes; his basic Romanticism comes out in his ideal love for Mme de Couaën, and, like so many Romantics, he is disgusted with life before tasting it, not blasé in true decadent style: his very ennui, like René's (in whom he recognizes himself "tout entier"[28]), is more distress and personal unhappiness than downright boredom.

We get much closer to the real thing in the poems and novels of Gautier. During the first part of his career, before he took up weight-lifting and began to frequent the Greek rooms in the Louvre, decadent sensibility interested him so much that he did everything he could to imitate it (or rather to initiate it, for it scarcely existed when he began to write). He describes himself in the preface to his *Poésies* (1830) as a "jeune homme frileux et maladif," who spends days on a sofa: "le manteau de la cheminée est son ciel; la plaque, son horizon... Il aime mieux être assis que debout, couché qu'assis." The content of the poems is of a piece with this: the poet's soul has no "fatal" secrets; it is moribund and precociously exhausted: "poussière infecte et noire

[25]*Ibid.*, 196, 215.   [26]*Ibid.*, 200–201.

[27]A number of interesting parallels exist between *Volupté* and *L'Education senti-mentale*: Amaury, for example, becomes Frédéric Moreau; Mme de Couaën, Mme Arnoux; Mlle de Limiers, Louise Roque; Mme R., Mme Dambreuse; the Paris whores, Rosanette. The tone of the two novels, and their respective conclusions, however, are totally different: Sainte-Beuve was designing a complacent portrait of the Romantic temperament, Flaubert was analysing it.

[28]*Volupté*, 157.

ordure, ossements jaunis aux décombres mêlés." Nor is this state, like Amaury's, the result of disappointed love. It comes from ennui: Barbier's abstract ennui is incarnated in a personality. Albertus, in "L'Ame et le péché"—the name, like the D'Albert of *Maupin*, represents Gautier himself—has lost his faith through too much reading and lapsed into pessimism: "L'Amour n'était qu'un mot pour lui... En cherchant il avait usé ses passions... A vingt ans l'on pouvait le clouer dans sa bière, cadavre sans illusions." All idea of revolt is abandoned: the poet accepts and even welcomes his spiritual bankruptcy. Such are the themes of poem after poem: "Le Cavalier poursuivi," "Ténèbres," "Thébaïde," "Le Trou du serpent," "Tristesse," "In Deserto." There is scarcely a "morbid" idea in *Les Fleurs du Mal* that Baudelaire could not have found in Gautier's volumes.

The Chevalier d'Albert (*Mademoiselle de Maupin*, 1834) is a more detailed portrait of the same type. He does not put his decadence into practice to any extent: he has Gautier's love of physical beauty, and the story retells the old Romantic search for an ideal passion. Yet there is throughout a deliberately nurtured corruption which is quite foreign to Romanticism. In his letters to his friend Silvio, D'Albert sketches his past life and explains the state of depravity he has reached. His childhood was chaste and strict, in the bosom of a respectable and ancient family. But: "Dans cette atmosphère de pureté et de repos... je me pourrissais petit à petit... J'étais parvenu à un degré de dépravation horrible... N'est-ce pas là une chose inexplicable qu'un enfant né de parents vertueux... se pervertisse tout seul à un tel point ?... Je ne suis pas de ma famille; je ne suis pas une branche de ce noble tronc, mais un champignon vénéneux, poussé par quelque lourde nuit d'orage."[29] His soul is like an Indian jungle, filled with poisonous flowers and filthy animals;[30] he is the victim of spiritual impotence (*impuissance*) which renders him incapable of any sort of action: "Je ne puis me mêler de rien... Si je veux prendre mon essor, l'air se condense autour de moi, et je reste pris, les ailes étendues sans les pouvoir refermer. Je ne puis ni marcher ni voler."[31] "Sous le premier duvet de l'adolescence, il cachait une corruption profonde," says his mistress Rosette. "Je fus effrayée... le vertige faillit me prendre en me

---

[29]*Mademoiselle de Maupin* (Fasquelle, 1834), 157.
[30]*Ibid.*, 270–1. The "flowers of evil" had begun to sprout long before Babou suggested a title for Baudelaire's volume. Louis Maigron (*Le Romantisme et les mœurs*, 177–8) quotes from the diary of Gustave B., who was twenty-eight years of age in 1845: "Chacun de nous peut être le jardinier de son âme, et il peut faire pousser dans son cœur des fleurs rares, des fleurs tourmentées, des fleurs inquiétantes."
[31]*Maupin*, 268–9.

penchant sur les noires profondeurs de cette existence."[32] The fact that no external cause is proposed to explain this state—no thwarted passion, illegitimate birth, "fatality" of any kind—is very remarkable. D'Albert is in the same sort of psychological condition that Barbier ascribed to Nero: he is satiated with life. Satiety has led to dissatisfaction and ennui, to escape which he longs for enormities: "Je verrais de sang-froid les scènes les plus atroces, et il y a dans les souffrances et dans les malheurs de l'humanité quelque chose qui ne me déplaît pas."[33]

Linked to this sadism is a craving for the *impossible* which Gautier was the first to define as a distinguishing mark of decadent sensibility. Its Roman origins (Caligula and Nero) appear in the following passage:

L'impossible m'a toujours plu. N'est-il pas singulier que moi, qui suis encore aux mois les plus blonds de l'adolescence... j'en sois venu à ce degré de blasement de n'être plus chatouillé que par le bizarre et le difficile?... Qu'un homme qui ne fait que s'asseoir à table... ne puisse toucher sans vomir qu'aux plats d'une saveur extrême et n'aime que les viandes faisandées, les fromages jaspés de bleu?... C'est un phénomène qui ne peut résulter que d'une organisation particulière... Je suis attaqué de cette maladie qui prend aux peuples et aux hommes puissants dans leur vieillesse : — l'impossible... Tibère, Caligula, Néron, grands Romains de l'empire, ô vous que l'on a si mal compris... je souffre de votre mal!... Moi aussi je voudrais bâtir un pont sur la mer... j'ai rêvé de brûler des villes pour illuminer mes fêtes ; j'ai souhaité d'être femme pour connaître de nouvelles voluptés... Néron... Héliogabale... colosses du monde antique, il bat sous mes faibles côtés un cœur aussi grand que le vôtre.[34]

The same theme appears in *Une Nuit de Cléopâtre*, written eleven years later. The Queen's debauchery is described as "cette large et puissante débauche qui ne craint pas de mêler le sang et le vin... ces furieux élans de la volupté inassouvie se ruant à l'impossible."[35] Cleopatra is a typical decadent type, a woman whom boredom has led to sadism; satiated, she is looking for new pleasures in sanguinary depravity. She complains of her ennui to her maid Charmion, who attributes it to the fact that the Queen has not had a new lover *nor had anyone killed* for over a month. "Cléopâtre... demandait un plaisir nouveau, une sensation inconnue... Elle songeait que le nombre des sens est bien borné... Essayer des poisons sur des esclaves, faire battre des hommes avec des tigres... tout cela est fade et commun.[36] Like

32*Ibid.*, 172. 33*Ibid.*, 197.
34*Ibid.*, 153–155. 35*Nouvelles* (Lemerre, 1898), 494–5.
36*Ibid.*, 473–4.

D'Albert's interest in Caligula, Nero, and Heliogabalus, this is decadent time-exoticism as opposed to the Romantic variety: Romanticism
sought distant lands and epochs because they were more picturesque
than the nineteenth century; Gautier seeks them because they are
more corrupt.

This search for historic decadence is another symptom of *impuissance*; it suggests an interest in abnormal eroticism as we find (in
relatively anodyne form, it is true) in D'Albert's relations with Rosette.
For D'Albert is no longer interested in humdrum sensuality; he must
have something spicier to stir his jaded palate: "J'ai eu ma maîtresse
au bain... la nuit, au clair de lune, dans une gondole avec de la
musique... dans sa voiture lancée au grand galop, au milieu du bruit
des roues, des sauts et des cahots... Je suis entré chez elle par la fenêtre,
ayant la clef dans ma poche. Je l'ai fait venir chez moi en plein jour."[37]
There is a hint of waning sexual power in these eccentricities; they
are part of a strong tendency in D'Albert towards perversion; a tendency which assumed such gigantic proportions in the novels of fifty
years later.

To wish to become a woman in order to taste new pleasures, and
then to refer to Nero and Heliogabalus, is a discreet way (not so very
discreet either) of admitting homosexual tendencies; and in fact
homosexuality is one of the principal themes of much of Gautier's
work. It springs partly from his cult of art, which makes the enjoyment
of any kind of beauty legitimate, and partly from his interest in the
artificial, the unnatural, the anti-natural, the abnormal. Nearly all his
heroes are androgynous; and when we consider the role played by the
androgyne in the literature of the end of the century, this is extremely
significant. Fortunio, despite his herculean strength, has a face of
feminine purity; his eyelids look as though he had touched them with
paint, his arms are like those of Antinous, he looks like the Indian
Bacchus, etc. Ctésias (in *La Chaîne d'or*) is as beautiful as Hyacinthe,
and his legs would make Diana herself jealous. The same ambiguous
charm distinguishes Meiamoun (*Une Nuit de Cléopâtre*): he joins
"la beauté de la femme à la force de l'homme."[38] This preoccupation
with the androgynous even appears in Gautier's portraits of his
friends: Baudelaire's neck was white and smooth as a woman's;[39]
Celestin Nanteuil had "ce sexe indécis de l'éphèbe et de la jeune
fille";[40] the singer Fanny Elssler is described twice, and each time she
is compared with the Hermaphrodite of the Louvre, that "ravissante

[37]*Maupin*, 101–2.   [38]*Nouvelles*, 468.
[39]"Notice," ii.   [40]*Histoire du Romantisme*, 47.

chimère de l'art grec."[41] The statue even inspired a poem in *Emaux et camées*, "Contralto," which sums up Gautier's interest in this type of beauty. It was written in 1849 and dedicated (a curious detail) to his mistress, Ernesta Grisi:

> Chimère ardente, effort suprême
> De l'art et de la volupté,
> Monstre charmant, comme je t'aime
> Avec ta multiple beauté!

In *Mademoiselle de Maupin* this vaguely aesthetic treatment becomes open homosexuality. The book is almost an apology for sexual inversion, both male and female, written a century before *The Well of Loneliness* or *Corydon*. From first to last, even when the subject is not actually under discussion, it is implied. Ambiguous situations abound: the plot is highly scabrous, dealing as it does with transvestitism. Even before D'Albert falls in love with what he believes to be a man, he has inverted tendencies, as his remarks on Nero and Heliogabalus show. His intense self-consciousness, a Romantic trait, but pushed in his case beyond the bounds of conventional Romanticism, leads him to elaborate these desires: "J'ai commencé par avoir envie d'être un autre homme; puis, faisant réflexion que je pouvais, par l'analogie, prévoir à peu près ce que je sentirais, et alors ne pas éprouver la surprise et le changement attendus, j'aurais préféré d'être femme... Aux instants de plaisirs j'aurais volontiers changé de rôle."[42] It is difficult to see how a perverted tendency could be expressed more clearly. True enough, when he finds himself on the way to realizing his wish by falling in love with a "man" (Mlle de Maupin disguised as Théodore de Serannes), he is horrified; but the horror sounds false somehow, as though it had been affected for benefit of the censor: "Quel malheur... quelle passion insensée, coupable et odieuse... J'ai horreur de moi-même," etc. The situation could be amusing, a quid pro quo of the *Charlie's Aunt* order, if Gautier did not lead D'Albert into a long justification of homosexuality. The argument is a further development of the cult of form; the connection between Gautier's neo-pagan aestheticism and homosexuality is very clear: "Ce qui est beau physiquement est bien, tout ce qui est laid est mal." "Comme on ne cherche que la satisfaction de l'œil, le poli de la forme et la pureté du linéament, on les accepte partout où on les rencontre. C'est ce qui

---

[41]*Souvenirs de théâtre, d'art et de critique* (Charpentier), 53, 130. The essays on Fanny Elssler are dated 1838 and 1844.
[42]*Maupin*, 100.

explique les singulières abérrations de l'amour antique." Before the
time of Christ, "on ne féminisait pas les dieux ou les héros que l'on
voulait faire séduisants... on faisait plus volontiers revenir à ce caractère
la beauté spéciale de la femme." "Ces amours étranges dont sont
pleines les élégies des poètes anciens... sont donc vraisemblables et
possibles. Dans les traductions... nous mettions des noms de femme
à la place de ceux qui y étaient... Les beaux garçons devenaient de belles
filles... C'était une forte galante occupation qui prouvait seulement
combien peu nous avions compris le génie antique."[43] This last quotation leads in a passage often quoted to illustrate Gautier's love of Greek
beauty and his devotion to classical art, form, and plastic perfection.
But that is only part of its significance. *In the context* it is a confession
of homosexuality, suggesting as it does that D'Albert had not mis-
understood the Greek genius: "Je suis un homme des temps homéri-
ques... Le Christ n'est pas venu pour moi; je suis aussi païen qu'Alcibiade et Phidias... ma chair n'entend point qu'on la mortifie."[44] Having
thus written a justification of pederasty, D'Albert is saved from putting
it into practice when Mlle de Maupin confesses to him that she is a
woman. But if he is thus spared a lapse into perversion, she herself
makes the full voyage to Lesbos. The novel is like a diptych:
pederasty on one side, Lesbianism on the other. Disguised as Théodore
de Serannes, Mlle de Maupin arrives at Rosette's château with a page.
Once in her room, she proceeds to undress the page, contemplates his
feet with admiration, kisses them, etc., all of which the page submits
to without surprise, which suggests that these caresses were habitual.[45]
However we look at this scene, it is homosexual: Serannes and the
page are dressed as men, yet, as we soon discover, both are women.
This motif is developed steadily through Rosette's passion for the
supposed Théodore. She has long been attracted by the Chevalier, and
shows considerable address in cornering "him" in isolated nooks. These
impromptu rendezvous are far from being unpleasant to Mlle de
Maupin. "Cet ardent désir m'échauffait de sa flamme," she writes of
one encounter, "et j'étais réellement fâchée de ne le pouvoir satisfaire;
je souhaitais même d'être un homme... afin de couronner cet amour."[46]
This wish corresponds to D'Albert's desire to become a woman. "Un
frisson me courut tout le long du corps," she writes of another occasion, "et les pointes de mes seins se dressèrent." "Je l'aimais réellement
beaucoup, et plus qu'une femme n'aime une femme... Je sentais une
grande volupté à parcourir ces formes pures et délicates... J'aurais, si

[43]*Ibid.*, 221, 223–5, 210.   [44]*Ibid.*, 210.
[45]*Ibid.*, 161.   [46]*Ibid.*, 338.

je n'avais craint de trahir mon incognito, laissé un champ libre aux élans passionnés de Rosette."[47] She concludes: "Beaucoup d'hommes sont plus femmes que moi... Je suis d'un troisième sexe à part qui n'a pas encore de nom... Ma chimère serait d'avoir tour à tour les deux sexes pour satisfaire à cette double nature : homme aujourd'hui, femme demain."[48] The book ends with a sapphic consummation between her and Rosette which, however discreetly veiled, is sufficiently explicit.[49]

The semi-historical character, Madelaine d'Aubigny, Madame (and not Mademoiselle de) Maupin, upon whose exploits Gautier based his novel, was well-suited as heroine for a romance dealing with sexual inversion. She was a seventeenth-century Chevalier d'Éon: dressed now as a man, now as a woman; had numerous love-affairs with both sexes, including an elopement with a Duc de Luynes, whom she had wounded in a duel, and an escapade with a nun; sang a role at the Paris opera (Campra's *Tancrède*, 1709) in an "ambiguous" contralto, etc. What is particularly interesting in Gautier's book, however, is less its actual borrowings from Madelaine d'Aubigny's chequered career, than the use of her legend to expound the author's own passion for plastic beauty—which takes the form of Mlle de Maupin's apology for Lesbianism and D'Albert's justification of pederasty. The novel's enormous vogue during the last three or four decades of the century (it was almost required reading for Péladan's characters) proves how thoroughly Gautier had anticipated and analysed the *fin-de-siècle's* interest in androgynism and perversion.[50]

Its influence, indeed, is traceable long before the eighties and nineties, in such works as Flaubert's *Œuvres de jeunesse*, where the passions of Romanticism are already beginning to fester. Had Flaubert not been caught up later by the great tradition of French realism, he might have ended with novels very different from *Madame Bovary* and *L'Education sentimentale. Novembre* (written in 1841–2) is in

[47]*Ibid.*, 339; 368–9.
[48]*Ibid.*, 398–9.
[49]*Ibid.*, 417.
[50]"*Mlle de Maupin* è responsabile.... della voga per l'Androgino che assumera proporzioni allarmanti solo nella seconda parte del secolo. Nel buon Théo l'eventuale accenno a motivi cruenti non era che posa, ma non era posa l'attrazione pel fascino equivoco di Lesbo." Praz, *La Carne*, 184. The sexual inversion of *Maupin* did not escape the notice of contemporaries. Louis Ménard, reviewing *Les Fleurs du Mal* in 1857, noted that if Baudelaire had treated Lesbianism, he had neglected pederasty—because he lacked Gautier's courage: "il n'a pas l'audace de son vénéré maître, l'auteur de *Mademoiselle de Maupin*." Quoted by J. Crépet in the Conard edition of the *Fleurs du Mal*, 363.

many ways a typical piece of Romanticism—the hero refers to "la fatalité qui m'avait courbé dès ma jeunesse,"[51] but the state of mind it reveals is quite distinct from René's. The hero is "las de vivre, las de désirer et las d'être dégoûté, las d'attendre et las d'avoir,"[52] a prey to sterility and boredom: "Je restais sans mouvement, aussi inerte qu'une statue";[53] his soul, like D'Albert's (the passage is almost certainly an echo of *Maupin*), is like an Indian forest, filled with monstrous plants and animals; he has no religious faith; he was born with a desire to die, resigned to be bored everywhere and bored by everything. "Usé par l'ennui, il n'ouvrait plus sa fenêtre pour respirer l'air, il ne se lavait plus les mains... la même chemise lui servait une semaine," etc. To relieve this tedium, he indulges in brandy and opium or meditates on becoming a Catholic priest. All these details are autobiographical, as is proved by numerous passages in Flaubert's letters; and as usual, this persistent boredom produces a desire for enormities: "Il me prit contre la vie, contre les hommes, contre tout, une rage sans nom... Je devins plus féroce que les tigres; j'aurais voulu anéantir la création et m'endormir avec elle dans l'infini du néant; que ne me réveillais-je à la lueur des villes incendiées! J'aurais voulu entendre le frémissement des ossements que la flamme fait pétiller... être Gengiskan, Tamerlan, Néron, effrayer le monde au froncement de mes sourcils."[54] The fact that a man between the ages of seventeen and twenty-one could shut himself up with such reveries is symptomatic of much; the reference to Nero is particularly significant, and is by no means isolated: Flaubert had something of a cult for the emperor. "C'était Rome que j'aimais," we read elsewhere, "la Rome impériale, cette belle reine se roulant dans l'orgie, salissant ses nobles vêtements du vin de la débauche, plus fière de ses vices qu'elle ne l'était de ses vertus. Néron! Néron, avec ses chars de diamant... ses amours de tigre... Je me reportais vers tes immenses voluptés, tes illuminations sanglantes, tes divertissements qui brûlent Rome."[55] And again: "Vous ne rêverez rien de si terrible et de si monstrueux que les dernières heures de l'Empire; c'est là le règne du crime... il se farde encore pour être plus beau... Les imaginations de dix grands poètes ne créeraient pas quelque chose qui vaudrait cinq minutes de la vie de Néron...

[51]"Novembre," *Œuvres complètes de Gustave Flaubert, Premières œuvres* (Edition du Centenaire, Librairie de France, 1923), 397.
[52]*Ibid.*, 390.
[53]*Ibid.*, 393.
[54]*Ibid.*, 397.
[55]"Mémoires d'un fou" (1838), 281–2.

Tibère, le premier, est atteint du malaise intime qui torture les entrailles de la société à ses vieux jours."[56] "Ils s'appelaient Caligula, Néron, Domitien... on égorge des hommes pendant qu'ils s'enivrent... Le crime est une volupté comme les autres... Néron... penché en avant sur les poitrines ouvertes des victimes, regardait le sang battre dans les cœurs, et il trouvait, dans ces derniers gémissements... des délices inconnues, des voluptés suprêmes... Oh! les âmes sublimes dans le crime! Ils insultent à la nature dans leurs débauches... Ils assassinent leurs mères, ils épousent leurs valets."[57] The same note sounds in *Passion et vertu* (1838), which is particularly interesting because it gives us the first sketch of Emma Bovary, and shows from what kind of soil Flaubert's later masterpieces sprang. The heroine, Mazza Willer, is a Romantic who loves "la poésie, le théâtre, la mer, Byron"; but her latent degeneracy comes out in an adultery with Ernest Vaumont (a name obviously derived from Laclos). Their rendezvous leave her unsatisfied: she wants "une plus vaste jouissance, car elle avait une soif inépuisable d'amours infinies, de passions sans bornes." Dissatisfaction leads to ennui, and ennui—the familiar pattern—to perversions. "Il y avait chez elle... une telle soif de délices et de voluptés... qu'elle aurait voulu faire sortir son amour des bornes de la nature."[58] She seeks inspiration for her perversity in the atmosphere of Paris: "Il y avait dans les grandes cités une atmosphère corrompue et empoisonnée... quelque chose de lourd et de malsain, comme ces sombres brouillards du soir qui planent sur les toits. Mazza aspira cet air de corruption à pleine poitrine, elle le sentit comme un parfum, et la première fois, alors, elle comprit tout ce qu'il y avait de large et d'immense dans le vice, et de voluptueux dans le crime."[59]

Any of these passages would fit without difficulty into the novels of fifty years later. "Faire sortir son amour des bornes de la nature" is the rule of the characters of Mendès and Rachilde: Flaubert's youthful efforts prove how sultry the literary climate had become by the late thirties—it even corrupted an earnest adolescent living in Rouen. Fifteen years afterwards, he rewrote Mazza as Emma Bovary; and it is extraordinary how much of the first heroine survives in the second.

[56]"Rome et les Césars" (1839), 337, 338.
[57]*Ibid.*, 339.
[58]"Passion et vertu," 217.
[59]*Ibid.*, 224–5. Coming from the Flaubert of 1838 (a Romantic adolescent if ever there was one) this exclamation shows how much the "decadent" view of Paris owes to Romanticism. Flaubert reached a much saner appreciation in *L'Education sentimentale* (Conard, 148), thirty years later: "Frédéric l'aspira de toutes ses forces, ce bon air de Paris qui semble contenir des effleuves amoureux et des émanations intellectuelles; il eut un attendrissement en apercevant le premier fiacre."

Emma's disappointments in marriage, her sophistication, her sloven-
liness (during her last days at Tostes she spends weeks in her room,
without dressing, without moving, making the tongs red hot and
watching the rain falling), her craving for new and keener pleasures,
above all her adultery with Léon, in which every trace of the poetic
veil she had spread over her affair with Rodolphe falls away: "Léon...
devenait sa maîtresse plutôt qu'elle n'était la sienne... Où donc avait-
elle appris cette corruption, presque immatérielle à force d'être profonde et dissimulée ?"[60] All this, besides looking backward to Mazza
and even Mme de Merteuil, looks forward to the madwomen of the
eighties and nineties. Later decadents recognized the affinities. Ernest
Raynaud in an article "Les Origines du mouvement décadent" (Le
Décadent, 15 janvier 1889) called Emma "un système nerveux,
malade, détraqué," a prototype of the females of contemporary fiction.
Baudelaire (in 1857) pointed out how her lust for domination, her
dandyism, raised her above the "animal level" of the ordinary woman:
she unites, in fact (and the same is true of Mazza, whose lover abandons her for the same reasons that Léon deserted Emma), the two
types of Romantic, the languid and the dynamic, and turns them into
something which approaches neurosis and decadence. The fact that
she is the heroine of a great novel, and not the spectral vampire of a
penny-dreadful is a proof of Flaubert's genius: without it he would
almost certainly have foundered in those literary swamps which
claimed so many victims from 1830 on. The man who wrote Novembre
could sit down for thirty years to analyse his own hypertrophied sensibility in novels like Madame Bovary, L'Education sentimentale and
Bouvard et Pécuchet—this is perhaps the greatest tribute French
classic realism has ever received.

A full discussion of the decadent potentialities of the dandy was
first made by Barbey d'Aurevilly in 1844. Dandyism, he says, "est
toute une manière d'être, entièrement composée de nuances, comme il
arrive dans les sociétés très vieilles et très civilisées ... où la convenance
triomphe à peine de l'ennui":[61] it is the fruit of corruption, born at
the court of Charles II as a protest against the rigours of Puritanism.
The dandy is surfeited and indifferent; he has had all the experiences,
and become "trop dégoûté pour s'animer." He seeks to astonish the
vulgar, but he has no passions: they would destroy his balance; a true
dandy must remain cold. Dandyism is another form of artificiality, a
flower that grows in the hot-houses of an advanced civilization, "ces

[60]Madame Bovary (Conard), 383–4.
[61]Du dandysme et de G. Brummel (Lemerre), 24–5.

salons où la richesse, le loisir, et le dernier degré de civilisation pro-
duisent des affectations charmantes qui ont remplacé le naturel."[62] It
is the product of a society in decadence, a society "horriblement blasée,
savante, en proie à toutes les fatigues des vieilles civilisations." The
very success of a dandy like Brummell proves how "refined" and
"secretly corrupt" his age was: "Est-ce que la grâce simple, naïve,
spontanée, serait un stimulant assez fort pour remuer ce monde épuisé
de sensations?"[63] As we shall see in chapter v, Barbey uses the same
terms to justify the dandy as Gautier used to excuse the risqué tone of
Maupin and *Les Fleurs du Mal*.[64] For that matter, the idea that the
nineteenth century was growing more and more corrupt had become
extremely popular. We find it in some of Stendhal's novels; men like
Julien Sorel and Lucien Leuwen, with their domination of women
and their cold detachment, are perfect dandies. Lucien also has a
taste for corruption which is very *fin-de-siècle*: tired of France, he
thinks of emigrating to America, but gives up the idea because
America is too virtuous. "Je préférerais cent fois les mœurs élégantes
d'une cour corrompue... Washington m'eût ennuyé à la mort, et
j'aime mieux me trouver dans le même salon que M. de Talleyrand...
J'ai besoin des plaisirs donnés par une ancienne civilisation... Il me
faut les mœurs élégantes, fruits du gouvernement corrompu de
Louis XV."[65] This preference for the corrupt is streaked with religious
tendencies which, in more favourable circumstances, were to produce
that mixture of brothels and confessionals so characteristic of Huysmans and Verlaine. "Quand on possède une âme comme la mienne, à
la fois faible et impossible à contenter," meditates Lucien, "on va se
jeter à la Trappe."[66]

Dandy and decadent are fused in Baudelaire's work and life. He
affected an English coldness and reserve, and a sobriety of dress which
was in contrast with the ebullience of the contemporary Bohemia. His
conception of the dandy, as he admits,[67] was based on Stendhal and
D'Aurevilly; and he saw the two artists he admired most, Delacroix
and Poe, as examples of the type. Both despised the democratic and
progressive theories of their age, and both, beneath a philosophic calm,
nourished an ardent passion for art and beauty.[68] Dandyism thus

---

[62]*Ibid.*, 54.   [63]*Ibid.*, 95–6.
[64]*Maupin*, préface, 15; *Les Grotesques*, préface, ix–x; *Les Poètes français*, IV,
595–6; "Notice," xv–xvi. I have quoted these passage, *infra*, 125 *et seq.*
[65]*Lucien Leuwen* (N.R.F.), I, 92–5.   [66]*Ibid.*, II, 472 and 511, 599.
[67]"Le Salon de 1846," *Œuvres*, II, 134; "Delacroix," *ibid.*, 309.
[68]"Delacroix," *Œuvres*, II, 309–10; "Notes nouvelles sur Edgar Poe," *Œuvres*
complètes (Conard), V, viii.

becomes, as D'Aurevilly had suggested, something more than a nice taste in dress. It is an affirmation of superiority, a moral prophylaxis which saves soul and intellect from contamination: "C'est le plaisir d'étonner et la satisfaction orgueilleuse de ne jamais être étonné." "C'est une gymnastique propre à fortifier la volonté et à discipliner l'âme."[69] It derives from Byron and the Satanic aspects of the fatal man; for the dandy, like Satan, however frustrated by circumstances, keeps his will intact and commands both himself and his environment. Dandyism and Satanism are thus closely allied; the unbroken determination of Milton's Satan was, for Baudelaire, a proof of dandyism; Baudelaire's thought describes a rigorous parabola between cosmetics, dandyism and Satan. The "modern heroism" he describes is itself a form of dandyism—the heroism of a decadence: "Le dandysme apparaît surtout aux époques transitoires... Dans le trouble de ces époques, quelques hommes déclassés, dégoûtés, désœuvrés, mais tous riches de forces natives, peuvent concevoir le projet de fonder une espèce nouvelle d'aristocratie... Le dandysme est le dernier éclat d'héroïsme dans les décadences... Un soleil couchant, superbe, sans chaleur et plein de mélancolie."[70]

Dandyism is thus a positive reaction against the frustrations of nineteenth-century life, turning on occasion into sadism and Satanism; *impuissance* and sterility are the negative reactions. Baudelaire wrote both these aspects of the matter into his own work. Samuel Cramer, in *La Fanfarlo* (1847), besides having points of resemblance with D'Albert and Amaury, carries decadent sensibility to an almost *fin-de-siècle* point. He loves the impossible: "Il n'a jamais réussi à rien, parce qu'il croyait trop à l'impossible. — Quoi d'étonnant? Il était toujours en train de le concevoir."[71] He is a victim of *impuissance*: "Samuel fut...l'homme des belles œuvres ratées; — créature maladive et fantastique... qui... m'est toujours apparu comme le dieu de l'impuissance, — dieu moderne et hermaphrodite, — impuissance colossale et si énorme qu'elle en est épique!"[72] "Les enfants maladifs qui sortent d'un amour mourant," he tells Mme de Cosmelly of himself, "sont la triste débauche et la hideuse impuissance."[73] He takes a morbid delight in his own corruption, through a sort of depraved cerebralism, itself a sign of decadence: "Nous nous sommes tellement appliqués à sophistiquer notre cœur, nous avons tant abusé du microscope pour étudier les hideuses excroissances et les honteuses verrues dont il est couvert...

[69]"Le Peintre de la vie moderne," *Œuvres*, II, 340; 350–1.
[70]*Ibid.*, 350–1.   [71]*La Fanfarlo*, *Œuvres*, I, 529.
[72]*Ibid.*, 527.   [73]*Ibid.*, 536–7.

qu'il est impossible que nous parlions le langage des autres hommes.
Ils vivent pour vivre, et nous, hélas! nous vivons pour savoir. Tout le
mystère est là." "Samuel fut une imagination dépravée, et, à cause de
cela même, l'amour était chez lui moins une affaire des sens que du
raisonnement."[74] Amaury spiced his sexual promiscuity with Thomas
à Kempis and Bourdaloue, Samuel reads Swedenborg and pornography, volumes of which lie side by side on his desk. Baudelaire's
tastes were very similar. Samuel writes sonnets to one mistress as a
Muse and a Madonna, to another as a symbol of vice: Baudelaire did
the same in his relations with Mme Sabatier and Jeanne Duval. *La
Fanfarlo*, in short, gives us decadent sensibility, particularly its two
alternatives, the positive and the negative, with remarkably lucidity.
Its tone is ironic—strangely so; there was always a detached, critical
intelligence in Baudelaire, examining the ecstasies and the passions
and the poses with a clear eye. Yet the fact remains: he spent the best
of his talent developing and describing the sensibility he had analysed
in Cramer. He notes *impuissance* as one of the main characteristics
of Poe's psychological studies,[75] and it occupies a large place in *Les
Fleurs du Mal*, appearing now as complete despair, a cessation of all
hope and all desire ("La Cloche fêlée," "L'Ennemi," "Le Mauvais
Moine"), now as ennui, to escape which the victim turns to drugs,
sadism and Satanism.

The positive and negative reactions, as can be seen, are closely
allied; and the way Baudelaire popularized them is of great importance, if only because his genius enabled him to put them over better
than Gautier, Sainte-Beuve or Barbier had done. This lyric presenta-
tion of despair and evil certainly explains, at least in part, the strange
fascination of *Les Fleurs du mal*. It is, after all, one of the elements
of human experience, as authentic as Browning's muscular optimism;
it invades and penetrates the reader, so that Baudelaire's admirers are
much more addicts than disciples: his poetry is like one of those drugs
which alters the faculties, adding depth and colour to normal vision,
distorting subtly the perspectives of everyday experience, so that the
patient never sees them in quite the old way again.

This curious sorcery may very well be the determining factor in
Baudelaire's literary immortality. The efforts that have been made
in France and elsewhere this past half-century to fit him into a classical
or traditional pattern are doubtless legitimate enough; it is good to
know that he was something more than an eccentric. But fortunately

---

[74]*Ibid.*, 534, 554.
[75]"Edgar Poe, sa vie et ses œuvres," *Œuvres complètes* (Conard), IV, xxviii–xxix.

for Baudelaire they will never succeed entirely. He was somewhat unhealthy; it is part of his charm; it saves him from being banal. His chapel is made for the half-light and the shadow; an opalescent miasma lies over *Les Fleurs du Mal*; we brush it away, it is so tenuous that it can scarcely be seen, like a shade on the edge of the retina; but it is always there, impregnating poem after poem and the effect can hardly be called classical or Catholic or Jansenist.

In "Au Lecteur" ennui, the work of Satan, leads to sadism: "l'œil chargé d'un pleur involontaire, / Il rêve d'échafauds"; ennui explains the sadism of the poet's mistress: "L'ennui rend ton âme cruelle... Il te faut chaque jour un cœur au râtelier." Barbier's verse about "femmes que l'ennui mène à la cruauté" is here elaborated into a whole poem. To relieve his ennui, the poet threatens Jeanne Duval with a sado-masochistic orgy ("L'Héautontimorouménos"):

> Je te frapperai sans colère
> Et sans haine, comme un boucher...
>
> Je suis la plaie et le couteau !
> Je suis le soufflet et la joue !
> Je suis les membres et la roue !
> Et la victime et le bourreau !

The same idea forms the basis of "A Celle qui est trop gaie," where cruelty is called in as a relief from *atonie*. In "La Destruction," Satan conducts the poet to ennui and thence to sadism; the corpse described in "Une Martyre" had known ennui and, as a result, sexual perversions; the young king in the third "Spleen" is bored, and can therefore find pleasure in nothing—not even in the wholesale execution of his subjects and the blood-baths of Roman decadence. Satanism flourishes in such poems as "L'Irrémédiable," which lists the symbols of frustration: a fallen angel, men bewitched or damned, ships frozen in the ice, etc., all of them the work of Satan, and the solution lies in acknowledging the power of Evil:

> Tête-à-tête sombre et limpide,
> Qu'un cœur devenu son miroir !
> Puits de Vérité, clair et noir,
> Où tremble une étoile livide.
>
> Un phare ironique, infernal,
> Flambeau des graces sataniques,
> Soulagement et gloire uniques,
> — La conscience dans le Mal !

Such also is the solution proposed in "Le Reniement de Saint-Pierre":

the worship of Satan is a means of escape from "un monde où l'action n'est pas la sœur du rêve." Durtal and his friend Des Hermies were later to endorse this judgment.

Dandyism, perversion, Satanism: a fourth form of evasion lies in drugs—they supply their addicts with a means to "emporter le Paradis d'un seul coup," as Baudelaire says, quoting Barbier.[76] Drug-addiction, like Satanism, is a "dépravation du sens de l'infini," another result of frustration, the frustration of man's dual nature, drawn between the extremes of absolute good and absolute evil. Baudelaire thought that modern man was especially liable to this type of psychosis because of his ill-balanced emotional state: he is a creature of nerves, subject to mental and moral disease: "Un tempérament moitié nerveux, moitié bilieux, tel est le plus favorable aux évolutions d'une pareille ivresse; ajoutons un esprit cultivé, exercé aux études de la forme et de la couleur; un cœur tendre, fatigué par le malheur... des fautes anciennes... une nature facilement excitable... Le goût de la métaphysique, la connaisance des différentes hypothèses de la philosophie sur la destinée humaine... Une grande finesse de sens... [et] je crois que j'ai rassemblé les éléments généraux les plus communs de l'homme sensible moderne."[77] Modern women, as depicted by Delacroix, are essentially of the same order: "Elles portent dans les yeux un secret douloureux... Leur pâleur est comme une révélation des batailles intérieures... Ces femmes malades du cœur ou de l'esprit ont dans les yeux le plombé de la fièvre ou la nitescence anormale et bizarre de leur mal..."[78] Nineteenth-century humanity, in a word, is sickly; Baudelaire contrasts it with the physical perfection of Greek antiquity and describes its degeneracy with relish:

> O pauvres corps tordus, maigres, ventrus ou flasques,
> Que le dieu de l'Utile, implacable et serein,
> Enfants, emaillota dans ses langes d'airain!
> Et vous, femmes, hélas! pâles comme des cierges,
> Que ronge et que nourrit la débauche, et vous vierges,
> Du vice maternel traînant l'hérédité
> Et toutes les hideurs de la fécondité!
>
> Nous avons, il est vrai, nations corrompues,
> Aux peuples anciens des beautés inconnues :
> Des visages rongés par les chancres du cœur,
> Et comme qui dirait des beautés de langueur...

---

[76]Les Paradis artificiels, Œuvres, I, 275.
[77]Ibid., 304–5.
[78]"L'Exposition universelle de 1855," Œuvres, II, 161–2.

Another of Baudelaire's contributions to decadent sensibility must be mentioned, although it belongs more properly to the realm of comparative literature—his translations of Poe, more especially of stories like *Morella, Ligeia, Berenice,* and *The Fall of the House of Usher.* The characters of those tales are very complete types of the phenomenon; they bear an unmistakable similarity to early examples like D'Albert and Amaury, and, owing to the popularity of Poe in France (at least as Baudelaire had translated him), they had much influence on the *fin-de-siècle.* Roderick Usher, Morella, Ligeia, and Egaeus are all the last scions of ancient and decayed families; they live in crumbling ancestral mansions, are prodigies of learning (generally of an esoteric and mystical kind), and spend days on end in their libraries; and most of them suffer from some variety of mental or nervous disease—epilepsy or catalepsy—which leads them to perversion and insanity. Their ancient lineage is sometimes called in to explain this incipient madness; and the atmosphere is charged with an intellectual (as distinct from emotional) perversity which is entirely decadent. Egaeus's necro-sadism is the best example: "Dans l'étrange anomalie de mon existence," he says, "les sentiments ne me sont *jamais* venus du cœur, et mes passions sont *toujours* venues de l'esprit."[79] These studies in degeneracy fascinated Baudelaire. He first read Poe in 1846 or 1847, at about the time he was writing *La Fanfarlo*; it is very probable that Samuel Cramer's eccentricities owe something to Poe—certainly Egaeus's phrase and the definition of Samuel as an "imagination dépravée" are of the same order. Baudelaire may also have been thinking of Egaeus, Usher and the rest when he wrote in his diary: "Mes ancêtres, idiots ou maniaques, dans des appartements solennels, tous victimes de terribles passions":[80] the phrase, at any rate, recalls Usher's house or the bridal chamber in *Ligeia.* For it is almost certain that Baudelaire's ancestry contained nothing so terrible. His father, François Baudelaire (1759–1827), was an eighteenth-century philosophe, a friend of Cabanis and Condorcet, the descendant of a line of farmers and peasants. As for Caroline Aupick (his mother), aside from the fact that she died of general paralysis (a not uncommon fate), there is no evidence that her antecedents were anything but unexceptionable.

Hippolyte Taine's conception of decadence, like his views on artificiality, is remarkably akin to Baudelaire's, and shows how general the

---

[79]"Bérénice," *Œuvres complètes* (Conard), V, 83. Cf. with Samuel Cramer, "l'amour était chez lui moins une affaire des sens que du raisonnement."
[80]"Fusées," *Œuvres* (Pléiade), II, 636.

idea of the nineteenth century's corruption had become by 1850; it was no longer a whim of the lunatic fringe of contemporary letters. Taine's reputation nowadays is somewhat austere and dusty; he survives as the author of *De l'intelligence*, of the *Histoire de la littérature anglaise*, (or rather, of one sentence in the preface to that work, a sentence about vice and virtue, sulphuric acid and sugar), and of the respectably solid *Origines de la France contemporaine*. But in others of his books, particularly the early ones (*Lafontaine et ses Fables*, 1853, *Essais de critique et d'histoire*, 1855–60, *Graindorge*, 1867), he showed a marked taste for the more alluring aspects of decadence, and did much to fix it as a formula.

Decadence, he thought, was characteristic of modern man, the victim of too much culture.

Quand on a trop longtemps regardé l'homme on ne souhaite plus de le regarder... Il est trop intelligent, il a trop travaillé... Chez lui rien n'est donné, tout est acquis. Chaque geste, chaque trait de visage, chaque pli d'un vêtement rappelle un labeur immense: nous sommes opprimés sous le poids de notre expérience... Il n'y a pas jusqu'aux petits enfants qui par la finesse de leurs traits, de leurs proportions... n'indiquent les altérations profondes que la civilisation a fait descendre des individus dans le type. L'homme aujourd'hui ressemble à ces grandes capitales qui sont les chefs-d'œuvre et les nourrices de sa pensée et de son industrie; le pavé y couvre la terre, les maisons offusquent le ciel, les lumières artificielles effacent la nuit, les inventions ingénieuses et laborieuses encombrent les rues, les visages actifs et flétris se pressent le long des vitrines; les souterrains, les égouts, les quais, les palais, les arcs de triomphe, l'entassement des machines étalent et multiplient le magnifique et douloureux spectacle de la nature maîtrisée et défigurée. Nous en voulons sortir. Nous sommes las de ces coûteuses merveilles.[81]

A cat or a goose is better off ("au fond, toutes les bêtes sont nobles") because it is simple, happier and better balanced than man, who must bear the yoke of civilization: "Leur cou ne porte pas les marques de la déformation que nous impose le métier, ni des flétrissures dont nous salit l'expérience. S'ils [the cat and the goose] sont plus bornés, ils sont plus purs."[82] Man's ills result from his own culture; he cherishes the memory of primitive nature like a lost paradise. Nature reposes and refreshes his soul; the intellect has led him into a kind of slavery. Taine, for all his intelligence, never perceived that he was writing the reductio ad absurdum of Rousseau's ideas: "Ces objets," he says, by which he means Nature, "sont affranchis de la forme, comme la plante est affranchie de la pensée, comme l'animal est

[81]*Lafontaine et ses fables* (Hachette), 168–9.   [82]*Ibid.*, 171.

affranchi de la raison. A mesure que l'on descend d'un degré, l'être devient plus libre."[83]

La Vie et Opinions de M. Frédéric Thomas Graindorge (which began to appear as *Notes sur Paris* in January 1863) elaborates these theories under a thin fictional disguise. Graindorge is a Frenchman who made a fortune in salt pork and oil in the United States and retired to France to finish his days. The book is thus constructed on the same principle as the *contes* of Voltaire and Montesquieu, where a Persian or a Chinese comes to judge French society. Graindorge examines the Paris of Napoleon III from a half-American point of view, and finds it over-civilized, artificial and decadent. There are a number of comparisons, *à la* Lucien Leuwen, between the hyper-refinement of the Parisians and the primitive vigour of the Americans; and while Taine was too subtle to write unreserved praise of the Noble Savage, such praise is implied. "Trop de travail et trop de plaisirs," says Graindorge after an evening at the theatre: "Paris est une serre surchauffée, aromatique et empestée, un terreau âcre et concentré, qui brûle et durcit l'homme." The women produced by the city are contemporary versions of Gautier's Cleopatra: "Des Cléopâtres; la pourriture et la culture égyptiennes faisaient pousser, il y a dix-huit siècles, des fleurs aussi enivrantes et aussi splendides, aussi maladives et aussi dangereuses que ce terreau parisien où nous puisons notre sève et nos maux... Ce sont des sphinx... La plus jeune demeure immobile ... les nerfs tendus... Ses joues maigrissent; ses prunelles avivées par le blanc intense, ses yeux imperceptiblement caves distillent le désir et la volonté... Surtout le sourire est alarmant. Elle a tout goûté, elle a sucé toutes les délices épicées de notre âpre littérature moderne... Elle a multiplié et exaspéré ses sensations, par le spectacle du monde, par l'habitude du théâtre, par les rivalités de la toilette... L'ironie parisienne a passé le tout à l'alambic."[84] The theatre, in fact, is the spot where modern

[83]*Ibid.*, 174. Cf. with Anatole France's remark: "C'est l'effet de la civilisation d'affaiblir peu à peu les énergies naturelles"—a review of Yriarte's *César Borgia*, 1892, in *La Vie littéraire*, IVe série (Calmann-Lévy), 48.

[84]*Graindorge* (Hachette), 141–3. Gautier, as quoted by the Goncourts (*Journal*, 11 avril 1864), gives the same picture of the high society of the period: "Le sentiment de la modernité... dont Gautier se proclame *pourri*. Là-dessus Gautier esquisse le type des femmes qu'il a vues, au dernier lundi de l'Impératrice; des femmes maigres, décharnées, plates, osseuses, minces... au teint de chlorose à l'apparence fantasmatique et malsaine, — avec seulement de l'esprit sur la figure." The Goncourts' own description of the female denizens of the Casino Cadet (16 mars 1865) and Huysmans' strumpets at the Folies Bergère (*Croquis parisiens*) are later versions of the same thing. Modernity—artificiality—decadence: the fact that the whole society of the Second Empire (from the Empress Eugénie's drawing-room to the dance halls of Montmartre) was depicted by different hands in the same terms is extremely curious.

decadence can be best observed: people going to their boxes at the Opera recall the Greeks and Romans of the decadence: "Quand je les vois défiler, l'idée de la vieille Rome et de la vieille Alexandrie se représente toujours à mon esprit... Ces têtes modernes m'apparaissent comme des bustes et il me semble que je revois vivants ceux du ıve siècle... En ce temps-là comme aujourd'hui, l'homme avait été raffiné et étriqué par la culture, par l'étalage des jouissances et par la concentration de l'effort; les grandes capitales avaient exaspéré les désirs; l'âme infiniment compliquée avait cessé de sentir le vrai beau qui est simple, et l'art réaliste... copiait les déformations et les bassesses dont nous aussi nous regorgeons."[85]

Similar passages occur in "Les Beaux Arts en France," an essay written in April 1868: "Les Parisiens... ne semblent vivre que le soir sous cent bougies. Artificiels et agités... c'est bien ainsi que nous sommes. Les rues sont trop pleines, les visages trop affairés. Au soir, le boulevard fourmillant et lumineux, les théâtres étincelants et malsains, partout le luxe, le plaisir et l'esprit outrés aboutissent à la sensation excessive et apprêtée. La machine nerveuse est à la fois surmenée et insatiable." "Les corps musculeux et héroïques, les figures fortes et saines du xvıe siècle, seraient déplacés parmi les fauteuils capitonnés, les idées compliquées, les sourires artificiels du nôtre."—"On vit ici, et même on vit trop; la flamme brûle... en salissant et en usant sa lampe... Voyez toutes ces femmes... Ce sont des délicatesses d'imagination que le monde avive comme une serre chaude."—"Ainsi nourri, la créature ardente et nerveuse souffre et se répand de tous côtés en idées violentes, en visions troubles. On n'a jamais senti plus à fond... le drame douloureux de la vie."[86]

Delacroix was the great painter of this contemporary decadence (Taine's criticism is very like Baudelaire's): "Il ne songeait pas à recréer ses yeux, à suivre des dehors voluptueux... Il nous voyait nous-mêmes, avec nos générosités et nos angoisses... Il faisait sortir la pitié, le désespoir, la tendresse, et toujours quelque émotion déchirante ou délicieuse, de ses tons violacés et étranges, de ses nuages vineux brouillés de fumées charbonneuses, de ses mers et de ses cieux livides comme le teint fiévreux d'un malade... de ses chairs frémissantes et sensibles d'où transpire l'orage intérieur, de ses corps ou redressés par le ravissement ou par le spasme."[87]

A further cause of modern decadence, Taine thought, was the spiritual imbalance brought about by the downfall of paganism: "Une tour-

[85]Ibid., 147.
[86]Essais de critique et d'histoire (Hachette), 379, 382, 387.   [87]Ibid., 388-9.

mente de quinze siècles a troublé la pensée humaine," he wrote in March 1868, "et l'homme moderne en retrouve encore aujourd'hui les atteintes persistantes dans l'exagération de sa sensibilité, dans la disproportion de ses désirs et de sa puissance, dans la déraison de ses rêves, dans la discorde profonde de ses facultés. Pour s'affiner, il s'est détraqué."[88]

Taine expresses more succinctly than Gautier or Baudelaire (whose point of view was almost purely literary) the social and political aspects of decadence, and tacks the label to contemporary society—the Second Empire. During the last three decades of the century, this was to become the main political idea of the decadent movement. Napoleon III's régime was, indeed, an easy target. It presented itself as a continuation of the First Empire, and the contrast was not difficult to make between "Augustus" and "Augustulus," as Hugo made it in *Les Châtiments*. From the beginning, its political ascendancy was shaky, its elegance suspect and feverish; it moved in an atmosphere of frivolity and scandal—shady financial doings, adventurers and adventuresses, backstairs imperial mistresses of doubtful vintage like La Castiglione, brassy strumpets like Hortense Schneider, La Païva and Cora Pearl, Offenbach waltzes and opera bouffe; and it ended in the disgraceful collapse of Sedan. Already in 1866 Henri Rochefort had published a series of articles entitled *Les Français de la décadence*,[89] which give a chatty account, rather like the social column in a smart modern newspaper, of the café society of the period—politics, racing, fashion, expensive gallantry. Contemporary decadence became a stock subject to break a pen upon: it is always cropping up, particularly in discussions of Baudelaire. "La profonde originalité de Charles Baudelaire," wrote Verlaine in 1865, "c'est de représenter puissamment et essentiellement l'homme moderne... tel que l'ont fait les raffinements d'une civilisation excessive : l'homme moderne, avec ses sens aiguisés et vibrants, son esprit douloureusement subtil, son cerveau saturé de tabac, son sang brûlé d'alcool... le *bilio-nerveux* par excellence, comme dirait H. Taine."[90] "Baudelaire accepta tout l'homme moderne," Ban-

---

[88]*Ibid.*, 411. The identification of refinement with decadence—another commonplace. Compare with the Goncourts (*Journal*, I, 185, mai 1858): "La délicatesse d'esprit est une corruption, longue à acquérir, et que ne possèdent jamais les peuples jeunes. Ce ne sont que les peuples usés, les peuples auxquels ne suffisent plus les sièges de fer et les bains de marbre, les peuples au corps douillet et lassé, les peuples mélancoliques et anémiés, les peuples attaqués de ces maladies de vieillesse qui viennent aux arbres fruitiers qui ont trop porté."

[89]Henri Rochefort, *Les Français de la décadence* (Librairie centrale, 1866). Essays written between 27 novembre 1864 and 14 janvier 1866.

[90]Verlaine, *Œuvres posthumes* (Messein 1913), II, 9–10.

ville said two years later, "avec ses défaillances, avec sa grâce maladive, avec ses aspirations impuissantes."[91] Two other judgments of the time are "le Prométhée des mœurs énervées de notre décadence" and "un être nerveux, né d'une époque nerveuse."[92] Baudelaire, in fact, served his contemporaries as a sort of yard-stick with which to measure decadence; the criticisms multiplied as the century aged. They are usually highly coloured: anyone who set to work on an article on Baudelaire let himself go in a flood of purple prose which swept along Roman reminiscences, painted trollops, gas-light, medical theories and aesthetic creeds in mad confusion. The most characteristic of them is Gautier's "Notice."

This was doubtless inevitable. Prepared as he was by long interest in decadence, Gautier was simply expanding his own ideas, and he presents Baudelaire from first to last as a decadent poet. The idea is the leit-motiv of the entire study:

les civilisations qui vieillissent (xvi); le terreau noir et saturé de pourriture comme un sol de cimetière des civilisations décrépites, où se dissolvent, parmi les miasmes méphitiques, les cadavres des siècles précédents (xx); les civilisations très avancées et très corrompues (xxv); un poète de *décadence* auteur des *Fleurs du mal* (xxvi); la dernière heure des civilisations (xxviii); ce livre consacré à la peinture des dépravations et des perversités modernes (xxx); il aimait... le sentiment profond ce que nous appellerons *décadence* (liii).

He says that Baudelaire used a decadent style, designed to analyse every kind of mental and moral disease: "Les confidences subtiles de la névrose, les aveux de la passion vieillissante qui se déprave, et les hallucinations bizarres de l'idée fixe tournant à la folie ... les larmes des superstitions, les fantômes hagards de l'insomnie, les terreurs nocturnes, les remords, les rêves monstrueux, les fantaisies obscures, et tout ce que l'âme récèle de ténébreux, de difforme et de vaguement horrible." The characters portrayed in *Les Fleurs du Mal* are ennui-haunted neurotics, seeking new thrills in sadism and excess, longing for the ferocious debauchery of Nero and Heliogabalus; the women are nineteenth-century versions of Mme de Merteuil, "d'une corruption froide, savante, et perverse... transposant le vice du corps à l'âme... hautaines, glaciales, amères, ne trouvant le plaisir que dans la méchanceté satisfaite, n'ayant que des fantaisies hystériques et folles."[93]

[91]"Discours aux obsèques de Baudelaire," reprinted in *Charles Baudelaire* (Pincebourde, 1872), 136–7.
[92]Quoted by W. T. Bandy, *Baudelaire Judged by His Contemporaries* (New York, Columbia University Press), 137, 99.
[93]"Notice," xvi–xvii, xxviii–xxix, xxxiv.

All these passages show what a change had come over literature since 1830—a growing perversity, a conviction that the age was depraved, or at least tending that way. A young poet starting in to write around the middle years of the century found new material to his hand—that is, if he wanted to be *avant garde* and original. Inevitably, his work would be very different from that of the great Romantics, and such indeed is the poetry of two writers whose books, although they did not attract much attention until after 1870, began to appear at this time—Verlaine and Mallarmé. Verlaine's essay on Baudelaire gives some indication of his state of mind; he followed his own precepts in most of the volumes he published from *Poèmes saturniens* onward. The constant references to *impuissance* are highly characteristic: "Lassitude," "L'Angoisse," "Promenade sentimentale," "Chanson d'automne," "Nevermore"—the last title comes from Poe, but Poe would never have written:

> Allons, mon pauvre cœur...
> Vieillard prématuré, mets du fard sur tes rides...
> Le ver est dans le fruit, le réveil dans le rêve.

There is a sophisticated tone which is quite foreign to Romantic exuberance.

Sterility is one of the main themes of Mallarmé's poetry—"Le Guignon," "Les Fenêtres," "Renouveau," "Angoisse," etc. The dancer in "Hérodiade" (written 1864–7) is a complete expression of it: she appears in her boudoir, heavily jewelled, surrounded by perfumes and cosmetics; her very chastity is a form of decadence—it is not the result of conventional virtue, but a refinement of dandyism: sexuality implies abandoning the dandy's self-sufficiency, ceasing to be egocentric and sterile, or at least running the risk of fecundity, and also it is *natural* ("c'est-à-dire abominable," to add the Baudelairean tag), a denial of the cult of artificiality. The "Hérodiade" reads as if Mallarmé had written it as a variation on Baudelaire's maxim, "Un dandy doit passer sa vie devant un miroir"—which is impossible, since the phrase was not published until 1887. The Hérodiade adopts an extreme form of Narcissism (she is, in fact, one of the first manifestations of the Narcissus-theme which later became so popular), satisfying a neurotic temperament by the sterile contemplation of her own beauty: "Un baiser me tûrait," she declares; "je ne veux rien d'humain... c'est pour moi, pour moi, que je fleuris, déserte... j'aime l'horreur d'être vierge." And she orders her nurse to shut the windows against the sky which (as elsewhere in Mallarmé) represents life, effort, even art—a trait we have already noticed in the Gautier of the *Poésies* and the Flaubert of *Novembre*. From first to last Mallarmé was half in love with his own easeful sterility: he elevates it into a sort of doctrine. "Muse moderne de l'Impuissance," we read in an essay of 1864, "qui m'interdis depuis longtemps le trésor familier des Rythmes, et me condamnes (aimable supplice) à ne faire plus que relire — jusqu'au jour où tu m'auras enveloppé dans ton irrémédiable filet, l'ennui... — les maîtres inaccessibles... ; mon ennemie, et cependant mon enchanteresse, aux breuvages perfides et aux mélancoliques ivresses, je te dédie... ces quelques lignes de ma vie écrites dans les heures clémentes où tu ne m'inspiras pas la haine de la création et le stérile amour du néant."[94] Silence, he concludes, is best, since the human voice is an error.

The curious *Igitur, ou La folie d'Elbehnon* (1867–70), a fragment, is perhaps the most complete expression of the decadent type before Zola and Huysmans. The influence of Baudelaire and particularly Poe is very great. Igitur, haunted by neurosis, spends his life in the heavily curtained rooms of his ancestral château: "Ecoutez, ma race," he apostrophizes his ancestors, "le compte que j'ai à vous rendre de ma vie... névrose, ennui (ou Absolu!)... J'ai épaissi les rideaux, et comme j'étais obligé pour ne pas douter de moi de m'asseoir en face de cette glace, j'ai recueilli précieusement les moindres atomes du temps dans des étoffes sans cesse épaissies." All this is obviously borrowed from Usher, Egaeus and Ligeia; and like them, Igitur is the decadent scion of a once-great race. But, as in Verlaine's poetry, his ennui, his sophistication adds an element foreign to Poe's lush sentimentalism: "Le passé de sa race qui pèse sur lui en la sensation de fini, l'heure de la pendule précipitant cet ennui en temps lourd... forment du temps pur, ou de l'ennui : ... cet ennui ne pouvant être, redevient ses éléments ; ... et Igitur... se cherchant dans la glace devenue ennui et se voyant vague et près de disparaître... puis s'évoquant ; puis lorsque de tout cet ennui, temps, il s'est refait, voyant la glace horriblement nulle... Et quand il croit être redevenu lui, il fixe de son âme l'horloge, dont l'heure disparaît par la glace, ou va s'enfouir dans les rideaux, en trop plein, ne le laissant même pas à l'ennui qu'il implore et rêve. Impuissant de l'ennui."[95]

L'ennui qu'il implore et rêve... sterility and powerlessness become ends in themselves, desirable states: an extreme development of what was, in Sainte-Beuve, Gautier, Flaubert and Baudelaire, a nervous malady, always recognized as such. Mallarmé loves in nature and

[94]*Œuvres complètes* (Pléiade), 261–2.
[95]*Ibid.*, 439–40.

literature only those languid, dying effects which correspond to his own state of mind. His prose-poems, written in 1864, explain this in some detail: "Le Phénomène futur" contains such phrases as "un ciel pâle, sur le monde qui finit de décrépitude," "la pourpre usée des couchants," "les arbres s'ennuient," etc. "Plainte d'automne" links this cultivated languor with the style of the decadent Latin authors: "J'ai passé de longues journées seul... avec un des derniers auteurs de la décadence latine... car... j'ai aimé tout ce qui se résumait en ce mot : chute... La littérature à laquelle mon esprit demande une volupté sera la poésie agonisante des derniers moments de Rome, tant, cependant, qu'elle ne respire aucunement l'approche rajeunissante des Barbares... Ces chers poèmes (dont les plaques de fard ont plus de charme sur moi que l'incarnat de la jeunesse)..."

Barbey d'Aurevilly's *Prêtre marié* contains an interpretation of decadent sensibility in metaphysical or Roman Catholic terms; it will be a convenient point upon which to terminate our discussion of the matter before we see how psychopathology added new elements. As in *Igitur*, Poe's influence can be traced. *Un Prêtre marié* was published in 1865, but D'Aurevilly had worked at it for some years before (there are frequent references to it, as *Calixte*, in the letters to Trébutien from 1855 on); and it was during this period that he first read Poe—in 1853 in a translation of *The Gold Bug* and *Hans Pfaall*; two years later in Baudelaire's version of the *Histoires extraordinaires*. He was sufficiently impressed to write an essay on the American in which he calls him "un cerveau étrange, puissant, et malade," "un talent individuel, anormal... qui... plonge sa racine dans quelque sombre et fixe manie, comme une fleur qui gagnerait des couleurs et des taches inconnues, si on en trempait le pied dans quelque poison," and notes that while Poe was born in the anti-literary and materialistic civilization of the United States, he had "les yeux retournés et dilatés du voyant." He added a chapter to this study in 1856; it shows the influence of Baudelaire's preface, but allotted much more space to Poe's decadence than Baudelaire had done: "Malgré ses prétentions à la jeunesse, l'Amérique, cette fille de l'Europe, est née vieille comme tous les enfants de vieillards, et elle a les épuisements spirituels de sa mère. Littérairement, c'est une impuissante... Tous les écrivains de ce pays vivent sur le fond commun des littératures de l'Europe. Quand les choses en sont là partout... les Claudiens de nos décadences — en Amérique ou autre part — doivent être plus étranges et plus compliqués que ceux des sociétés qui n'avaient pas usé sous elles autant d'idées que nous, quand elles croulèrent... Edgar Poe serait-il un Claudien, un énorme

Claudien du XIXe siècle, un de ces produits exubérants et corrompus d' une civilisation développée à outrance et qui en est arrivée à chercher la complexité comme la cherche la Barbarie, ou serait-il véritablement un grand poète ? ... On ne trouve [chez lui] que de la matière malade, anormale, *désaccordée*. Edgar Poe est un poète pathologique..."[96] This interest in Poe, coinciding with the composition of *Un Prêtre marié*, doubtless explains the Poe-like, morbid tone of the book.

The "married priest" of the title is the Abbé Sombreval, who, during the Revolution, "engourdi par le serpent de la Science," abandoned the priesthood, took up scientific studies, and married. His pious wife, who knew nothing of his past, finds out the secret during her pregnancy. This causes a nervous attack, and she dies after giving premature birth to a daughter, Calixte. From the beginning, the sin of her birth is stamped physically and morally upon Calixte. She bears the red mark of a cross on her transparently white forehead, and she is the victim (like Poe's heroines) of complicated neuroses leading to cataleptic attacks. She has "une beauté effrayante, une pâleur sépulcrale, et deux yeux caves et éblouissants comme deux brasiers"—the spectral beauty of Ligeia or Berenice. Under her father's guidance she becomes a prodigy of learning; but her intellectual attainments do not cure the neurosis—quite the reverse: "L'intelligence s'alluma plus tôt et plus fort...que la vie elle-même, et des convulsions fréquentes préludèrent à la névrose qui s'empara d'un organisme toujours à la veille d'une excitation suraiguë."[97] The malady reaches an acute stage when a priest tells her the truth about her birth and converts her: "La névrose dont elle était atteinte multiplia ses phénomènes et finit par dépayser le savoir et le coup d'œil des médecins de l'Europe les plus renommés." The moral nature of her illness, as distinct from anything of a purely pathological character, is constantly stressed: "Sous l'effroyable désordre sanguin causé par la violence d'une émotion ... il y avait, permanente et tenace, la névrose indomptable ... cette névrose de toute sa vie dont la cause était encore plus dans le moral de la malade que dans son physique." "Cette enfant," says one of the physicians consulted, "est malade d'une idée."[98] During the course of her brief life, Calixte has attracted the love of a local noble, Néel de Néhou; it is one of those sexless, half-incestuous passions typical of Poe's couples: she calls him her "frère d'élection" and herself his "sœur." This dehydrated lubricity is shot with streaks of brutal real-

---

[96]*Les Œuvres et les hommes* (Lemerre), 347, 348, 361–2, 370.
[97]*Un Prêtre marié* (Bernouard), I, 41.
[98]*Ibid.*, I, 49 and II, 188.

ism—during her death agony Calixte's face becomes first black then white; her mind goes; decomposition sets in almost before she is dead, etc. After her death, Néel, remembering her catalepsy, and fearful that she might be buried alive, decides, on consultation with the priest who has administered Extreme Unction, to burn her feet with a red-hot iron. The following description is a subtle mixture of sexual desire, sadism and perverted religiosity (the burns are likened to the Stigmata): "Une fumée monta avec un bruit navrant... Néel, qui cherchait la vie avec rage et qui voulait la faire jaillir par la douleur ... brûlait avec un acharnement égaré les beaux pieds insensibles que le feu rongeait... Bourreau par tendresse, il s'enivrait de son action."[99] The novel ends on a turgid episode with hints of incestuous necrophilia. Sombreval returns after the funeral. Convinced that his daughter has been buried alive, he digs up the corpse and tries to recall it to life: "Sombreval labourait convulsivement de son front, de ses lèvres, de son visage tout entier le cadavre qu'il tenait et levait dans ses bras. Il plongeait sa tête désolée au giron de cette chère fille morte."[100] There are no less than three pages of this; and the father's caresses (we are told) make Néel, who is looking on ... *jealous*. When he finds that Calixte is really dead, Sombreval throws himself into a lake with the corpse in his arms.

[99]*Ibid.*, II, 210–15.

[100]*Ibid.*, II, 230–2.

CHAPTER 3

NERVE-STORMS AND BAD HEREDITY

> La plupart des individus doués d'une intelligence supé-
> rieure... comptent parmi leurs ascendants ou parmi les mem-
> bres de leur famille, soit des aliénés, soit des personnes
> sujettes à des affections du système d'organes.
>
> Moreau de Tours, 1859

> C'est avec de la moelle épinière et des nerfs que nous expli-
> quons l'homme tout entier.
>
> Barbey d'Aurevilly, 1884

THERE IS ONE FACT about the decadents thus far examined which
strikes the reader at once: they are all "literary"; their vices are too
abstract and deliberate to be altogether real. All borrow much from
Romanticism's egoistic and emotional hypertrophy and graft onto this
common trunk fantasies and whimsies of their own. A number of
species can be distinguished: the aesthetic decadent (D'Albert, Samuel
Cramer), the metaphysical decadent (Amaury, Egaeus, Calixte), the
over-civilized decadent (Taine's Parisians); and they tend to fuse and
run together so that in several (like Mallarmé's Igitur) we find various
characteristics existing side by side. Most of them, however—D'Albert
is a good example, and might be taken as the type-decadent of the first
half of the century—never put their "depravity" into practice to any
extent. It remains abstract, a source of morbid day-dreaming; they
shut themselves up in elaborate rooms and indulge in drugs and
meditation to get the proper atmosphere. But at bottom very few are
seriously deranged; and their creators—Gautier, Baudelaire, Barbey—
seem to have realized the slightly rootless nature of all this perversity:
their constant harking back to Imperial Rome was one result—they
were looking for suitably disreputable predecessors.

Baudelaire especially, by cultivating his hysteria "avec jouissance et
terreur," by his cult of Poe (whose characters are among the few

before 1860 whose symptoms are explained as logical syndromes of neurosis—epilepsy and catalepsy), and by providing himself with a line of tainted but purely imaginary ancestors, tried to create a charged background. The fact that in his essay on *Madame Bovary* he recommended psychopathology as a means of studying character is very interesting: "L'hystérie! Pourquoi ce mystère physiologique ne ferait-il pas le fond et le tuf d'une œuvre littéraire, ce mystère que l'Académie de Médecine n'a pas encore résolu, et qui, s'exprimant dans les femmes par la sensation d'une boule ascendante et asphyxiante ... se traduit chez les hommes nerveux par toutes les impuissances et aussi par l'aptitude à tous les excès ?"[1] This suggestion is almost a résumé of the entire Naturalist programme as Zola and his followers understood it; but Baudelaire made no effort to use it in his own work. The deliberate corruptions of *Les Fleurs du Mal* frequently suggest late-Romantic posing. Baudelaire's conception of decadence was entirely metaphysical—he thought of it as Evil, "une dépravation du sens de l'infini," "un goût de l'infini qui partout, dans le mal lui-même, se proclame." It is hard to imagine what he would have said of Zola's novels, written according to the formula he had suggested. The same is even truer of Barbey D'Aurevilly: he tells us nothing of Sombreval and his wife to explain Calixte's neurosis on logical grounds. Her derangement is due to the fact that her father was a priest who had forgotten his vows. Unless one is a believer, and an orthodox Catholic believer, this situation is simply incredible.[2]

Neither Barbey nor Baudelaire had any real knowledge of the pathology of degeneracy; nor had any of the other writers up to the middle of the century. It is not until after the fifties and sixties that this ignorance is remedied. A new influence then appears—due to the medical publications of the time. The emotional hypertrophy of Romanticism, and the theoretical perversities of Gautier and Baudelaire, are no longer presented as the fruits of aspirations towards the infinite or thwarted idealism. They are symptoms of neurosis. We are still dealing with decadent sensibility—its characteristics remain the same. But they are attributed to other causes: a man is decadent because he is psychotic. Poets and novelists begin to explain their heroes

---

[1] *Œuvres* (Pléiade), II, 447.
[2] Characteristically, Zola found it so. In his review of *Un Prêtre marié* ("Le Catholique hystérique"—by which he means D'Aurevilly) he says "cette œuvre m'a exaspéré" : "Calixte est le produit d'une imagination déréglée, un cas curieux de catalepsie et de somnambulisme qu'un médecin étudierait avec joie... Que vient faire cette folle, cette figure de légende, dans un livre qui a la prétention de discuter les faits contemporains?" *Mes Haines* (Bernouard), 36, 42.

and heroines in terms of psychopathology. For, by a curious chance, literature's interest in such matters coincided with a similar development in medical science. The nineteenth century laid the foundations of psychosomatic medicine, and a number of the treatises of the period exercised considerable influence on the evolution of decadent writing and on the whole theory of decadence. The chief point to be noticed is that at a very early date doctors began to equate genius with insanity.

The idea that great wits are sure to madness near allied is not new, as any conscientious editor of Dryden will usually point out with quotations from Aristotle and Seneca.[3] But it assumed new vigour during the nineteenth century, a fact which speaks volumes for the period's intellectual bias, prone to consider civilization in a dubious light. Most psychopathologists from 1800 on, if they did not actually dub genius madness, at least showed an increasing tendency to insist upon the exceptional, abnormal, or morbid nature of any outstanding talent—whether in literature, art, philosophy or mysticism.

Philippe Pinel,[4] in a series of articles published between 1784 and 1798, studied madness, neurosis, eroticism, etc., and was one of the first to take a scientific interest in such phenomena as Lesbianism. In his *Traité médico-philosophique sur l'aliénation mentale* (1801), he divided insanity into a number of categories, "mélancolie ou délire exclusif," "manie sans délire," "manie avec délire," "démence ou abolition de la pensée." As examples of the first variety he cites Tiberius and Louis XI because of their gloom, timidity, perfidy, retirement from the world, etc., and also "des mélancoliques d'un caractère opposé," who shine in art, science or letters, but who, while charming society with their genius, "ne sont que trop habiles à faire leur propre tourment et celui de tout ce qui les approche, par leurs ombrages et leurs soupçons chimériques."[5] The passage refers to Rousseau, but it would have done as well for the early Romantics, whose work was about to appear (*Atala* was published in the same year as the *Traité*); and it is particularly interesting because it is perhaps the first time psychiatry was applied to literature. During succeeding years, the method was used more and more. The first quarter of the century saw the appearance of a number of medical works which attempted to

---

[3]"Nullum magnum ingenium sine mixture dementiae fuit." *De Tranquillitate animae*, XV.

[4]Pinel (1745–1826) was director at Bicètre (1792–5), then at the Saltpêtrière from 1795 to his death. He occupies an honourable place in the history of psychiatry. For details of his life, see *Lettres de Pinel précédées d'une notice plus étendue sur sa vie par son neveu, le Dr. Casimir Pinel* (Masson, 1859). The reference to Sappho is on page 30.   [5]*Traité* (Richard, Caille et Ravier, an IX), 138–9.

show that genius was "sujet à l'hallucination et même à la monomanie"[6]: the influence of such theories in an atmosphere charged with
the nervous exaltation of Rousseau, Chateaubriand and Byron, and
later of Gautier, Baudelaire and Poe, may be easily imagined. Dr.
Joseph Moreau, who later styled himself "de Tours," began his career
in 1830 with a thesis De l'influence du physique sur le moral, in which
he resolutely denied the metaphysical or moral nature of insanity:
"Nulle différence essentielle n'existe ... entre la folie et toute autre
affection de l'organisme."[7] He followed this up in 1836 with Les
Facultés morales, which contains a discussion of heredity, and a note
to the effect that the most brilliant families, with the largest proportion
of geniuses, also contain the largest number of neurotics and mad-
men.[8] These ideas are further developed in Etudes psychiques sur la
folie (1840), Du haschisch et de l'aliénation mentale (1845), Mémoires sur les causes prédisposantes héréditaires de l'idiotie et de l'imbécilité (1853), De l'identité de l'état de rêve et de la folie (1855), and
La Psychologie morbide (1859), of which the argument is thus summed up in the preface: "Les dispositions d'esprit qui font qu'un
homme se distingue des autres hommes par l'originalité de ses pensées
et de ses conceptions ... prennent leur source dans les mêmes conditions
organiques que les divers troubles moraux dont la folie et l'idiotie sont
l'expression la plus complète."[9] This was an equation of genius with
madness which, as we shall see, was to become extremely popular.
There follows (chapter I, part II) a study of the laws of heredity, pur-
porting to show that certain hereditary defects, such as insanity, may
produce a variety of morbid symptoms: crime, prostitution, sexual
perversions, and religious fanaticism, mysticism, genius. The state of
inspiration, Moreau says, is the nearest a sane man can come to madness. "La plupart des individus doués d'une intelligence supérieure,"
he adds by way of conclusion, "comptent parmi leurs ascendants ou
parmi les membres de leur famille, soit des aliénés, soit des personnes
sujettes à des affections du système d'organes ..." and he gives a list of
historical and literary figures to prove his point, maintaining that they
all owe their eminence to some form or other of insanity, ranging from

[6]The titles are given by Lombroso in L'Homme de génie (Alcan, 1889), 4 et seq.
[7]Such is his résumé of it in Traité pratique de la folie névropathique (Baillière,
1869), vii.
[8]Les Facultés morales considérées sous le point de vue médicale, de leur influence
sur les maladies nerveuses, les affections organiques (Librairie des Sciences Médicales,
1836), 26.
[9]La Psychologie morbide dans ses rapports avec la philosophie de l'histoire ou de
l'influence des névropathies sur le dynamisme intellectuel (Masson, 1859), v.

simple eccentricity to actual cerebral lesions. Amongst them we find Socrates, Aristotle, Queen Elizabeth, Cromwell, J.-J. Rousseau, Dr. Johnson, St. Francis of Assisi, Chateaubriand and Joan of Arc.[10]

Meanwhile, other men had been busy in the field. Dr. Prosper Lucas wrote a study of heredity, *L'Hérédité naturelle* (1850), which was later read by both Taine and Zola; and B. H. Morel published (1857) his *Traité des dégénérescences physiques, intellectuelles et morales de l'espèce humaine*, partly based on the early experimental work of Claude Bernard. It is an effort to examine "jusqu'à quel point la physiologie expérimentale pouvait éclairer la question des dégénérescences."[11] There was, Morel says, an accepted idea at the time that the human race was in degeneracy from a primitive type, itself "le chef d'œuvre et le résumé de la création." He agrees with this premise, and bases his definition of degeneracy (or decadence) upon it: "Les dégénérescences ne peuvent donc être que le résultat d'une influence morbide, soit de l'ordre physique, soit de l'ordre moral... La dégénérescence de l'espèce humaine est... *une déviation maladive d'un type primitif*... Dégénérescence et déviation maladive du type normal de l'humanité sont donc dans ma pensée une seule et même chose."[12] One thinks at once of D'Albert lamenting the difference between himself and his ancestors. Seven years later Morel discussed the hereditary nature of degeneracy in *De la formation du type dans les variétés dégénérées*, a sequel to his first book. Bits of it read like a summary of Zola's *Rougon-Macquart*—which indeed they are, since the volume was one of those Zola consulted when planning his work. For example: "La théorie des dégénérescences dans l'espèce humaine repose sur ce fait général et important qu'étant donné un principe maladif qui s'attaque à la constitution des ascendants, ce principe ... devient pour les descendants le premier terme d'une série de phénomènes pathologiques ... qui finissent par amener la décadence progressive de telle ou telle famille, et parfois même de telle ou telle race. Cette décadence est fatale..."[13]

During the rest of the century works on degeneracy, tainted heredity, insanity, sexual perversions, etc., appeared in great profusion and in most of the principal European languages. There is Huchard's *L'Etat mental des hystériques* (1852) which insists on the *impuissance* characteristic of hysteria; Letourneau's *Physiologie des passions* (1868); Axenfeld's *Des Névroses* (1879); Féré's *La Famille névropathique* (1884, rewritten in an even thicker volume ten years later);

[10]*Ibid.*, 576.   [11]*Traité* (Baillière, 1857), xiii.
[12]*Ibid.*, 1–5.   [13]*De la formation du type* (Baillière, 1864), 17.

Déjérine's *L'Hérédité dans les maladies du système nerveux* (1886); Boinet's *Les Parentés morbides* (1886, in which the author says he agrees with Moreau de Tours that "le génie est une névrose"); Orchansky's *L'Eredità nelle famiglie malate* (1895); Krafft-Ebing's classic *Psychopathia sexualis*, and the long and important series of studies by Lombroso: *Genio e follia* (1863, which also equates genius with madness), *L'Uomo delinquente* and *L'Homme de génie* (French translation, 1889). The last calls for special mention. Dr. Ch. Richet, who wrote a preface for the French edition, says that he had often heard his master, Moreau de Tours, say that "le génie et la folie se touchent," and he sums up the argument of Lombroso's book with the remark that "le génie ne concorde pas avec une santé intellectuelle irréprochable, et... dans les formes de l'intelligence qui sont propres aux aliénés, on rencontre certains caractères psychologiques communs aux fous et aux hommes de génie."[14] The book itself is of a piece with this précis: there is a discussion of contemporary literature—the Parnassians and the Symbolists are defined as "mattoïdes," an intermediary type between sanity and madness; Symbolist poetry "serait celle d'un solitaire, d'un névropathe, et presque d'un fou."[15] Baudelaire is dismissed on the basis of Brunetière's article of 1887, more especially the passage in which Brunetière called his photographs typical portraits of a madman;[16] reference is made to the legends current about him at the time (such as the episode in "Le Mauvais Vitrier"); his own note about his ancestors is quoted with the remark that "Baudelaire descendait d'une famille de fous et d'excentriques."[17] This was taking Baudelaire seriously with a vengeance! Other insane geniuses referred to are Poe, Hoffman, De Quincey, Hugo, Lucretius, Blake, Zola and Virgil (because of his homosexuality).[18] Mysticism is also identified with nervous disease. The conclusion is that "la fréquence et la multiplicité des délires, des caractères de dégénérescence... la dérivation et plus encore la descendance d'alcooliques, d'imbéciles, d'idiots, d'épilep-

[14]*L'Homme de génie*, traduit sur la vie édition italienne, préface de Ch. Richet (Alcan, 1889), v.

[15]*Ibid.*, 313–14.

[16]*Revue des Deux Mondes*, 1 juin 1887: Baudelaire's photograph resembles the "images classiques et les représentations consacrées à des mégalomaniaques dans nos traités des maladies mentales". The Italian edition of Lombroso's book (Torino, Fr. Bocca editori, 1888) has a reproduction of the Carjat photograph of Baudelaire on its cover.

[17]*L'Homme de génie*, 92.

[18]*Ibid.*, 157 *et seq.* Lombroso devotes some space (168) to the homosexual tendencies frequently observed in men of genius, and apropos of Virgil refers (706) to Valmaggi's "Psicopatia sessuale di Virgilio" (*Revista di Filologia*, 1890, fasc. 7, 9).

tiques, et surtout le caractère spécial de l'inspiration, montrent que le génie est une psychose dégénérative du groupe épileptique."[19]

A final expression of these preposterous theories occurs in Max Nordau's *Entartung* (1892; French translation, *Dégénérescence*, 1894), which enjoyed a certain vogue during the last years of the century. Nordau gives Morel credit for first conceiving and defining the idea of degeneracy which, he says, now dominates all psychiatric science,[20] and refers also to Féré and Lombroso. Most contemporary authors, he declares, particularly Frenchmen like Baudelaire, Verlaine, Mallarmé and Huysmans, would, if examined, be found to have degenerate parents or relatives; and he lists certain stigmata of degeneracy—excessive emotionalism, "folie morale," "aversion pour toute action... qui peut aller jusqu'à l'horreur d'agir et l'impuissance de vouloir (aboulie)," "rêverie creuse," "la stigmate capitale du dégénéré ... le mysticisme," and as a cause of much of this disorder, life in the great city. "L'habitant de la grande ville... aspire un air chargé de détritus organiques, il mange des aliments flétris, contaminés, falsifiés, il se trouve dans un état perpétuel de surexcitation nerveuse... Avec la croissance des grandes villes s'augmente parallèlement le nombre des dégénérés de toute espèce."[21] The book closes with a repetition of Moreau's dictum, "le génie n'est qu'une névrose," and a list of prominent recent or living decadents: Baudelaire, the Pre-Raphaelites, Verlaine, Mallarmé, Moréas, Laforgue, Tolstoy, Wagner, Ibsen, Barbey d'Aurevilly.[22]

It must be admitted that these treatises make heavy reading nowadays. They occupy a worthy place in the history of psychiatry, but their absurdity as literary criticism is self-evident, and did not escape contemporary censure.[23] None of the doctors, whatever their eminence in pathology, had much flair in the field of aesthetics. Irony, *blague*,

[19]*Ibid.*, 490.
[20]*Dégénérescence* (Alcan, 1894), I, 31.
[21]*Ibid.*, 64. Mortality in cities, he says, is 25 per cent higher than in other regions.
[22]*Ibid.*, 218.
[23]Mallarmé (*Œuvres*, Pléiade, 651); Huysmans, preface to Verlaine's *Poésies religieuses* (Messein, 1904, xiv); René Doumic, *Revue des Deux Mondes*, 14 janvier 1894; even medical opinion was not unanimous on this point: "Une conception aussi simpliste, aussi rudimentaire de la dégénérescence mentale n'est pas extrêmement séduisante," wrote Dr. Louis Danel apropos of the Morel-Moreau-Lombroso-Nordau thesis of ranging geniuses like Pascal and Rousseau amongst the degenerates: "La Notion de dégénérescence particulièrement dans l'étude du mouvement littéraire et artistique contemporain," *Revue de Lille*, avril 1907. Danel's paper was read at "la section d'anthropologie et de biologie de l'Université libre de Lille" on March 1, 1907; it contains a sharp criticism of Nordau. By the twentieth century, a reaction had set in.

and all the delicate shades of meaning and intention slipped through their heavy fingers like minnows. Nordau was particularly obtuse, and Moreau's incomprehension almost passes belief. He seems to have taken Swift's *Modest Proposal* seriously, as an actual invitation to cannibalism: "L'idée d'une pareille composition," he tells us gravely, "ne pouvait germer que dans le cerveau d'un futur aliéné."[24] As for Lombroso, his remarks on Baudelaire are a good example of slipshod research, and vitiate the argument of his book. However, from the standpoint of decadent sensibility, all this solemn buffoonery is of considerable interest. Most of the doctors accepted without question (as Nordau says) the idea that nineteenth-century man was decadent. Zola did not simply find a theory of heredity in the medical works he read to plot the Rougon-Macquart family tree: he found a theory of decadent heredity. Literature and medicine were in agreement on contemporary decadence, and they borrowed from each other. From Pinel down, the doctors used contemporary writers as living examples of degeneracy, and more and more as the century aged, writers began looking for themes and ideas in the findings of the doctors. It is possible that Gautier and Baudelaire had read some of the books which appeared before the middle sixties, such as Moreau de Tours' works. Baudelaire had looked through his treatise on hashish (1845) before writing his own essays on the drug, and did not agree with its conclusions, as he says in a note.[25] Since Moreau drew liberally on an article by Gautier when writing his book, Gautier may have read him in turn, if only out of curiosity. The medical vocabulary of the "Notice," while not very extensive, suggests that Gautier had some acquaintance with the literature of pathology.

Whatever the case may be for Gautier and Baudelaire, however, there is no doubt at all about Zola. He was not, of course, the first; medical theory had been used in fiction before: Balzac, among other things, had attempted to write the natural history of his period. The Goncourts, Zola's immediate predecessors in the Naturalist field, produced a series of novels in which morbid states play a considerable role. "Songez que notre œuvre, et c'est peut-être son originalité ... repose sur la maladie nerveuse," they wrote Zola in 1870.[26] The

[24]*La Psychologie morbide*, 539.

[25]*Du vin et du haschisch*, 1851, *Œuvres*, I, 629. Moreau suggested hashish as a cure for insanity. "Le fou qui prend du haschisch," says Baudelaire, "contracte une folie qui chasse l'autre. Le médecin qui a inventé ce beau système n'est pas le moins du monde philosophe." It is curious to find Baudelaire defending conventional morality against a member of the faculty.

[26]Quoted by Paul Bourget, *Nouveaux essais de psychologie contemporaine* (Lemerre, 1886), 168.

dénouement of *Renée Mauperin* (1864) results from the heroine's heart-disease. *Germinie Lacerteux* (1864) is a study of nymphomania and hysteria in a servant. *Charles Demailly* (1868) ends in insanity. *Madame Gervaisais* (1869) depicts a case of morbid religiosity culminating in tuberculosis. *La Faustin* (1881) is the portrait of an actress, all nerves and caprice, and her lover Lord Annandale: he dies of nervous disease, the result of decayed lineage complicated by sexual perversions. The Goncourt brothers occasionally visited hospitals to document themselves (as they note in their *Journal* on December 18, 1860, and April 17, 1864). According to the *Journal*, sexual and nervous aberrations were the usual subjects of conversation at the famous "Dîners Magny": Taine, Flaubert, Gautier, and the other guests showed an extraordinary interest in all the manifestations of decadence and degeneracy, especially the sexual manifestations. Flaubert's taste for the Marquis de Sade is noted in November 1858; pederasty was discussed at his house on February 22, 1863; on May 17, 1863, the Duc de Morny is quoted as praising Lesbianism, "qui, selon lui, raffine la femme, la parfait, l'accomplit." Sexual perversions were discussed again on May 4, 1862: "On descend aux mystères des sens, à l'inconnu des goûts bizarres, des tempéraments monstrueux. Les fantaisies, les perversions, les toquades, les démences de l'amour charnel sont étudiées, creusées, spécifiées. On philosophe sur de Sade, on théorise sur Tardieu." This Tardieu is doubtless the Dr. Ambroise Tardieu with whom the brothers mention talking four years later, in 1866.[27] His *Manuel de pathologie et de clinique médicales* appeared in 1848, and contains nearly two hundred pages on nervous disorders, including satyriasis, nymphomania, hysteria, etc. The section on nymphomania seems to have furnished the documents for *Germinie Lacerteux*.[28]

The Goncourts have also left a number of sketches of decadent types which recall earlier examples and look forward to the *fin-de-siècle*. One depicts a sado-masochist, a young sprig of the English aristocracy: "C'est un jeune homme d'une trentaine d'années, chauve, les tempes renflées comme une orange, les yeux d'un bleu clair et aigu, la peau extrêmement fine et laissant voir le réseau sous-cutané des veines, la tête ... d'un de ces jeunes prêtres émaciés et extatiques... Un élégant jeune homme ayant un peu de raideur dans les bras, et les mouvements du corps, à la fois mécaniques et fiévreux d'une personne

[27]*Journal*, III, 42.
[28]Compare Tardieu, *Manuel* (Ballière, 1848), 450 with *Germinie Lacerteux* (Charpentier), 191–2, 228–9.

attaquée d'un commencement de maladie de la moelle épinière."[29] He was drawn from life, and his mania consists of practising sexual perversions while watching executions. One finds traces of him in *La Faustin*, in the characters of George Selwyn and Lord Annandale. Some details of his appearance and eccentricities, like his collection of pornography, splendidly bound (sometimes in human skin), suggest Des Esseintes. George Selwyn has "un front hydrocéphale," and his old woman's face is continually distorted by a nervous twitch. He describes himself as a "cas pathologique": "C'est, disent les médecins, la prépondérance du cerveau annihilée par l'influx nerveux de la moelle."[30] He adds that his friend, Dr. Burnett, is going to devote a paragraph to him in a forthcoming study of nervous disease.

The main contribution of the Goncourts to decadent literature, however, is less their use of psychopathology than the purple passages which occur here and there in their books, and which, when the *fin-de-siècle* turned away from a purely medical explanation of decadence towards something more glamorous and metaphysical, exercised considerable influence. Ernest Raynaud, in an article on the origins of the decadent movement, praised the brothers for analysing "ce besoin de destruction, cette cruauté froide, qu'a la femme... tout ce mécanisme de méchanceté et de bêtise."[31] The portraits of La Crécy (*Charles Demailly*) and La Faustin, both of them actresses, bear him out. The description Mme Faustin gives of Lord Annandale's castle in Scotland, with its ruined halls, huge park, white peacocks, etc., reads like something from Poe.[32] On the whole, the Goncourts used psychopathology rather sparingly in their books as an explanation of character. Of course all illness is a form of degeneracy or decadence. But if this point be waived, people like Renée Mauperin are not really decadent at all. It is true that in Germinie, Mme Gervaisais, Selwyn and Lord Annandale, we have an approach to degenerative neurosis; but it is not until Zola that the theme is carried out fully.

Degeneracy is the very basis of the twenty novels which compose the *Rougon-Macquart*; and some of the medical titles we have just quoted (*La Famille névropathe, L'Eredità nelle famiglie malate*)

[29]*Journal*, 7 avril 1862.

[30]*La Faustin* (Charpentier, 1882), 310–11.

[31]"Les Origines du mouvement décadent: Les Frères de Goncourt," *Le Décadent*, 1–14 janvier 1889.

[32]*La Faustin*, 5. These peacocks were so much to the taste of subsequent decadent writing that we find them again and again during the rest of the century: Jean Lorrain, "Les Paons blancs pour M. Edmond de Goncourt," *Les Griseries*, 1887; Gustave Kahn, *Les Palais nomades*, 1887; Maurice Maeterlinck, "Ennui," *Les Serres chaudes*, 1889.

would do as subtitles for that "Histoire naturelle et sociale d'une famille sous le Second Empire." Furthermore, for some years before he set to work on his magnum opus of tainted heredity, Zola had been interested in decadence, nervous disease, and their manifestations in contemporary literature. As early as 1866, in an essay "La Littérature et la gymnastique," he spoke of "notre génération d'esprits affolés et hystériques," and defined nineteenth-century man in the same terms Taine and Baudelaire had used: "Le corps... est singulièrement en déchéance chez nous. Ce n'est plus l'âme qu'on exalte, ce sont les nerfs, la matière cérébrale... Nous sommes malades... de progrès. Il y a hypertrophie du cerveau, les nerfs se développent au détriment des muscles... L'équilibre est rompu entre la matière et l'esprit."[33] Taine's thought is especially strong in such a passage. Though Zola later, in 1893—at the time of *Les Trois Villes* and *Les Quatre Evangiles*— declared that he had adopted only the austere, intellectual elements of Taine ("En le lisant, le théoricien, le positiviste qui est en moi s'est développé... J'ai utilisé dans mes livres sa théorie sur l'hérédité et sur les milieux"[34]), he saw something else in 1866. Taine, he says, "appartient bien à notre siècle de nerfs... C'est un esprit malade et inquiet... Il vit de notre vie nerveuse et affolée, il frissonne, il a l'appétit léger et l'estomac étroit, il porte le vêtement sombre et étriqué de notre âge."[35] He applied much the same terms to the Goncourts when reviewing *Germinie Lacerteux*: "Il y a... une relation intime entre l'homme moderne, tel que l'a fait une civilisation avancée, et ce roman du ruisseau... Cette littérature est un des produits de notre société qu'un éréthisme nerveux secoue sans cesse. Nous sommes malades de progrès, d'industrie, de science; nous vivons dans la fièvre, et nous nous plaisons à fouiller les plaies... avides de connaître le cadavre du cœur humain."[36] The passage might have been signed by Taine, Gautier or Verlaine.

The insistence on nerves is very familiar; and neurosis is the main theme of Zola's work. If we take his remarks on *Germinie* literally (and it is difficult to see how else to take them) the Second Empire

[33]"La Littérature et la gymnastique," *Mes Haines*, 47. Compare with Taine's "nos corps mal venus ou gâtés de plébiens ou de penseurs," *Philosophie de l'art* (1865), 74.
[34]An interview in *Le Figaro*, 6 mars 1893; quoted by H. Martineau, *Le Roman scientifique d'E. Zola* (Baillière, 1907), 140.
[35]"M. H. Taine, artiste," *Mes Haines*, 159; compare with Baudelaire's description of nineteenth-century dress—"l'habit nécessaire de notre époque, souffrant et portant sur les épaules noires et maigres le symbole d'un deuil éternel," *Œuvres*, II, 134.
[36]"Germinie Lacerteux," *ibid.*, 66.

was a decadent period, and the scientific method was of value in exploring and defining this decadence. That is how he used it in his own novels, beginning with *Thérèse Raquin*, his first Naturalist effort, in 1867. "J'ai choisi des personnages souverainement dominés par leurs nerfs et leur sang," he wrote in the preface, "entraînés à chaque acte de leur vie par les fatalités de leur chair." In the preface of *La Fortune des Rougon* four years later this becomes: "Physiologiquement, ils [les Rougon-Macquart] sont la lente succession des accidents nerveux et sanguins qui se déclarent dans une race, à la suite d'une première lésion organique, et qui déterminent, selon les milieux, chez chacun des individus de cette race, les sentiments, les désirs, les passions, toutes les manifestations humaines, naturelles et instinctives, dont les produits prennent les noms convenus de vertus et de vices."[37] Some of these phrases are repeated in the last of the series, *Le Docteur Pascal* (1893): "Notre famille," says Pascal, "pourrait... suffire d'exemple à la science, dont l'espoir est de fixer un jour... les lois des accidents nerveux et sanguins qui se déclarent dans une race à la suite d'une première lésion organique."[38] The tone of all these passages is resolutely medical: Zola is at pains to show that the decadence of his characters is no mere affectation. But—and this is how they interest us from the point of view of decadent sensibility—their symptoms, their personalities, are identical in nearly every way with the characters of Gautier, Baudelaire and Poe, and later of Rachilde, Mendès, Péladan and Lorrain. The only difference lies in the causes proposed—causes drawn from Zola's medical readings. He spent the winter of 1868–9 at the Bibliothèque Nationale (then Impériale) documenting himself, and we have a list of the books he consulted: Claude Bernard, Letourneau, Lucas, Moreau de Tours, Morel. For some reason, Zola attributed most of his medical ideas to Claude Bernard, and subsequent criticism has followed his lead and accepted Bernard's *Introduction à l'étude de la médecine expérimentale* (1865) as the main (medical) source of *Les Rougon-Macquart*. In my opinion, Zola got much less from it than from Moreau or Morel. Amongst his notes occurs the familiar "le génie n'est qu'une névrose," and a sketch of the syndromes of degeneracy taken directly from *Les Facultés morales*, *La Psychologie morbide*, and the *Traité des dégénérescences*: "Famille atteinte de défectuosité morale, il y a un vice névropathique dans l'ascendance, ou folie, ou hystérie, ou convulsions... Etat mixte dans l'enfance. Etat

---

[37] Prefaces to *Thérèse Raquin* and *La Fortune des Rougon*.
[38] *Le Docteur Pascal* (Bernouard), 115.

mixte chez les adultes. Hommes femmes, Henri III, Hermaphrodites moraux. Un homme qui a besoin de tuer... Causes qui développent l'intelligence: anesthésie, névropathie, fièvre, exaltation maniaque, agonie, névroses."[39]

Every student of nineteenth-century fiction knows the pathology of the Rougon-Macquart family. The original *tare* comes from the genetrix of the race, Adélaide Fouque, the famous Tante Dide, a neurotic and semi-imbecile, subject to attacks of hysteria. "Il y avait en elle un manque d'équilibre entre le sang et les nerfs, une sorte de détraquement du cerveau... Elle fut sujette à des crises nerveuses qui la jetaient dans des convulsions terribles... Les médecins qui furent consultés, répondirent qu'il n'y avait rien à faire."[40] These crises return throughout the novel, labelled epilepsy or catalepsy; and behind the medical phraseology we catch glimpses of more than one familiar figure—Hérodiade, Madeline Usher, Calixte Sombreval: Tante Dide's case is identical with theirs, down to the shrugs of the medical men; but it is explained, not in aesthetic or metaphysical, but in physiological terms. The same method is applied to her descendants.

She is the founder of two lines: the Rougons, fruits of her marriage with a dull-witted peasant, and the Macquarts, results of her concubinage with the village drunkard (the Macquarts thus inherit a lurid combination of neurosis and alcoholism). Degeneracy haunts both branches, although there are exceptions to it—Eugène Rougon, Tante Dide's grandson, a capable intriguer and politician, a pillar of the Second Empire, who knows how to dominate his passions for the sake of power; his brother Pascal who devotes his life to science and becomes a sort of lay saint; Octave Mouret who, though his ancestry is an unwholesome combination of Rougons and Macquarts, succeeds in making a fortune and dominating the commercial world of his time (*Pot Bouille*, 1882; *Au bonheur des dames*, 1883). But most of the other characters succumb to some form or other of the hereditary neurosis—vice, crime, perversion, and (according to the doctrines of contemporary psychopathology) heroism, mysticism and genius.

In Nana, Tante Dide's great-grand-daughter on the Macquart side, vice is the main characteristic, turning to nymphomania ("hystérie") and Lesbianism; she personifies the corruption of the Second Empire; in his notes Zola described her as an example of "hérédité de l'ivrog-

---

[39]Quoted by H. Martineau, *Le Roman scientifique*, 65.
[40]*La Fortune des Rougon* (Charpentier), 51. Similar attacks occur on pages 140, 231-2, 363. On 163, it is suggested that her catalepsy was aggravated by enforced chastity: "Ses besoins d'amour, après la mort de Macquart, cet homme nécessaire à sa vie, avaient brûlé en elle, la dévorant comme une fille cloîtrée."

nerie se tournant en hystérie."[41] This sexual aberration assumes a more sinister note in two of her half-brothers, Etienne and Jacques Lantier: both are a prey to homicidal mania. Etienne is obliged to forego alcohol, which unchains his blood-lust: "Quand je bois, cela me rend fou... Je ne peux pas avaler deux petits verres sans avoir le besoin de manger un homme." "Une voix abominable, en lui, l'assourdissait... un besoin de goûter au sang... Et il luttait contre le mal héréditaire."[42] Jacques' mania is more exclusively erotic: normal sexual desire has become sadism: "Tuer une femme, tuer une femme! Cela sonnait à ses oreilles du fond de sa jeunesse... Comme les autres... rêvent d'en posséder une, lui s'était enragé à l'idée d'en tuer une... fêlure héréditaire."[43] In a third brother, Claude, this hereditary lesion becomes artistic genius, complicated by decadent *impuissance*: "Il s'énervait... arrivait à une véritable paralysie de la volonté. Etaient-ce donc ses yeux, étaient-ce ses mains qui cessaient de lui appartenir, dans le progrès des lésions anciennes qui l'avait inquiété déjà?"[44] This is Zola's interpretation of the impotence and the languor which Baudelaire, Gautier, Mallarmé and the young Flaubert describe. The end of the novel shows Claude hanging himself in front of the painting he cannot finish.

Catalepsy, homosexuality, blood-lust, genius: to make the picture of degeneracy complete, heroism and mysticism were needed; and heroism and mysticism therefore crop up amongst the Rougon-Macquarts. Silvère, the unfortunate hero of *La Fortune des Rougon*, owes his Republican and democratic idealism to the same nervous disease which leads Nana to abandon herself to vice or Etienne to strangle a woman. His uncle Pascal, the biologist, recognizes this in a characteristic interview with the young man: "Ah! tu es bien le petit-fils de ta grand'mère... Hystérie ou enthousiasme, folie honteuse ou folie sublime. Toujours ces diables de nerfs!... La famille est complète... Elle

[41]Zola, for all the atrocities of his books, had a strong streak of middle-class puritanism (which probably explains the atrocities, by a process of fascinated repulsion). His thesis on the French Revolution was the same as Carlyle's: France paid with the Terror for her loose living under Louis XV (see the quotation given by Auriant, *La Véritable Histoire de "Nana,"* Mercure de France, 1942, 17); and he thought that 1870 was the direct result of the corruption of the Second Empire— of which Nana herself was a symptom. *Nana* (Charpentier), I, 236.

[42]*Germinal* (Charpentier), 48, 358.

[43]*La Bête humaine* (Bernouard), 55–6.

[44]*L'Œuvre* (Bernouard), 226. The situation between Claude and his wife Christine is (apart from Claude's hereditary neurosis) identical with that between Tiburce and Gretchen in Gautier's *Toison d'or*: both ladies complain, and in nearly the same terms, that their men neglect them for the unreal, artificial creatures of painting and sculpture.   [45]*La Fortune des Rougon* (Charpentier), 257.

aura un héros."[45] Of the same order is the mysticism which flits through the twenty volumes, lighting up this or that character with a sickly gloss:[46] Marthe Mouret (*La Conquête de Plassans*), her son Serge (*La Faute de l'abbé Mouret*), and Angélique (*Le Rêve*). Zola said of Marthe that she was "encore une détraquée: chute dans la religion... Du moment qu'elle est dévote, elle peut se détraquer à son aise."[47] She also suffers from catalepsy. Serge is "prédestiné à la prêtrise, à être eunuque par le sang, par la race et par l'éducation."[48] Angélique's piety is of exactly the same kind: it is due to the hereditary taint which, in other circumstances, would have made her a Nana: "Elle triomphait dans une flambée de tous les feux héréditaires que l'on croyait morts."[49] She dies in a nervous crisis the day of her wedding, as she is leaving the church on her husband's arm.

The familiar identification of modern civilization (which Zola calls "affinement") with decadence occurs more than once. Its ravages are supposed to increase from one generation to the next, like hereditary syphilis. The children of the first batch of neurotics, brought in contact with the hot-house corruptions of Paris, are invariably more degenerate than their parents. From one novel to the next, the reader is constantly meeting sickly adolescents who sprout like toad-stools in the damp rot of a cellar, lead a poisonous existence complicated by neurotic ailments, and die prematurely (Nana's son Louis; Jeanne Grandjean in *Une Page d'amour*). The best examples flourish in the Rougon-Saccard line. Aristide Rougon, another of Tante Dide's grandsons, who takes the name of Saccard, is a shady financier, crooked but energetic. His son Maxime is merely corrupt, a physical and moral degenerate: "Un être pourri," Zola wrote in his notes, "glissant au mal sans volonté, faible et sensuel, s'abandonnant, inconscient presque de son ordure... si vicieux qu'il ne sent plus le vice. Le vice, c'est sa vie."[50] He had passive homosexual experiences as a student in boarding-school, and these vicious tendencies, partly (as ever) hereditary, reached full

---

[46]In a review of the Goncourts' *Madame Gervaisais* (1869), Zola said that a conversion to Catholicism was a sign of "amoindrissement du cerveau," *Mes Haines*, 298. He attributes Bernadette's visions to sexual neurosis (*Lourdes*, Charpentier, 586-7).

[47]Quoted by Martineau, *Le Roman scientifique*, 106.

[48]*Ibid.*, 110.

[49]*Le Rêve* (Charpentier), 261. Anatole France and Jules Lemaître demolished *Le Rêve* in two of the best reviews in literature (reprinted in *La Vie littéraire* and *Les Contemporains*).

[50]*La Curée* (Bernouard), appendice, 336. Another idea of Taine's, who thought spleen a characteristic result of this hyper-refinement: "le signe des siècles descendant la pente d'une civilisation ... des sociétés décadentes," he calls it. Quoted by the Goncourts, *Journal*, II, 141-2.

development in the hectic, artificial atmosphere of his father's house in Paris. For all the medical jargon, his true sources are not hard to trace: he is another version of Gautier's Hermaphrodite: "Ses cheveux bouclés achevaient de lui donner cet 'air fille'... La race des Rougon s'affinait en lui, devenait délicate et vicieuse... Il était un produit défectueux, où les défauts des parents se complétaient et s'empiraient. [Une] créature frêle, chez laquelle le sexe avait dû hésiter... hermaphrodite étrange venu à son heure dans une société qui pourrissait... Il était le dieu de cet âge, avec ses hanches développées, ses longues mains fluettes, son air maladif et polisson... Il avait certainement rêvé les ordures les moins usitées. Le vice chez lui... [était] une floraison naturelle et extérieure."[51] In his incestuous adultery with his step-mother, Renée, he plays the passive role: "Renée était l'homme... Maxime subissait. Cet être neutre, devenait aux bras curieux de la jeune femme une grande fille, avec ses membres épilés, ses maigreurs gracieuses d'éphèbe romain. Il semblait né et grandi pour une perversion de la volupté. Renée... pliait sous sa passion cette créature où le sexe hésitait toujours... Cette fille manquée... se trouva être, aux mains de Renée, une de ces débauches de décadence qui, à certaines heures, dans une nation pourrie, épuise une chair et détraque une intelligence."[52]

This would seem to be degeneracy carried to its furthest point. Yet in Maxime's son Charles (by a serving-wench, herself afflicted with an alcoholic ancestry), we go a step further. The child is described as having "une beauté d'ange, avec l'indéfinissable corruption de toute une race... un de ces petits dauphins exsangues, qui n'ont pu porter l'exécrable héritage de leur race, et qui s'endorment de vieillesse et d'imbécilité." He is a cretin, "ni cerveau ni cœur, rien qu'un petit chien vicieux,"[53] and dies of haemophilia.

Presumably if one chooses a decadent family as subject for a series of novels, one has to study its decadence. From this point of view, Zola's passion for *félures*, *lésions* and *flammes héréditaires* is legitimate enough. But, as the echoes from Gautier suggest, he had more than a mere scientific interest in the subject; his preoccupation with it is as much in the period as Mallarmé's, or later Huysmans' and Lorrain's; and comes very close to a morbid fascination, although his essentially robust talent saved him from the worst consequences of this tendency. Two things betray his secret inclinations: the decadence and perversity

---

[51]*La Curée*, 146–7. Other relevant passages are on pages 123, 128–9.
[52]*Ibid.*, 230.
[53]*Le Docteur Pascal* (Bernouard), 213, 215.

of many characters who have no blood-connection with the Rougon-Macquarts, and the fact that in his last books (*Les Trois Villes* and *Les Quatre Evangiles*) the themes of nymphomania, hysteria, degeneracy, etc. occur again and again.

Sometimes the Rougon or the Macquart of this or that novel is the least degenerate person of the book—for example, Octave Mouret in *Pot-Bouille*. Son of Marthe and brother of Serge, his degeneracy should have been a foregone conclusion. Yet it is characters like Auguste and Théophile Vabre, Judge Duveyrier, and Saturnin Josserand who are the typical fruits of a decayed lineage: plagued by nervous attacks, headaches, skin-disease, insanity. Théophile's wife Valérie is the nymphomaniac of the book, as she confesses to Octave: "Elle faisait ça sans le vouloir souvent, uniquement parce qu'il lui venait dans la tête des choses dont elle n'aurait pu expliquer le pourquoi. Tout se cassait, elle tombait malade, elle se serait tuée. Alors, comme rien ne la retenait, autant cette culbute-là qu'une autre."[54] This is a Rougon-Macquart confession from a woman who is neither a Rougon nor a Macquart. As for Renée Saccard, if her step-son Maxime recalls Gautier's Hermaphrodite, she is like the Queen in *Une Nuit de Cléopâtre*. Her first words, like Cleopatra's, are "Je m'ennuie!" She has "mordu à toutes les pommes," and satiety and boredom lead her to dream of new pleasures, perverted pleasures. Her decadent possibilities, in fact, are carried far beyond those of Gautier's heroine, whose affair with Meiamoun is almost idealistic. Renée's incestuous adultery with Maxime is "une nécessité de son ennui, comme une jouissance rare et extrême qui seule pouvait réveiller ses sens lassés... Elle voulait le mal, le mal que personne ne commet... Elle se remit à son rêve d'un plaisir sans nom."[55] This emotional erethism brings her to insanity and death from cerebral meningitis. If Zola had attached her to the Rougon-Macquart family tree, she would have been one of its most characteristic sprouts. Hyacinthe Duvillard (*Paris*, 1898) is pale, slight, elegant and hermaphroditic, interested in occultism and decadent verse, conniving at his father's orgies and his mother's adulteries, squandering fortunes in depraved pleasures—a perfect copy, at twenty-seven years' distance, of Maxime.

It is typical of the Rousseauism *à rebours* which characterizes the decadent idea that the cure Zola proposes for his festering world is a return to primitivism. Both the *Rougon-Macquart* and the *Quatre Evangiles* end in a back-to-the-land movement. Dr. Pascal's great hope

[54]*Pot-Bouille* (Charpentier), II, 151.
[55]*La Curée*, 226–7.

for the regeneration of the family is in Jean Macquart, who has settled down on a farm and married a peasant. His first-born son, "un gros garçon, semblait apporter le renouveau, la sève jeune des races qui vont se retremper dans la terre."[56] And the last scene of *Fécondité* (one of the *Evangiles*) represents three generations of women all nursing their new-born children amongst the freshly tilled pastures of a "New France" somewhere in the African colonies. The episode has an unconscious humour, an almost hallucinatory quality; it was the logical conclusion, not only of Rousseau's ideas, and Taine's, but of the psychiatric theories of the whole century, which had made anything but a bovine, half-vegetable existence seem depraved. We find very similar pictures in subsequent decadent writing. The most interesting thing about Zola's conception of decadence is that it shows an evolution characteristic of the time: it begins as something literary and aesthetic (his essays on Taine and the Goncourts), acquires a medical and scientific tone from his readings in psychopathology, and ends in a revival of the nature-cult. The medical treatises he consulted supplied him with a method of investigating and explaining the complicated psychological states which form the basis of *Mademoiselle de Maupin*, *Les Fleurs du Mal*, Poe's stories, *Un Prêtre marié*: epilepsy, catalepsy, monomania, and all their side issues, from hyper-refinement and mysticism to madness, perversion, strange sins and strange crimes. And, however "scientific" his analysis may be, it is distinctly tinged with Romanticism.[57] He was too near Romanticism, or at least too near men like Barbier, Gautier and Baudelaire, to be entirely scientific; he borrowed nearly all his matter from them. Some of his disciples achieved a more clinical approach to decadent sensibility—notably Henri Céard, in *Terrains à vendre au bord de la mer* (1906).

Céard began his career as a contributor to the Naturalist manifesto *Les Soirées de Médan* (1880), for which he wrote a characteristic study of Second Empire corruption, *La Saignée*. *Terrains*, laid in a somnolent seaside village in Britanny (Kerahuel), presents the whole province in terms of Morel and Moreau de Tours. A doctor, Laguépie, spends all his spare time on the coast, studying the degeneracy of its inhabitants, whom he treats gratis in order to accumulate documents. He believes that Brittany is suffering from hereditary hysteria, complicated by mysticism (*folie mystique*, as he calls it). Such is the background; and while the main characters, Laguépie himself, Malbar

---

[56]*Le Docteur Pascal*, 118.
[57]He recognized this himself: "Je hais le Romantisme et j'en suis." Quoted by Henri Massis, *Comment Emile Zola composait ses romans* (Fasquelle, 1906), 99.

(a journalist) and Mme Trénissan (a concert singer) are neither decadent nor degenerate, the old Naturalist preoccupation with disease crops up ubiquitously in people who have nothing to do with Kerahuel. The worst of them is Mme Vincent Trois, a Parisian who has come for the sea air, and who might have stepped out of the *Rougon-Macquart*. She is the victim of "une hérédité très chargée," walks in jerks like an automaton, has nervous attacks, suffers from nymphomania (all the more inflamed because neurosis has made her incapable of any sort of normal sexual relations); and in her frustration she longs for perversions. Her "orgueil de dégénérée" takes the form of exalted mysticism ("Je suis l'Immaculée Conception," she declares during one of her crises) and sadism: "Pour tromper la police qui éloigne les femmes de l'échafaud, une fois, afin d'assister de près à une exécution capitale, elle s'était déguisée en homme, et elle souhaitait se dévouer à l'heure des catastrophes, dans l'espoir de contempler la souffrance et de prendre plaisir à la vue des agonies."[58] Once again we meet the heroines of De Sade and Gautier and Baudelaire—not to mention those of Rachilde, Mendès, Lorrain, etc., many of whom had displayed their perversity in print long before Céard's novel was published. *Terrains*, in fact, is a curious piece of *naturalisme attardé*: it appeared many years after such characters as Mme Vincent Trois had ceased to be explained, or uniquely explained, as the results of hysteria or heavily charged heredity. The reaction against Zola's theories began more than a quarter of a century before 1906.

We can trace its first stirrings, ironically enough, in another of Zola's disciples, J. K. Huysmans—in *Les Sœurs Vatard* (1879) and *À Rebours* (1884). Both books are in many ways central points in the evolution of decadent sensibility: a perfect equilibrium between the aesthetic decadence of Gautier and Baudelaire and the naturalistic decadence of Zola and Céard.

If decadent sensibility before Zola was too literary, it may be argued that Zola's conception of it is not literary enough. A distinction ought to be made between degeneracy and decadence—although Zola and others used both terms synonymously—the one being pathological, the other aesthetic. Characters like Tante Dide and Mme Vincent Trois are more degenerate than decadent; they are neurotic "cases"; they do not relish their corruption and seek to nourish it on poetry, art and fiction. The same is true of most of the Rougon-Macquarts. The river of degeneracy that washes through that massive work, while it touches decadence at so many points, is not self-conscious enough to be truly

[58]*Terrains à vendre au bord de la mer* (Charpentier), 261–2.

decadent: the balance between science and literature is upset; we do not find it restored until the novels of Huysmans. *A Rebours* especially shows how Zola's psychopathology, when applied to the D'Albert type, gave a finished portrait of the species. The Duc des Esseintes is both degenerate and decadent, both neurotic and aesthetic.

His composite nature is not surprising, if we consider the literary influences that played upon J. K. Huysmans. He began to write as a disciple of Gautier and Baudelaire, had a special admiration for *Maupin*, and called Gautier "notre maître à tous, au point de vue de la forme."[59] The judgment stresses the technique rather than the content of *Maupin*, but hardly precludes the possibility—rather the certainty—that Huysmans relished the aesthetic corruption of D'Albert. Such, at all events, was what attracted him in Baudelaire; for if Baudelaire (he says) was the great innovator, the creator of a new poetry distinct from Hugo's, he was also "l'abstracteur de l'essence et du subtil de nos corruptions."[60] Corruption, indeed, exercised a strange fascination on Huysmans. In an autobiographical sketch (1885) he calls himself "un être d'exception, un écrivain bizarre et maladif, capricant et osé," with none of that "belle santé de l'idée" which produces such true masterpieces as Balzac's novels.[61] The phrases recall Gautier's preface to the *Poésies* of 1830, except that they are much more intellectual and deliberate than emotional and sentimental. Huysmans' preference of the modern to the ancient, and his habit of identifying both with artificiality and decadence, certainly came from Gautier and Baudelaire; while from Zola he learned to interpret decadence in psychopathological terms. The neurosis of the Rougon-Macquart family so impressed him that in his article of 1876 on Zola he practically reproduced the preface of *La Fortune des Rougon*.[62] He was fascinated by Renée Saccard ("une hystérique" as he calls her); and here and there in his own books we find Naturalistic sketches of degenerates as distinct from decadents: Jacques Marles' wife in *En Rade* (1887) for example: "La santé de sa femme égarait la médecine depuis des ans; c'était une maladie dont les incompréhensibles phases déroutaient les spécialistes... Des douleurs étranges... tout un cortège de phénomènes aboutissant à des hallucinations, à des syncopes, à des affaiblissements."[63] He first fused the two kinds of sensibility—aes-

[59]"Emile Zola et *l'Assommoir*" (1876), *Œuvres complètes de J. K. Huysmans* (Crès), II, 176.
[60]The preface to Hannon's *Rimes de joie*.
[61]"J. K. Huysmans," an autobiographical essay signed A. Meunier (1885), reprinted in *En Marge* (Lesage, 1927), 59–60.
[62]"Emile Zola et *l'Assommoir*," 167.   [63]*En Rade* (Stock, 1887), 3.

thetic and degenerate—in the painter Cyprien Tibaille, the hero of
Les Sœurs Vatard, "un homme excellemment désorganisé." Cyprien's
dilapidated nervous system explains his taste for the modern and the
decadent: "C'était d'ailleurs un homme dépravé, amoureux de toutes
les nuances du vice, pourvu qu'elles fussent compliquées et subtiles...
Frêle et nerveux à l'excès, hanté par ces sourdes ardeurs qui montent
des organes lassés, il était arrivé à ne plus rêver qu'à des voluptés
assaisonnées de mines perverses et d'accoutrements baroques. Il ne
comprenait, en fait d'art, que le moderne." And in the modern he
sees nothing but prostitutes: "Il ne tentait de peindre que des filles...
Leurs senteurs énergiques, leurs toilettes tourmentées, leurs yeux fous,
le ravissaient." "Il dessinait avec une allure étonnante les postures
incendiaires, les somnolences accablées des filles à l'affût... il arrivait...
à une intensité de vie furieuse... La Vénus de Médecis lui semblait
imbécile... Au fond, la fille, jeune et vannée, au teint déjà défraîchi...
la figure alléchante et mauvaise, polissonne et fardée, l'attirait."[64] This
aesthetic depravity comes from Gautier and Baudelaire, and so does
Cyprien's eroticism: like D'Albert and Samuel Cramer, he flavours
his sexual adventures with perversity: "Il souhaitait de faire du navre-
ment un repoussoir aux joies. Il aurait voulu étreindre une femme
accoutrée en saltimbanque riche, l'hiver, par un ciel gris et jaune, un
ciel qui va laisser tomber sa neige, dans une chambre tendue d'étoffes
du Japon pendant qu'un famélique quelconque viderait un orgue de
barbarie des valses attristantes dont son ventre est plein."[65]

The Duc des Esseintes is an enlarged portrait of Cyprien, plus all
the decadent characteristics as we have met them from Gautier down.
He is a dandy, affecting a cold demeanour and attempting to astonish
his friends and servants; he gives eccentric banquets, and indulges in
fantastic clothes and furniture.[66] The dandy's lust for domination
appears with refined viciousness (the episode was probably borrowed
from De Sade) in his relations with a boy, Auguste Langlois, whom
he takes to a brothel for a systematic course of depravity. His purpose,
as he explains to the bawd, is to create a murderer and thus take
revenge on modern society.[67] This hatred of the nineteenth century
shows itself most in Des Esseintes' time-exoticism, his desire to escape
from the platitude and ugliness of the contemporary world. It is the
fundamental contradiction of decadent sensibility which we have
already noted, running counter to the professed enthusiasm for the

[64]*Les Sœurs Vatard* (Calmann-Lévy), 60–1, 61–2.
[65]*Ibid.,* 61.
[66]*A Rebours* (Charpentier), 15–16.
[67]*Ibid.,* 95. Compare with *Justine,* III, 53–4.

modern; and it is much more marked in *A Rebours* than in Huysmans'
earlier works. Not a word is said in praise of modern painting—or at
least of painting which draws inspiration, like Cyprien's, from modern
life: Des Esseintes' modernism is entirely confined to his cult of
artificiality; his preferred artists are either ancients, or those who deal
with timeless or non-modern subject-matter—Jan Luyken, Odilon
Redon, El Greco, Gustave Moreau. As such, they indicate a return to
something very like Romantic time-exoticism; except that, after fifty
years of cultivated perversity, it was not the same exoticism that had
fascinated Hugo and Vigny, or even Gautier. As Des Esseintes sees it,
it is entirely neurotic—part of the decadent's search for sharper titilla-
tions. He wants "une peinture subtile, exquise, baignant dans un rêve
ancien, dans une corruption antique... Quelques œuvres suggestives ...
lui ébranlant le système nerveux par d'érudites hystéries, par des
cauchemars compliqués, par des visions nonchalantes et atroces"—such
as Gustave Moreau's "Salomé," "accessible seulement aux cervelles
ébranlées, auguisées, comme rendues visionnaires par la névrose," Jan
Luyken's "abominables imaginations, puant le brûlé, suant le sang,
donnant la chair de poule," Odilon Redon's "effroi du rêve tourmenté
par la congestion... fantastique de maladie et de délire."[68] All his other
tastes are of the same kind: in colours he loves orange, which suits
"les yeux des gens affaiblis et nerveux dont l'appétit sensuel quête des
mets relevés par les fumages et les saumures, les yeux des gens
surexcités et étiques"; in jewels, stones which are "opaques, sulfu-
reuses, comme jaunies de bile, aux lueurs vitreuses et morbides, aux
jets fiévreux et aigres, aux scintillements mystérieux et pervers"; in
interior decoration, the Louis XV style, made for people "épuisés surtout par des éréthismes de cervelle"; in music, harmonies which leave
him "étranglé par l'étouffante boule de l'hystérie"; in literature, works
"mal portantes, minées et irritées par la fièvre... les caprices de la
psychologie les plus morbides, un style perspicace et morbide."[69] Baudelaire was of this sort: he analysed "la psychologie morbide de
l'esprit," and Poe dealt with "ces impulsions irrésistibles que la pathologie cérébrale explique maintenant d'une façon à peu près sure."[70]

As the last phrases suggest, Huysmans' conception of decadence is
psychopathological: like Zola, he is at pains to show that his hero's
manias are no mere pose. Des Esseintes is as much the product of

[68]*Ibid.*, 70, 74–5, 82, 85.
[69]*Ibid.*, 20, 59, 87 (in 1885 he wrote of the eighteenth century: "Cette époque
érotisa le meuble d'une façon charmante, aphrodisia l'industrie des tapissiers et des
ébènistes," *Certains*, 84), 273–4, 209, 244.
[70]*Ibid.*, 188, 253.

diseased heredity as any Rougon-Macquart: he differs only from Zola's characters in so far as he exploits his degeneracy as a source of morbid pleasure. His decadence is aesthetic, as aesthetic as D'Albert's or Samuel Cramer's, with a medical explanation thrown in. The last scion of a decayed race, he suffers from too much lymph in the blood (the result of generations of consanguineous marriages) complicated by the homosexual taint of a sixteenth-century ancestor, a *mignon* of Henri III. His parents both died of racial degeneracy ("la mère... mourut d'épuisement; à son tour le père décéda d'une maladie vague,"[71]) and Des Esseintes' childhood was plagued by scrofula and fever. When the novel opens, he is "un grêle jeune homme de trente ans, anémique et nerveux, aux joues caves, aux yeux d'un bleu froid d'acier, au nez éventé et pourtant droit, aux mains sèches et fluettes"; his appearance and his tastes are very similar to those of Henri III's favourite; and he suffers from beginning to end from "cette singulière maladie qui ravage les races à bout de sang."[72] This is the novel's theme. His flight from Paris was the result of a nervous collapse following depraved sexual excesses; we are given a list of his gallantries: all of them were abnormal in one way or other, all haunted by impotence and peppered with eccentricities beside which the timid inventions of D'Albert and Samuel Cramer seem pale. There was Miss Urania, an American acrobat, a sort of Amazon, with whom he hoped to achieve an inverted sort of pleasure. There was a ventriloquist, who had to recite verses while she lay in his arms, or, if that failed, imitate the thunderings of an outraged husband on the door and thus stimulate Des Esseintes' impotence with fright. Another woman was as much a neurotic decadent as Des Esseintes himself: "Une femme détraquée et nerveuse, aimant à faire macérer la pointe de ses seins dans les senteurs, mais n'éprouvant, en somme une délicieuse et accablante extase, que lorsqu'on lui ratissait la tête avec un peigne ou qu'elle pouvait humer, au milieu des caresses, l'odeur de la suie, du plâtre des maisons en construction, par les temps de pluie, ou de la poussière mouchetée par de grosses gouttes d'orage, pendant l'été."[73] His inherited homosexuality comes out in his relations with a youth he meets on the Avenue de La Tour Maubourg. It is described as the most seductive of all his experiences: "Jamais il n'avait supporté un plus attirant et un plus impérieux fermage; jamais il n'avait connu des périls pareils, jamais aussi il ne s'était senti plus douloureusement satisfait."[74]

71Ibid., 3.   72Ibid., 2, 148.
73Ibid., 160.   74Ibid., 146.

This turbid sensuality is generously laced with mysticism, which becomes both another spice and a symptom of hereditary neurosis. The homosexual episode especially is presented in this light. "Parmi les rappels qui l'assiégeaient," Huysmans writes, "celui de ce réciproque attachement dominait les autres. Toute la levure d'égarement que peut détenir un cerveau surexcité par la névrose, fermentait... En faisant naître un idéal extrahumain dans cette âme qu'elle avait baignée et qu'une hérédité datant du règne de Henri III prédisposait peut-être, la religion avait aussi remué l'illégitime idéal des voluptés."[75] In a previous chapter we pointed out the connection between Des Esseintes' cult of artificiality and his Catholic tendencies—tendencies which later (as described in En Route) led Huysmans to the Church. And as the last quotation shows, neurosis, to which all his other tastes are attributed—paintings, jewels, music, literature—is given as a cause of this one also: it explains his hankering after both perversions and faith. It is true that during most of the novel Des Esseintes is an agnostic; he declares more than once that "le moment de la grâce ne viendrait jamais pour lui";[76] but his psychopathic condition guides him inevitably towards a mystic conclusion, through a combination of artificiality and algolagnia. His religious tendencies are based entirely on depravity—he conceives faith in terms of sacrilege: Satanism, sadism, the Black Mass, the Witches' Sabbath; he wants a "mysticisme dépravé et artistement pervers," which he knows in advance no orthodox priest would tolerate.

His neurosis develops in the hot-house atmosphere of his retreat at Fontenay like a melon under a bell-glass, leading to complete physical collapse. Hallucinations appear: he imagines that his rooms are perfumed with frangipane, that he hears noises and music. An inopportune heat-wave completes his ruin: "Semblable à tous les gens tourmentés par la névrose, la chaleur l'écrasait; l'anémie, maintenue par le froid, reprenait son cours, affaiblissant le corps débilité par d'abondantes sueurs."[77] We are back in pure psychopathology once more: a doctor is summoned: he examines "les urines où certaines traînées blanches lui révélèrent l'une des causes les plus déterminantes de la névrose," puts the duke on a course of peptone enemas to rest his stomach and get his digestion back in order, and informs him that unless he gives up his unnatural existence and returns to Paris for treatment, he will fall a victim to madness complicated by tuberculosis

[75]Ibid., 146–7.
[76]Ibid., 103.
[77]Ibid., 218; also 219, 267–8.

(the neurosis-tuberculosis combination of Mme Gervaisais and Ursule Macquart). The novel ends as Des Esseintes, cursing fate and reflecting that in religious faith alone can he find solace for the miseries of life, packs his bags.

As can be seen, he unites every characteristic of decadent sensibility: he has all the dandy's anti-socialism and lust for domination, and all the neurotic's fear of reality and love of artifice and sterile revery. He spends his days closed in his library, hating the nineteenth century and at the same time enjoying the corrupt beauties it produces. Like any Rougon-Macquart, he is the victim of hereditary neurosis. His resemblance to D'Albert, Fortunio, Poe's creatures, Igitur, Samuel Cramer, Amaury, Calixte Sombreval, is obvious from first to last; but is it possible to imagine such characters suffering from the ailments Huysmans describes in such crude detail?

Des Esseintes' composite nature did not escape the notice of contemporary criticism. Barbey d'Aurevilly[78] called him a perfect representative of nineteenth-century decadence—especially French decadence:

> Le héros de M. Huysmans... est un malade comme tous les héros de roman de cette époque malade... Il est en proie à la névrose du siècle. Il est de l'Hôpital Charcot... On a même inventé des maladies d'avant la naissance... Cela s'appelle l'atavisme et fait présentement le tour de la littérature. Le héros de M. Huysmans a des ancêtres sous Henri III, et c'est l'explication d'un de ses vices... Un tel livre [est] l'un des plus décadents que nous puissions compter parmi les livres décadents de ce siècle de décadence. Pour qu'un décadent de cette force pût se produire... il fallait vraiment que nous fussions devenus ce que nous sommes — une race à sa dernière heure!

D'Aurevilly also pointed out how psychopathology had altered the Romantic conception of personality: "C'est avec de la mœlle épinière et des nerfs que nous expliquons l'homme tout entier. Des Esseintes est soumis dans toute la durée du roman à cette fatalité terrible des nerfs... [Il] n'est plus un être organisé à la manière d'*Obermann*, de *René*, d'*Adolphe*, ces héros de romans humains, passionnés, coupables. C'est une mécanique détraquée." Jules Lemaître a year later[79] made a similar analysis of the difference between Romantic and Decadent: "Aujourd'hui René n'est plus mélancolique; il est morne et il est

---

[78]"*A Rebours* par M. Huysmans," *Le Pays*, 29 juillet 1884. He also noted the Catholic tendency of the book, and remarked that Huysmans now had to choose between conversion and suicide—the same terms he had applied to Baudelaire in 1857.

[79]"J. K. Huysmans," *Revue contemporaine*, 25 avril 1885.

âprement pessimiste. Il ne doute plus, il nie ou même ne se soucie plus de la vérité... Sa volonté est morte. Il ne se réfugie plus dans la rêverie ou dans quelque amour emphatique, mais dans les raffinements littéraires ou dans la recherche pédantesque des sensations rares... René n'était malade que d'esprit ; à présent il est névropathe. Son cas était surtout morale ; il est aujourd'hui surtout pathologique. Vous trouverez la plupart de ces traits chez Des Esseintes." Emile Hennequin also stressed the neurosis of Huysmans' characters, and thought *impuissance* its most striking symptom: "A mesure que M. Huysmans rend ses personnages plus nerveux... il est forcé d'atténuer leur force de volonté... Dans *A Rebours* cette dysénergie est consommée... De leur impuissance volitionnelle, on peut déduire leur incapacité de vivre dans la société... leur absolu pessimisme, leur misanthropie acerbe, leur dégoût de toute vie active."[80]

By the 1880's, indeed, the phenomena of decadence had become so wide-spread that we find critics trying more and more for a synthesis and a definition. Paul Bourget's *Essais de psychologie contemporaine* and *Nouveaux essais de psychologie contemporaine* (1881, 1885) are just such an effort, based on contemporary writers like Baudelaire, Renan, Flaubert, Taine and the Goncourts. Bourget pushed his criticism to the point of a system: nothing less than a demonstration that nineteenth-century civilization was completely decadent. His purpose was to examine "la philosophie dégoûtée de l'universel néant"[81] as it appeared in the authors under discussion; and, inevitably, he argues the case from the primitivist point of view. He thinks that the nineteenth century's unrest comes from the material perfection and excessive complication of its civilization: contemporary man has a *cœur raffiné*; he knows too much; and therefore his life is unhappy and devoured by ennui, that "ver secret des existences comblées." Hence his melancholy, his nausea, his violent reaction against the culture he has created: Russian nihilism, Germanic pessimism (Schopenhauer), Latin neurosis—they are all symptoms of that negation of life which is darkening more and more the horizons of the West. "Lentement, sûrement, s'élabore la croyance à la banqueroute de la nature, qui promet de devenir la foi sinistre du xxe siècle, si la science ou une invasion de barbares ne sauve pas l'humanité trop réfléchie de la lassitude de sa propre pensée." The sentence leads to a hackneyed comparison between the nineteenth century and Imperial Rome: "Par le mot de décadence,

[80]"J. K. Huysmans," *La Revue indépendante*, 4 juillet 1884. To create Des Esseintes, he says, Huysmans used "la symptomatologie de la névrose." Huysmans (*En Marge*, 57) approved this article.

[81]Essay on Stendhal, *Essais de psychologie contemporaine* (Lemerre), 322.

on désigne volontiers l'état d'une société qui produit un trop grand nombre d'individus impropres aux travaux de la vie commune... La société romaine produisait peu d'enfants; elle en arrivait à ne plus mettre sur pied de soldats nationaux... L'entente savante du plaisir, le scepticisme délicat, l'énervement des sensations, l'inconstance du dilettantisme, ont été les plaies sociales de l'empire romain, et seront en tout autre cas des plaies sociales destinées à miner le corps tout entier." The other case being, of course, the nineteenth century. Modern man's ills are the direct result of too much intellectualism: ever since the Middle Ages he has developed his mind more and more, leading to an "ébranlement de l'âme" and consequent "usure physiologique"—the passage is an echo of Taine—which manifests itself "par les déformations du type humain qui se rencontrent à chaque pas dans les grandes villes. L'homme moderne... porte dans ses membres plus grêles, dans la physionomie trop expressive de son visage, dans le regard trop aigu de ses yeux, la trace évidente d'un sang appauvri, d'une énergie musculaire diminuée, d'un nervosisme exagéré."[82] The fruits of this excessive cerebralism are impotence and perversion; sentiment—the true "natural" passion—is destroyed by thought and calculation; analysis "empêche le sourd travail de l'inconscience dans notre cœur et tarit la sensibilité comme à sa source"; "l'abondance des points de vue, cette richesse de l'intelligence, est la ruine de la volonté, car elle produit le dilettantisme et l'impuissance énervée des êtres trop compréhensifs." It would be difficult to imagine a more thorough attack on reason and the intellect: "La pensée... est comme un de ces périlleux agents chimiques, d'un maniement nécessaire sans doute, mais qui exige d'infinies précautions." Because the nineteenth century has not taken these precautions, it has become too refined, too cultured and therefore . . . decadent; and its civilization is condemned to extinction within the near future: "La haute société contemporaine... est parvenue à cette heure, coupable peut-être, à coup sûr délicieuse, où le dilettantisme remplace l'action... C'est encore ici une des formes de la décadence... Les sociétés barbares tendent de toutes leurs forces à un état de conscience qu'elles décorent du titre de civilisation, et à peine cette conscience atteinte, la puissance de la vie tarisse en elles."[83]

[82]Essay on Baudelaire, *ibid.*, 14–16, 24–5; essay on Flaubert, 150–1.

[83]Essay on Stendhal, *ibid.*, 307–8. In the *Nouveaux Essais* (1885) he takes the Goncourts (173–4) and Zola (177) as examples of decadent writers. Bourget's style borrowed ideas and phrases from Gautier: the nineteenth century is "une civilisation vieillissante," "une civilisation fatiguée," a "maladive époque," a "siècle caduc" (*Essais*, 23, 127, 144; *Nouveaux Essais*, 167, 179), the age of "les races cultivées et fatiguées" (*Essais*, 290), etc.

CHAPTER 4

FIN-DE-SIECLE

Il est vraiment trop facile de déclarer qu'une perturbation
des lobes cérébraux produit des assassins et des sacrilèges.
Huysmans, *Là-Bas*, 1891

THE SUMMARY which Hennequin, Lemaître and Barbey d'Aurevilly
give of Des Esseintes' character (nervous disease manifesting itself as
sterility and perversion) is not quite complete. It neglects one significant point—of primary importance in the development of decadent
sensibility after the middle eighties: neurosis is not the only explanation Huysmans proposes for Des Esseintes. The very fact that *A
Rebours* exploits all the possibilities of psychopathology so thoroughly
suggests that something new would soon have to be found. In Des
Esseintes himself the need is already manifest: the perverted Catholicism into which he falls at the end of the book has a touch of glamour
about it; it is almost Baudelairean, a "dépravation du sens de l'infini";
it gives the Duke's manias a metaphysical tone which is much nearer
to *Les Fleurs du Mal* than to the *Rougon-Macquart*.

This new trend was part of Huysmans' growing dissatisfaction with
Naturalism; he wrote *A Rebours* in half-conscious revolt against Zola's
method. The passivity of the Rougon-Macquarts, all in the grip of a
family *tare*, all acting instinctively and submissively according to its
dictates, reduced the dramatic possibilities. Baudelaire had admired
Poe's talent for depicting the exceptions of human life, but the whole
tendency of Zola's work was to prove that neuroses were not exceptional. By 1884, this was something Huysmans could no longer accept.
The Naturalist school, he says, "n'admettait guère d'exception ; elle se
confinait dans la peinture de l'existence commune, s'efforçant de créer
des êtres qui fussent aussi semblables que possible à la bonne moyenne
des gens."[1] The result was a literary blind alley in which he felt
himself suffocating. By giving so much space to exoticism and the

[1] *A Rebours*, préface de 1903, ii.

dandy type (the "exception") he opened a huge breach in the craft of fiction as Zola understood it.[2] None of Zola's degenerates, not even Renée Saccard, has the self-conscious taste for corruption which distinguishes the true decadent. The active sadism of Jacques Lantier is involuntary; he craves enormities not, like De Sade's characters or D'Albert or later Freneuse, as a means of procuring a fresh titillation of his senses or a supreme expression of his *moi*, but because he cannot help it, owing to the insanity he has inherited from Tante Dide and her drunkard lover. To some extent, heredity is proposed to explain Des Esseintes' perversities. But we tend to lose sight of this explanation as the novel progresses: his complicated anti-socialism and his sadistic debauches are not sufficiently attached to his family tree. The truth is that the literary schizophrenia we have seen before in decadent sensibility (love of the modern and hatred of the modern) had grown too strong by 1884 to be ignored any longer. By isolating his hero, representing him as "fuyant à tire-d'aile dans le rêve, se réfugiant dans l'illusion d'extravagantes féeries, vivant seul, loin de son siècle, dans le souvenir d'époques plus cordiales, de milieux moins vils,"[3] Huysmans resolved the problem against the modern.

This solution dominates the evolution of decadent sensibility during the rest of the century. Decadent literature deals with demonic characters who, while sometimes explained in terms of nervous disease, become more and more like the fatal men and women of Romanticism. At the same time artificiality, modernism and decadence had become so strongly identified with each other that space- and time-exoticism of a thorough-going kind like *Notre Dame de Paris* or *Contes d'Espagne et d'Italie* was more or less out of the question. The nineteenth century was decadent, and to be decadent one had to write about the nineteenth century. The result is that exceptional characters in the style of Hernani or Lucrèce Borgia make the necessarily modern backgrounds of most decadent writing seem anachronistic. The themes become so lurid that we look involuntarily for a perspective of Neronian amphitheatres and Renaissance palaces—embellishments which more than one writer took pains to supply.

It is illuminating to follow out these tendencies in Huysmans' next major work, *Là-Bas* (1891), even though such a discussion anticipates by a number of years a great deal of significant material. Modernism appears in *A Rebours* only as artificiality, but there is none at all in

---

[2]Zola saw at once what damage *A Rebours* would do to Naturalism, and reproached Huysmans bitterly for writing the book. *A Rebours*, préface de 1903, ii–v.
[3]*Ibid.*, vi.

Là-Bas. The book is an almost pure example of time-exoticism—an effort to escape from the contemporary world into the mysticism at once lusty, ascetic and depraved of the fifteenth century. Modern civilization is attacked as "cette vie moderne atroce, l'américanisme nouveau des mœurs, l'apothéose du coffre-fort," "un affreux temps," "un territoire américain," a Manichean scene, in degeneracy from the high times of the Middle Ages.[4] To avoid the sight of contemporary Paris, Durtal (the hero) keeps his eyes down when he walks the streets and tries to imagine himself back in the Middle Ages. Huysmans could scarcely have written a more complete denial of the modernism he had preached in *Croquis parisiens, Les Sœurs Vatard* and his artistic criticism. Durtal has stopped writing Naturalist studies of manners (his usual stock in trade) and is busy with a biography of Gilles de Rais, the fifteenth-century sado-masochist. The project is even represented as a necessary form of psychotherapy; he was a sick man until he set to work on Gilles. "Tu devrais reprendre haleine, et t'asseoir dans une autre époque," his friend Dr des Hermies tells him: "Cela explique bien facilement ton déssaroi spirituel pendant des mois et cette santé qui t'est subitement revenue lorsque tu t'es emballé sur Gilles de Rais."[5]

There are three decadents in the book: Gilles, Durtal, and Durtal's mistress, Mme Chantelouve, and not one of them is explained in medical terms.

Gilles is an exotic treatment of Des Esseintes: Huysmans even calls him "le Des Esseintes du xve siècle."[6] He has not the Duke's complicated refinements and decadent heredity (the documents were lacking for that); but, thanks to the immunity of a marshal of France in the fifteenth century, he is able to practise all the crimes and perversions Des Esseintes only timidly dreams about. He has a collection of Latin books and objets d'art and like any nineteenth-century decadent has run through conventional pleasures and arrived at perversions, the only means left of stirring his jaded appetites. After his debauches at the court of Charles VII, "il semble que le mépris des formes féminines lui soit venu. Ainsi que les gens dont l'idéal de concupiscence s'altère et dévie, il en arrive certainement à être dégouté par la délicatesse du grain de la peau, par cette odeur de la femme que tous les sodomites abhorrent."[7] He begins by debauching the choir-boys of his chapel, and this in turn leads to what modern psychiatry calls sadistic pedophilia: "La première victime de Gilles fut

4*Là-Bas* (Plon), 84–5, 169, 417. 5*Ibid.*, 24.
6*Ibid.*, 67–8. 7*Ibid.*, 233.

un tout petit garçon... Il l'égorgea, lui trancha les poings, détacha le cœur, arracha les yeux."[8] But what is chiefly remarkable about Gilles' crimes is less their atrocity than their depraved mysticism: Huysmans presents him as a religious man, fond of Church ceremonies, who committed his horrors for a Satanic purpose: "Du Mysticisme exalté au Satanisme exaspéré, il n'y a qu'un pas... [Gilles] a transporté la furie des prières dans le territoire des à rebours."[9] He dabbles in alchemy, offers the hearts and blood of his victims to Satan, whom he attempts to raise by celebrating the Black Mass. His perversity, in short, is not simply a neurotic syndrone; and the same applies to Durtal and Mme Chantelouve.

Durtal's book on Gilles is a side-product of his interest in Satanism —which in turn is the main symptom of his disgust with modern life. His spiritual condition is very much like Des Esseintes': he realizes that religious faith is the only solution to his spiritual disorders, but considers that the Church demands such an abdication of all common sense that he cannot accept her doctrines.[10] Curiously enough, he does not feel quite so strongly about Satanism: it has an evil glamour about it which contrasts very favourably with nineteenth-century mediocrity: "L'exécration de l'impuissance, la haine du médiocre," Des Hermies points out, "c'est peut-être l'une des plus indulgentes définitions du diabolisme."[11] It also provides a dramatic explanation of character. Durtal can no longer tolerate the humdrum thesis of pathology: it leaves too much out of account; he is almost ready to accept the mediaeval belief in demonic possession: "Toutes les théories modernes des Lombroso et des Maudsley ne rendent pas compréhensibles les singuliers abus du Maréchal de Rais. Le classer dans la série des monomanes, rien de plus juste... Mais pourquoi le Maréchal fut-il

[8]*Ibid.* A similar passage occurs in Lautréamont's *Chants de Maldoror* (Corti), 11–13, written in 1870. On sadistic pedophilia in general, see Paul de River's *The Sexual Criminal* (Springfield, Charles C. Thomas, 1949), chap. vi, "The Sadistic Pedophile," 75–86. Lautréamont and Huysmans, though writing fiction, give all the manifestations of this perversion; there is not a detail in their descriptions which is not confirmed by De River's observations of actual cases in the criminal courts of Los Angeles.

[9]*Ibid.*, 73. Gilles' crimes included necrophilia, which leads Huysmans (240) to compare him to Sergeant Bertrand, who was tried for mutilation of corpses in 1849. Baudelaire refers to him in his first article on Poe (1856), and when the Goncourts published their *Portraits intimes du* xviiie *siècle* (1857) a critic called them "les sergents Bertrand de l'histoire," a stricture which nearly sent Jules to bed with an attack of jaundice (*Journal*, I, 150). Bertrand's necro-sadism is now a classic of psychopathology: see Maurice Heine's *Confessions et observations psychosexuelles* (Crès, 1936), 194 *et seq.*

[10]*Ibid.*, 15–16.   [11]*Ibid.*, 76.

monomane, comment le devint-il ? C'est ce que tous les Lombroso de la terre ignorent. Les lésions de l'encéphale, l'adhérence au cerveau de la pie-mère ne signifient absolument rien dans ces questions. Ce sont de simples résultantes, des effets dérivés d'une cause qu'il faudrait expliquer et qu'aucun matérialiste n'explique. Il est vraiment trop facile de déclarer qu'une perturbation des lobes cérébraux produit des assassins et des sacrilèges."[12] Durtal is continually repeating these ideas, either in solitary meditation or in conversation with Des Hermies; *Là-Bas* opens with six or eight closely argued pages on the inadequacies of Naturalist psychology, with its denial of the super-natural and its mechanical dogmatism. Durtal (that is, Huysmans) was writing his own history backwards when he embarked on Gilles de Rais: the Marshal went from orthodoxy to Satanism; it is not hard to see that his biographer must go from Satanism to orthodoxy—as actually happened four years later in *En Route*. He doubts the exis-tence of God, but he is half-ready to believe in the Devil—the more so as mystic diabolism is a perfect symbol of the age, a complex fruit of a decadence, born of a desire to escape from an intolerable world and a craving for new sensations: "Ce sont ces sacrées études hors du monde, ces pensées cloîtrées dans des scènes ecclésiastiques et dé-moniaques qui m'ont ainsi détraqué, se dit-il... Toute l'efflorescence d'un mysticisme inconscient... partait en désordre à la recherche d'une atmosphère nouvelle, en quête de délices et de douleurs neuves."[13] For, like all the other decadents, Durtal is *blasé* and satiated: "Il manquait d'appétit, n'était réellement tourmenté que par l'éréthisme de sa cervelle. Il était usé de corps, élimé d'âme, inapte à aimer,... Il avait le cœur en friche et rien ne poussait... Il ne pouvait plus toucher à rien, sans le gâter."[14] His sterile satiety leads him to per-versions, and perversions are represented by Mme Chantelouve in whom he senses a mysterious depravity.

She is the most interesting decadent in the novel, a female counter-part of Gilles de Rais living in the nineteenth century, her degeneracy explained in terms of Satanism. "Tout un côté visible de femme du monde... et un autre côté alors inconnu de folle passionée, de romantique aiguë, d'hystérique de corps, de nymphomane d'âme."[15] Her dreamy, neurotic eyes reveal her spiritual corruption: they appear on page after page like a theme[16]; she has attacks of hysteria,

[12]*Ibid.*, 157–8. The same point is discussed on pages 159, 204, 211–13, 361–2 —an indication of how it preoccupied Huysmans.
[13]*Ibid.*, 136–7.   [14]*Ibid.*, 272–3.
[15]*Ibid.*, 149–50.   [16]*Ibid.*, 177, 180, 210, 226, 256, 270, 299, 301, 305.

laughing suddenly and without cause, even in public places—"Pardon
c'est nerveux, cela me prend souvent dans les omnibus."[17] Her love-
making is full of strange surprises, perverted caprices and sudden
nerve-storms which disconcert her partner. All this, of course, was
equally characteristic of Zola's women such as Valérie Vabre, but
with Mme Chantelouve it is not the result of bad heredity, but
of diabolic possession. "Savez-vous que vous êtes une jolie satanique!"
Durtal exclaims. "Cela se peut," she replies, "j'ai tant fréquenté
de prêtres."[18] Her greatest desire is to be constantly in a state of
mortal sin, and she practises the *incubat*, using a diabolic power
to summon whatever men she desires. The final revelation of her
character occurs in chapter XIX, the nerve-centre of the book. She is in
touch with a circle of diabolists led by the unfrocked priest, Docre,
and Durtal persuades her to get him admitted to a celebration of the
Black Mass. The ceremony takes place in a disaffected chapel on the
outskirts of Paris, in front of a congregation of Lesbians, nymphomaniacs and painted male prostitutes, and ends in a perverted orgy,
whipped by religious hysteria. Durtal escapes, dragging Mme Chantelouve with him. She tricks him into a sordid bar and then up to a
filthy bedroom. The episode is a nice combination of squalor and
sacrilege, both of which are necessary to unchain Mme Chantelouve's
passions: when Durtal finally tears himself from her, he sees fragments
of the Host, which Docre had consecrated, amongst her petticoats. He
later describes the evening to Des Hermies, who calls Docre's congregation a harem of hysteric epileptics and erotomaniacs, well known
in mental hospitals. *Là-Bas* thus ends on a medical note. But it is
impossible to read it without feeling that Huysmans saw much more
in Satanism than nervous disease—as indeed is proved by his later
novels.

I have dealt with *Là-Bas* in some detail, both because it shows the
fin-de-siècle search for a new interpretation of decadence, and because
it is the last decadent work of any value. Even before its publication
we enter the waste-lands of literature, a depressing expanse where
French genius burnt low, where even the greatest names (and they are
outside the decadent movement)—Barrès, France, Loti, Maupassant—
are scarcely stars of the first magnitude, and nobody could foresee the
brilliant renaissance of the twentieth century.

One of the gaudiest seed-pods of this weedy garden is Elémir
Bourges' *Le Crépuscule des dieux* (1883); it is even more luridly
neo-Romantic than *Là-Bas*. The story deals with the life of Duke

17*Ibid.*, 175.   18*Ibid.*, 305–6, and 224.

Charles of Blankenbourg and his children in the Paris of the Second Empire. Their heredity is ancient and tainted enough, and to make it more alluring, Bourges uses a paraphernalia of horrors which would not be out of place in a Romantic *drame*. The Duke is an aged debauchee, and his children, Otto, Hans Ulrich and Christiane, are the victims of sexual neurosis—attributed, it is true, to their ancestry, but presented in such feudal and almost legendary terms that, like Gilles de Rais' depravity, it is more like diabolic possession than a pathological state. The family is under the influence of an evil genius, the old Duke's mistress, Julia Belcredi. She has discovered that Hans Ulrich and Christiane have an unconscious passion for one another, and she encourages it until it culminates in incestuous intercourse, after which the young man shoots himself and Christiane becomes a nun. Otto, the eldest son, is a bloodthirsty degenerate: "Teint jaunâtre et pourri, grosse tête vacillante, une sorte d'âme rouge... qui brûlait dans ses yeux pleins de sang," "un prodige de perversité," spending his days in a harem of strumpets and pathics, a victim of nervous attacks which can only be assuaged by running naked in a thunder-shower. He plunges into an intrigue with Julia Belcredi, demanding "complaissances criminelles" from her "pour obtenir une preuve d'amour plus grande... Les deux amants se livrèrent enfin à des ardeurs et des désordres tels qu'ils eussent fait trembler les plus abandonnés. Elle s'y révéla complaisante, savante même... Tandis qu'Otto ... demandait à tous les secrets de débauche les plus énormes de quoi rassasier son âme."[19] At the end of the book, this pair try to poison Duke Charles. He discovers the plot and fires a pistol at his son, who falls. Julia, thinking him dead, poisons herself on his body. He was in reality only wounded and goes insane. Such a conclusion, as Praz says,[20] recalls the fifth act of an Elizabethan tragedy; but, without going so far afield, we may find very close resemblances in the last scenes of Romantic plays like *Antony*, *Marie Tudor* and *Lucrèce Borgia*.

Le *Crépuscule des dieux*, even more than *A Rebours* or *Là-Bas*, became the type of the *fin-de-siècle* novel: it set an example of glamorized neurosis that was followed by all the writers of the decadence proper—Mendès, Rachilde, Péladan and Jean Lorrain.

To the modern reader, Catulle Mendès' novels are very unattractive curiosities—both pretentious and unpleasant, like the buffets and whatnots of the period, carved with leering mahogany monsters. The

[19]*Le Crépuscule des dieux* (Stock, 1901), 161, 164, 228, 249.
[20]Mario Praz, *La Carne, la morte e il diavolo nella letteratura romantica*, terza edizione (Firenze, Sansoni, 1948), 343.

theme of *Zo'har* (1886) is incest, embroidered with all manner of baroque horrors which make the book very nearly unreadable. *La Première Maîtresse* (1887) describes an androgynous youth's love-affair with a depraved woman who leads him into every variety of vice, including trips through the Paris slums in search of "new sins" and an experiment in incestuous Lesbianism. Lesbianism is the theme of *Méphistophéla* (1890), mixed with every vicious detail, both neurotic and neo-Romantic, as if Mendès had drawn up a list and taken pains to leave no ingredient out. The heroine, Sophor d'Heme-linge, is the daughter of a prostitute and a degenerate Russian count, Stéphan Tchercélew, who suffers from hereditary neurosis, general paralysis and leprosy. "Le mal dont je souffre," he declares, "c'est le vice des miens, devenu lèpre en leur dernier héritier: la grimace qui crispe ma bouche est l'affreux rire amer de leur damnation... Le passé des miens est le joyeux étonnement de l'enfer! Si notre engeance eût été une dynastie... elle aurait laissé dans le souvenir consterné des peuples une traînée illustre d'abominations, comme les Césars et les Borgias... Chacune de nos générations, héritière et légatrice des hontes, eut des Caligulas et des Lucrèces, des Messalines et des Alexandres."[21] Sophor inherits this taint; it drives her to such atrocious perversions that Mendès suggests that they were something more than psycho-pathic: "Qui affirmera que les mystérieuses névroses sont autre chose que les Charmes, les Vénéfices, les Envoûtements pratiqués par les sorciers?... Une incarnation démoniaque?"[22] She is proud of her vices, practising them with a sort of diabolic *élan*: "Transgresser, étant humaine, l'humanité, quelle glorieuse audace!... Dire non à Dieu, c'est devenir une espèce de Dieu. L'être se recrée, s'égale au créateur. La femme éprise de l'homme, c'est la règle primitive... La femme éprise de la femme, c'est une nouvelle règle, plus superbe d'avoir vaincu l'autre."[23] This is the fatal dandyism of René, Manfred, Antony, etc., mixed with a deliberate perversity which Gautier, in the "Notice," indicated as a consequence of the cult of artificiality; and once again it leads to sadism: "Elle se saoula de la rougeur des blessures... Elle fut la diabolique réalisatrice des chimères qu'inventa la satiété des vieux rois et des impératrices lasses... Et elle s'ennuyait, intolérablement."[24] The society in which she lives is as depraved as she: Paris is a den of iniquity, the sort of town Nero would have delighted in. There is even a scene at the Opera, *à la* Graindorge; Dr Urbain Glaris, a psychiatrist, calls the theatre his clinic and never

[21]*Méphistophéla* (Dentu, 1890), 81–2.   [22]*Ibid.*, 11.
[23]*Ibid.*, 395.   [24]*Ibid.*, 500, 502.

misses a night: "N'est-ce pas qu'ils sont effrayants," he asks of the audience, "et qu'une salle d'hôpital est moins horrible à considérer que cette fête?... Pour s'oublier, pour s'ignorer, rien qu'ils n'entreprissent... Ils demandent aux drogues maudites, à l'opium, au haschisch, à la morphine, la mort du souvenir. Leurs nerfs, leurs sens, tout leur être... défaille."[25]

In an autobiographical sketch, Rachilde (Mlle Marguérite Eymery) tells us that the bizarre themes of her books were the result of her upbringing in the country, where she lived in an atmosphere of innocence and First Communions. By contrast, she got a taste for "tous les ridicules des névrosés malheureux": cosmetics, sultry perfumes, satin slippers stained with mud, and fell a victim to nervous attacks. The "literary" tone is evident. Mlle Eymery was a D'Albert, a Mazza Willer, an Emma Rouault—twenty years after: a Romantic whose native idealism had been contaminated by neurosis and artificiality.[26] Her books are everything this beginning suggests. *Nono* (1885) has as heroine Renée Fayor, *blasée, folle, un monstre*, a female dandy with "caprices worthy of a Roman Empress," who dominates her lovers and abhors love: "J'espère bien vivre sans amour toute ma vie. L'horrible chose que vos passions, l'horrible chose!"[27] This perverse dandyism does not keep her from promiscuity, however; she indulges in a number of affairs, and finally murders one of her lovers by dropping a large stone on him. *La Marquise de Sade* (1887) is a study of exacerbated Romanticism, spiced, as the title suggests, with the ideas of Sade and the usual Naturalistic insistence on neurosis. The heroine, Mary Barbe, whose mother was a tubercular neurotic, has an elongated "assassin's thumb" which later, when her proclivities have developed, leads her uncle, a learned biologist, to exclaim: "C'est une névrose que je devine enfin. Vous avez la monomanie des cruautés... Ah! ce pouce, long et mince... il est l'indice absolu."[28] But, as in the

[25]*Ibid.*, 245–6. All Mendès novels are of the same kind. In *Les Boudoirs de verre* (Ollendorff, 1884), he announced his programme on the first page: "Le poète flirtira ... pendant que les maris sont au cercle, avec les mondaines curieuses de péché, chercheuses d'inconnu, avides d'impossible." His taste in monstrous characters was more pronounced than Victor Hugo's, as Barbey d'Aurevilly pointed out (quoted by Praz, *La Carne*, 344): in *Le Chercheur de tares* (Charpentier, 1898), decadent sensibility itself—neurasthenia, bad heredity, anti-socialism—is swamped under a flood of black magic, demonic possession, hallucinations and lyric apostrophes: neo-Romanticism at its seedy worst. Even Mendès seems to have realized how excessive his books were: *Zo'har, Méphistophéla* and *Le Chercheur de tares* are all subtitled "roman contemporain," as if their frantic content might have led the reader astray.
[26]Preface to *À mort* (Mounier, 1886), xiii.
[27]*Nono* (Mounier, 1885), 15.
[28]*La Marquise de Sade* (Mounier, 1887), 327.

novels of Mendès and Bourges, these concessions to pathology are so brief as to be scarcely noticeable. Her career is a sadistic orgy: as a child she kills or disfigures her playmates; poisons her husband with cantharides and leads her lover (who is also her illegitimate step-son) to death by aggravating his tuberculosis with perverse sexuality. Under her uncle's guidance, she studies science and soon becomes proficient, but her learning is no check on her depravity: she abandons herself to a life of debauchery in the Paris slums. "Sa vie s'épanouissait en des exagérations à travers ce que les philosophes du siècle appellent la *décadence*, la fin de tout... Elle courut dans les lieux mal famés qu'on lui vantait comme endroits recelant de fortes horreurs, capables, en ébranlant ses nerfs, d'étancher sa soif de meurtre... espérant trouver dans un coin inexploré... la vision de la Rome terrible disputant les sexes sous des voiles de sang."[29]

Monsieur Vénus (1889) deals with Raoule de Vénérande and her two lovers, Jacques Silvert and Raittolbe, another trio of decadents. Raoule, the "Monsieur Vénus" of the title, is the last scion of an ancient family. Her father killed himself with debauchery, and she is variously described as "une hystérique," "une folle," "une nerveuse," "une créature pervertie," who suffers from nervous crises and "les dépravations d'une pensée ardente": "[Chez elle] l'activité cérébrale remplaçait presque toujours les situations positives."[30] She is also a dandy; she indulges in numerous intrigues but refuses to become emotionally involved: "Je n'ai pas eu de passions," she tells Raittolbe, "je représente l'élite des femmes de notre époque... Toutes nous désirons l'impossible... J'ai voulu l'*impossible*."[31] Raittolbe is infected by the century's corruptions, seeks low-class prostitutes because their corruption fascinates him, etc.; and as for Jacques Silvert, he is a potential homosexual, the son of an alcoholic and a prostitute. His androgynous beauty attracts Raoule and leads her to choose him as her "impossible": she will be, she says, not his mistress, but his lover; their affair will thus become "une dépravation nouvelle," undertaken "pour l'amour du vice." She marries him, dresses him as a woman and herself as a man, and after a number of farcical scenes (which would be extremely amusing if Rachilde, like most of the decadent writers, had not lacked all sense of humour) Jacques becomes involved in a duel with Raittolbe and is killed. Raoule has his corpse mummified and painted, and instals it on a couch in her boudoir.

[29]*Ibid.*, 372.
[30]*Monsieur Vénus* (Boissier, 1889), 23, 55, 138, 17, 15.
[31]*Ibid.*, 80, 83.

L'Animale (1893) is the story of Laure Lordès, daughter of parents who, too old when she was born, led an unhealthy existence between dining-room and kitchen, eternally stuffing themselves with rich dishes and liqueurs distilled from the angelica plants which flourished rankly in the garbage heaps of their yard. These angelicas appear more than once; they were the flowers of evil of Laure's childhood: "L'enfant... était pourrie... elle se montrait naturellement décomposée... Née sous les angéliques... elle charriait dans ses veines des ferments terribles."[32] Her career as a "pretty little Messalina" begins by seducing village boys under the angelicas; she then casts an eye on her father's clerk, whose monstrous ugliness appeals to her perverted senses, and finally on the village priest whom (in a scene which curiously foreshadows similar passages in George Bernanos' novels) she terrifies with her perversity. She finds country life dull: "Laure... éprouvait une inquiétude de ne pas aimer davantage, désirant toujours une autre sensation, une volupté plus aiguë."[33] She goes to Paris, "la ville maudite receleuse de toutes les hontes, de toutes les criminelles passions,"[34] to live with one of her lovers; and when he deserts her, consoles herself first with a young worker, then with a pet cat: "Abîmant son esprit dans la contemplation de l'impossible... une fois... elle osa jouer avec la mignonne corne de corail s'érigeant parmi les soies rousses de son ventre."[35] The novel ends when she falls from a roof during a fight with this cat and is killed.

This bestiality theme, only half-developed in *L'Animale*, is treated in greater detail in *La Princesse des Ténèbres* (1896). Madeleine Deslandes, who has "des yeux de pervers," is "détraquée," "une fille pervertie," "une névrosée," etc., falls victim to a mysterious stranger, Hunter, who afflicts her with lycanthropy. She calls him (with italics) her *impossible*; he comes to her at night accompanied by a large black dog,[36] and initiates her into various perversions, bestiality with the dog predominating. There is a suggestion throughout that all these episodes were hallucinations—a variety of insanity; but the general tone of the book is that of a mediaeval legend: Hunter and his dog are always accompanied by a mysterious red flame, and Madeleine's symptoms are never explained scientifically.

Paul de Fertzen, the hero of *Les Hors Nature* (1897), is such a characteristic decadent that one suspects Rachilde composed him like

[32]*L'Animale* (Empis, 1893), 21.
[33]*Ibid.*, 102.
[34]*Ibid.*, 198.
[35]*Ibid.*, 272–3.
[36]*La Princesse des Ténèbres* (Calmann-Lévy, 1896), 231, 241, 307, 17.

a literary cake-mix. He spends days before his mirror and has a passion for the impossible—loves "fleurs impossibles," is writing a poem entitled "Impossible" and composing a ballet on the theme of "l'impossible."[37] There are the usual hints of precious exhaustion, neurosis and androgynism: he has a voice "où revient tout le dandysme de sa perversion"; his brother Reutler calls him a combination of woman and Don Juan, and says he had sadistic tendencies in childhood; he is "un être singulièrement idéal... plus mince, plus pâle, plus fatigué, plus blasé encore, seulement ses yeux brillants disaient l'infatigue de son cerveau où galopaient des chimères furieuses... Il avait l'air d'une femme déguisée. Il gardait les deux ondulations naturelles de ses cheveux où l'on pouvait deviner les naissantes protubérances du démoniaque... La taille se ployait, et des tics nerveux s'ajoutaient lentement aux habitudes de la pensée."[38] Transvesticism plays a large part in his manias: a typical episode is his visit to a masked ball disguised as a Byzantine empress, an ambiguous situation which gives rise to a number of perverted incidents. He retires with his brother Reutler to their country estate, dresses himself as a woman and spends days on end in a boudoir, and is finally strangled by Reutler as the château burns beneath them and engulfs both in its smoking ruins.

Rachilde turned out novels indefatigably, until well into the twentieth century. L'Heure sexuelle (1898) is a study of neurasthenia and perversion, plus an episode dealing with Cleopatra which makes Gautier's story seem almost austerely reticent; La Jongleuse (1900) describes Eliante Donalger, "un cas pathologique, une femme nerveuse, superstitieuse, un peu folle"; Le Grand Saigneur (1922) deals with sadism; Jeux d'artifice (1932) repeats the androgynous and transvesticist themes of the earlier books.

The main argument behind the fourteen volumes of Joséphin Péladan's La Décadence latine (1884–1925) is that Latin decadence results from religious decay.[39] This conceit is mercilessly dunned into the reader: each novel has its mage, absurdly decorated with a Sumer-

[37]Les Hors Nature (Mercure de France, 1897), 7–8, 26, 83–4.

[38]Ibid., 236 (he is "la perpétuelle victime de ses nerfs," 56), 70, 194.

[39]Le Vice suprême (Flammarion, s.d.), 334—another idea inherited from Romanticism. Compare with H. Fierens-Gevaert, La Tristesse contemporaine (Alcan, 1899), 161: "Cette déploration du monde moderne où se confondent des cris d'espérance et de doute, ressemble étrangement au long soupir d'agonie qu'exhala le monde antique pendant la décadence du polithéisme gréco-romain. Alors, comme aujourd'hui, la règle religieuse s'affaiblissait d'année en année." And Emile Tardieu, L'Ennui (Alcan, 1903), 258: "Le départ de Dieu, de la foi, voilà les raisons peu générales, mais vraies, de l'ennui moderne." This loss of faith, he adds, resulted from eighteenth-century sceptical philosophy . . . "Dors-tu content, Voltaire...?"

ian or Babylonian name (Mérodack, Nebo, Tammuz) who, as a prophet of Rosicrucianism, preaches a return to faith. Unfortunately, it is a faith so tainted with depravity and bogus metaphysics that it is difficult to see just how it could reform either France or the Latin races as a whole. This is so obvious that it raises a question—how serious was Péladan? One is constantly tempted to see the whole monstrous work as a farce: the author might well have achieved a certain immortality as a master of parody, and it is a pity that he missed his chance. For the supposition must be abandoned. Péladan had no sense of humour, even less than Rachilde; the bathos of his situations quite escaped him. As a result, he produced one of the most monumental bores in literary history. The sight of so much perverse industry, elaborating volume after volume with sheer nonsense, is dismaying—all the more so because of Péladan's excruciating earnestness.

The heroine of the first of the series, *Le Vice suprême* (1884), is the Princess Leonora d'Este. Barbey d'Aurevilly called her a metaphysical monster,[40] which is a good definition: her resemblance to Poe's women is clear. She is a descendant of the ancient Dukes of Ferrara, and knows Greek, Latin, French, Italian, German and English (on page 47 we find her spending a quiet evening alone by the fire with a volume of Boethius). Like a number of other characters of the period, she had perverted sexual experiences during her education in a convent. Her husband, Prince Sigismondo Malatesta (of Rimini) is a debauched masochist who represents the dying civilization of the nineteenth century: "Il est des modernes," Péladan writes of him, "qui se font de perpétuelles et sanglantes blessures à l'âme. L'étude passionelle des décadences trouvé à peu près toujours un déterminisme illogique, irrationnel, absurde aux phénomènes psychiques. A cette heure des histoires où une civilisation finit, le grand fait est un état nauséeux de l'âme, et... une lassitude d'exister. Les absorptions de la volonté consenties, les accouplements qui dégradent... toutes ces lâchetés ont un but; l'immense soulagement d'abdiquer toute activité, le nirvana du passivisme; un désintéressement complet de la dignité de la vie. Pantin cassé aux ficelles pendantes, le décadent... pourrit sur place... Aux époques de dandysme, on fait bon marché de sa volonté."[41] After her husband's death in a duel, Leonora is free but devoured by ennui: "elle a secoué toutes les branches de l'arbre de science"; normal love no longer interests her—"dans la nuit

[40]*Le Vice suprême*, préface.
[41]*Ibid.*, 48–9.

des temps, Sodome et Gomorrhe l'attirent," and also diabolism, "le péché lettré, patricien et décadent par excellence."[42] The passage shows how the ideas of *Là-Bas* were in the air some years before Huysmans wrote his book. At the same time, while sexually obsessed, Leonora remains virtuous—"rester vertueuse par volupté" is her formula—in order that no man can say "je suis ton maître." This of course, is a variety of the dandy's narcissism, to which is added a sadistic touch: she amuses herself by torturing her admirers with her beauty (as she tortured her husband before his death), allowing them to see her naked in her bath while refusing anything else; she poses for an artist as a statue of "Perversité" which corrupts his talent ever after. "Vous avez débauché ma main," he cries, "Oh! l'obsession de l'Androgyne!" "Que mon corps soit androgyne et l'androgynat le vice plastique, je ne conteste pas," she replies.[43]

Androgynism is one of Péladan's favourite themes—as of all the literature of the period; he considered it a distinguishing mark of decadence. Princess Leonora is paralleled in this respect by La Nine, a courtezan: "La Nine n'avait pas de hanches: la Nine n'avait pas de gorge... Son costume, toujours d'homme, augmentait le trouble détestable que sa vue causait aux pervers. Elle était, consciemment, l'androgyne pâle, vampire suprême des civilisations vieillies, dernier monstre avant le feu du ciel."[44]

The mage of *Le Vice suprême* is Mérodack, a metaphysical development of the dandy. He is represented as a man of iron will—so much so that he is the only man to spurn Princess Leonora's advances. To obtain this self-control he has learned to conquer his desires: "Il me faut dompter les sept éléments du Mal, les sept péchés capitaux!"[45] He deals with Pride by allowing himself to be insulted without seeking revenge; with Luxuria, by reading carefully all obscene literature from the decadent Romans to the Marquis de Sade, examining obscene paintings and statuary, studying the brutal vice of the lower classes and the exquisite eroticism of the aristocracy, etc. Péladan compares him with Don Juan and Balzac's dandies which makes his literary

[42]*Ibid.*, 61, 63, 64.
[43]*Ibid.*, 99. Another of her victims appears "le regard fébrile, les traits décomposés, le teint terreux, en proie à un visible ramollissement de la moelle épinière," 91.
[44]*Ibid.*, 145–6. La Nine receives a circle of aristocratic debauchees who meet "pour profaner et souiller l'idée"; they are seeking a "new evil": "Où est le pire ... l'action criminelle ou la pensée perverse? Raisonner, justifier, héroïser le mal ... n'est-ce pas pis que le commettre?... Concevoir et théoriser exigent une opération calme de l'esprit, qui est le *Vice suprême*" (169). It is also, of course, the intellectualism of the dandy as distinct from the passionate *élan* of Romanticism.
[45]*Ibid.*, 123.

ancestry clear enough, despite the metaphysical verbiage in which he is displayed.

In *Curieuse!* (1886), the second volume of the series, the Leonora-Mérodack saga is taken up by Princess Paule Riazan and Nebo. The purpose of the book was to paint "les mœurs décadentes sous leur aspect parisien et public." Nebo defines the princess as an androgyne on the very first page: she is "l'être complet," he says, "possédant le double charme féminin et viril... androgyne, se suffisant à lui-même et n'aimant pas."[46] He explains to her that androgynes are of divine origin: they were originally "complete beings" until Zeus separated them; they now have to seek each other. He and she are partners reunited: "Appelez-moi Socrate et soyez mon Alcibiade; je vous instruirai aux arts libertins."[47] This instruction does not include any sort of sexuality since the androgyne must remain sterile: it consists uniquely of a theoretical instruction, a training of the will very much like Mérodack's in *Le Vice suprême*. Nebo will unveil every sort of vice and passion to the Princess until, *blasée*, she is no longer attracted by them. "Je lui ouvrirai le fruit pour qu'elle n'en mange pas," he writes of her to his master Mérodack: "Je lui ferai parcourir le cycle du mal et j'éteindrai dans le dégoût sa dernière curiosité... Je souillerai tellement cette âme qu'elle ne pourra plus respirer que dans le Beau et le Pur. Je nie la chair, je nie le sexe." Paule will become his *impossible*.[48]

Nebo is well suited to carry out this programme: he has indulged in every variety of metaphysical speculation, carved statues, works which show "la fin d'une civilisation et la décadence d'une race," has a "sourire Baudelairien," and his lubricious metaphysics are, like Mérodack's, an extreme development of the dandy's narcissism. "Au respir des alcaloïdes de la décadence... Nebo gardait une attitude de diamant... Il était calme et froid dans sa force... Etrange Brummel."[49] He lives in strict chastity, astonishes Paris by his eccentricities, is an admirer of *Maupin* (which he gives Princess Paule as a guide to her thinking). Together they make a tour of the dives of the capital to study "l'ignominie des mœurs décadentes." Their adventures make up the two following volumes of the series, *L'Initiation sentimentale* and *A Cœur perdu* (both of 1888). *A Cœur perdu* is supposed to be "un grand effort vers la sublimation de l'Amour"[50]—a strange phrase.

---

[46]*Curieuse!*, 8.
[47]*Ibid.*, 17.
[48]*Ibid.*, 34–5. "Nous nous prendrons la main pour nous mettre en route vers l'absolu!" 18. All this nonsense is defined as Platonism.
[49]*Ibid.*, 20, 21, 22.   [50]*A Cœur perdu*, préface, xiv.

Perhaps the most extraordinary thing about *La Décadence latine* is that it professes to be a reaction against nineteenth-century decadence, not a morbid delectation therein; Péladan even proposes a cure for decadence—the Rosicrucianism of which Mérodack and Nebo are adepts. Unfortunately for this high ideal, however, Péladan was too much attracted by the decadent themes of contemporary letters. He wrote at the same time as Huysmans, Mendès and Rachilde. Try as he would to inject the pure airs of Platonism into this atmosphere, he could not help breathing it, with the result that all his situations become obscene—the more grotesquely so because of their pretentiousness. This is particularly the case with *A Cœur perdu*. Princess Riazan falls in love with Nebo; he resists her advances; and there follow a series of episodes which, had they been treated in comic vein, would certainly be amongst the funniest things in fiction. The details are all but incredible. On one occasion, Nebo, dressed in nothing but a red silk robe, half Cardinal and half *tapette*, receives the Princess for metaphysical conversation; on another, she has his rooms carpeted with black bear-skins, comes to him squeezed into white silk tights, and they spend the evening drinking champagne and wrestling ("Dangereuses ivresses!" we are told on page 222): these "étreintes ophidiennes" go so far that he only saves himself from what is described as a rape by putting her to sleep with hypnosis. The supreme farce occurs when, having discovered that his androgyne is, after all, a woman, he consents to satisfy her passions. He steeps himself in an aromatic bath, puts on the robes of a Chaldean priest, and designs her a costume of precious stones. Then, after a prolonged session of swinging censers and chanting hymns, experiences what Stendhal called a *fiasco*. With unconscious humour, the 1888 edition of the book has a sketch of this scene on its cover: Princess Riazan, wrapped in bangles and portrayed according to the period's substantial ideal of feminine beauty, and Nebo emaciated and "mystic" in the background, form a picture which, had it been put in vaudeville, would certainly have brought down the house.

The same lascivious mysticism and Platonic hocus-pocus fill out the remaining volumes of *La Décadence latine*—*L'Androgyne*, *La Gynandre*, *Typhonia*, etc.—with, as their titles suggest, a generous spice of androgynism and perversity. Like *A Cœur perdu*, they are lugubriously comic, but this did not prevent them from exercising considerable influence, according to the principle that "Un sot trouve toujours un plus sot qui l'admire."

Remy de Gourmont's *Le Fantôme* (1891) is a curious Péladan derivative, glazed with Poe. Its two characters, Damase and his wife Hyacinthe, were it not for their itching libidinousness, might have emerged from *Ligeia* or *The Fall of the House of Usher*. He is a sterile narcissist, and she, the last of an ancient race: "Hyacinthe sortait d'une race morte au monde, depuis des siècles. Fleur d'automne et la dernière, elle accumulait en son parfum tout l'esprit de cette sève tardive." Both of them crave "d'exceptionelles voluptés," to find which they begin indulging in perversions—with the highest moral ends in view: "Pour que tu sois vraiment sans espoir charnel," Damase says, "pour que tu connaisses l'humiliation d'avoir un sexe insatiable et menteur."[51] The perversions include sacrilege, sadism and masochism —all practised "mystically"; and, as in *La Décadence latine*, this mysticism is so contaminated that it is nothing but a perversion the more: Damase and Hyacinthe end in "le plus mémorable abîme de divagations voluptueuses."[52]

Sexual perversions, in fact, are the chief ingredient of all these works—usually appearing as androgynism and Lesbianism, both described as symptoms of decadence. By the eighties, Romanticism's *mal du siècle* had become androgynism: "A quels cultes mystérieux vont-ils donc se vouer, ces hommes et ces femmes que *l'amour de soi* écarte l'un de l'autre?" asked Maurice Barrès in a preface he wrote for *Monsieur Vénus*. "La maladie du siècle... est faite en effet d'une fatigue nerveuse, excessive" which leads to "le dégoût de la femme" and "la haine de la force mâle," so that certain minds "rêvent d'un être insexué"—the androgyne.[53] The evolution, however startling, can be traced quite easily; it is a further development of dandyism, owes a good deal to the anti-naturism of the cult of artificiality, and even more to psychopathology which, by its investigation of abnormal nervous and sexual states, opened new fields to literature and made accessible subjects until then reserved for pornography. It also took colour from the Imperial Roman parallel: sexual perversions occupy so much space in Latin authors of the decadence that they were naturally introduced onto the contemporary scene.

A final statement of what the nineteenth century was looking for in ancient Rome is to be found in Lombard's *L'Agonie* (1888). The novel is set in the reign of Heliogabalus. The timid hints of previous

[51]*Le Fantôme* (Mercure de France), 83, 86–7.
[52]*Ibid.*, 149.
[53]*Monsieur Vénus*, xix–xx.

writers like Gautier are developed in detail and supported by an elaborate apparatus of scholarship derived from Lampridius and Dio. Lombard sees Heliogabalus' perversions as a Roman anticipation of nineteenth-century androgynism. Atillius, the chief character, follows the Emperor's teachings because they agree with his own tastes; both men aim at "la Révolution sexuelle du monde romain" in order to establish "l'universalisation de l'Amour Androgyne."[54] Atillius' arguments are the same as Nebo's, from which they are probably derived: the new cult, he thinks, "par la poursuite acharnée du sexe mâle par le sexe mâle, inutiliserait le sexe femelle ou plutôt la bisexualité humaine, et aussi aiderait à la création... de l'ANDROGYNE, l'être qui se suffit à lui-même parce qu'il renferme les deux sexes, et établirait l'unité de la Vie là où sa dualité s'étalait"[55]—a definition which strips the metaphysical veil from Nebo's latent pederasty. This sort of plot furnishes an excuse for an indefinite number of lurid scenes; and L'Agonie in fact is little else but a long fresco of depraved eroticism. All the characters, furthermore, are presented in terms of nineteenth-century degeneracy, like a group of Rougon-Macquarts. Heliogabalus has "les yeux cerclés de noir, terribles, ennuyés; les traits fins, tirés"[56]; his mother, Soemias, practises Lesbianism and takes Messalina as her model; her nymphomania is supposed to be the result of tainted heredity: "L'ancestralité violemment amoureuse de cette mère, cette ancestralité qui de crimes avait accablé le monde, maintenant perçait, rouge fleur aux pétales de sang, en aventures frénétiques, en débordement névrotiques."[57] Atillia (Atillius' sister) is "très gracile, très nerveuse et électrisante avec, dans le regard, une lueur d'égarement... comme si le surmènement de sa vie flottant en de l'artificialité l'eût déséquilibrée."[58] Another character, Madeh, uses rouge and dresses as a woman, is "très sensitif parce que très maladif," lives a perverted life and ends by becoming a Christian. His conversion is part of a turbid Christian atmosphere which exists throughout L'Agonie, and which is much more *fin de siècle* than third-century Roman. Heliogabalus favours the Christians, and Atillius himself is drawn to the new cult; after a particularly depraved orgy in the imperial palace, the scene changes to a Christian meeting in the catacombs where the faithful draw blood from one another's breast and communicate in it.

[54]*L'Agonie* (Ollendorff, 1901), 162.
[55]*Ibid.*, 22.
[56]*Ibid.*, 136. Heliogabalus is defined as "androgyne comme le destin ... riche des deux sexes," 134.
[57]*Ibid.*, 75.
[58]*Ibid.*, 177. She is unbalanced for the same reasons as Lorrain's Freneuse.

The book concludes with a universal slaughter: Heliogabalus is overthrown, and heterosexuality triumphs over androgynism, "l'amour artificiel."

Perversion occupies a large place in Verlaine's later work (his earlier poetry was relatively pure in this respect). In "La Dernière Fête galante" (*Parallèlement*, 1889) he announced that he has given up the Watteau style for "un embarquement pour Sodome et Gomorrhe" and proceeds to illustrate the new programme with poems like "Les Amies," "Ballade Sapho," "Explication," "Sur une statue de Ganymède," "Laeti et errabundi," and particularly "Ces Passions":

> Ces passions qu'eux seuls nomment encore amours
> Sont des amours aussi, tendres et furieuses,
> Avec des particularités curieuses
> Que n'ont pas les amours certes de tous les jours.

The poem was later reprinted in *Hombres*, a collection of verse which leaves no doubt as to Verlaine's tastes.[59] He was also fond of the sterility theme, and finally wrote it down in a sonnet, "Langueur," which summed up the whole decadent idea:

> Je suis l'Empire à la fin de la décadence
> Qui regarde passer les grands Barbares blancs,
> En composant des acrostiches indolents
> D'un style d'or où la langueur du soleil danse.
>
> L'âme seulette a mal au cœur d'un ennui dense.
> Là-bas on dit qu'il est de longs combats sanglants.
> O n'y pouvoir, étant si faible aux vœux si lents,
> O n'y vouloir fleurir un peu cette existence!
>
> O n'y vouloir, ô n'y pouvoir mourir un peu!
> Ah! tout est bu! Bathylle, as-tu fini de rire?
> Ah! tout est bu, tout est mangé! Plus rien à dire!
>
> Seul, un poème un peu niais qu'on met au feu,
> Seul, un esclave un peu coureur qui vous néglige,
> Seul, un ennui d'on ne sait quoi qui vous afflige!

"Langueur" was first published in *Le Chat noir* on May 26, 1883. Like a fine bell, it contains echoes of the previous fifty years—the *impuissance* and ennui of Gautier and Baudelaire, the long conversations of Amaury with Mme de Couaën, the decadent style recommended in *Franciscae meae laudes* and the "Notice," the whole set

[59]*La Trilogie érotique de Paul Verlaine, Amies — Femmes — Hombres* (A Paris et à Londres, 1907, édition limitée à 235 exemplaires).

against a background of the dying Roman empire, the world of the Finis Latinorum, which becomes the post-1870 world, when the big white barbarians had once again invaded the Latin city. The period after the Franco-Prussian war was well conditioned to understand such analogies: "Il y avait certainement une curiosité vers des époques qu'on disait faisandées... Il y avait aussi l'idée que les Prussiens de 70 avaient été les barbares, que Paris c'était Rome ou Byzance; les romans de Zola, *Nana*, avaient souligné la métaphore, et il y avait donc des décadents."[60]

The influence of this sonnet was seen at once. Gabriel Vicaire produced his good-humoured travesty of the decadent movement in 1885, *Les Déliquescences, poèmes décadents d'Adoré Floupette*. The introduction, written by "Maurius Tapora," a friend of Adoré's, describes an evening at the Panier Fleuri, a café frequented by the decadents. The conversation is an amusing burlesque on most of the novels and poems we have been examining. Love, at least normal love, is tedious: "Pour y trouver quelque piment," says one of the poets, "il faudrait imaginer des complications invraisemblables," such as existed in decadent Rome. "La décadence romaine... a bien compris l'amour. A force d'inventions perverses et d'imaginations Sataniques, elle est arrivée à le rendre tout à fait piquant. Oh! la décadence, vive la décadence!"[61] Another poet shows a lingering Romanticism, combined with sacrilege: "Luther était bien heureux, il était le mari d'une religieuse. Je voudrais être l'Antéchrist."[62] Still another prefers Thomas à Kempis to *even* the Marquis de Sade. Somebody else declares himself "hystérique," and so on. Tapora and Floupette leave together, the latter declaiming: "De la perversité, mon vieux Tapora. Soyons pervers; promets-moi que tu seras pervers."[63] Parodies of Huysmans and Hannon appear here and there: Adoré's rooms are decorated with an engraving of a spider by "Pancrace Buret," which corresponds to the description of a plate by Odilon Redon in the house at Fontenay; "Liminaire," a little prose introduction by Adoré himself, calls his book "la basilique parfumée d'ylang-ylang et d'opoponax, le mauvais lieu saturé d'encens"—certainly a parody of *Rimes de joie*. Mysticism, depravity, sterility and ennui are the themes of the poems. "Décadents," the last sonnet, is typical:

[60]Gustave Kahn, *Symbolistes et décadents* (Vanier, 1902), 37–8.
[61]*Les Déliquescences* (Byzance, chez Lion Vanné, 1885), xxxiv, xxxv.
[62]See the Romantic examples quoted by Louis Maigron, *Le Romantisme et les mœurs* (Champion, 1910), 183, 185.
[63]*Les Déliquescences*, xxxix.

Nos pères étaient forts, et leurs rêves ardents
S'envolaient d'un coup d'aile au pays de Lumière.
Nous, dont la fleur dolente est la Rose Trémière,
Nous n'avons plus de cœur, nous n'avons plus de dents !

Pauvres pantins avec un peu de son, dedans,
Nous regardons sans voir la ferme et la fermière,
Nous renâclons devant la tâche coutumière,
Charlots trop amusés, ultimes Décadents.

Mais, ô Mort du Désir, Inappétence exquise !
Nous gardons le fumet d'une antique Marquise
Dont un Vase de Nuit parfume les Dessous !

Etre Gâteux, c'est toute une philosophie,
Nos nerfs et notre sang ne valent pas deux sous,
Notre cervelle, au vent d'Eté, se liquéfie !

All this is highly amusing. But its full importance as parody can only be realized when it is understood that such writing was taken quite seriously by young authors of the time—as I pointed out in connection with the cult of artificiality. Anatole Baju's little periodical, *Le Décadent*, which appeared from April 10, 1886, to April 15, 1889, contains little else. Its very title was inspired by Verlaine's sonnet, and the first number has an article by Baju, "Aux Lecteurs !" which is a synthesis of everything we have read thus far: "Se dissimuler l'état de décadence où nous sommes arrivés serait le comble de l'insenséisme. Religion, mœurs, justice, tout décade... La société se désagrège sous l'action corrosive d'une civilisation déliquescente. L'homme moderne est un blasé. Affinements d'appétits, de sensations, de goût, de luxe, de jouissances; névrose, hystérie, hypnotisme, morphinomanie, charlatanisme scientifique, schopenhauérisme à outrance, tels sont les prodromes de l'évolution sociale." Another essay signed Villatte in the issue of November 15–30, 1888, equates the dandy with the decadent in terms borrowed word for word from Aurevilly and Baudelaire: "Un Décadent n'aime pas, n'a pas de passions, ou, s'il en a, il les modère à son gré et ne leur obéit jamais... Le Décadent est responsable de tous ses actes; il ne fait rien qui ne soit prémédité, posé, préparé en vue d'un but unique: l'enquête personnelle." One can trace a line which runs without a break from the Don Juan and the roué of classicism through the fatal man, the dandy, the decadent, the Gidian Prometheus down to the existentialist heroes of J.-P. Sartre and the *mauvais garçons* of Jean Genet.

As for the type of literature suited to the decadent, it would seem to be almost entirely perverted (at least if we are to judge from the contents of *Le Décadent*). The first number contains a serial (which was not continued beyond the first instalment) *La Grande Roulotte*, by Luc Vajarnet. It is stuffed with material from *Maupin*, and describes the Lesbian relations of a neurotic Countess and her maid. *L'Espado negro* by Paul Pradet and *Le Sceptique* by Lucien de Sably deal with pederasty. The issue of January 15, 1888, has three sonnets by Jean Lorrain entitled "Retour de Lesbos"; two deal with Sappho, the third, "Narcisse," presents sexual chastity in the manner of the *Hérodiade*, as the last refinement of dandyfied perversion. An article by Ernest Raynaud (June 15, 1888), "Causerie morale," stresses the role played by Gautier and Baudelaire in introducing homosexual themes into literature. Both were "nerveux détraqués," and both sought in ancient Rome decadent elements, "de subtils préoccupations saphiques et sadiques." But they used their discoveries timidly; Gautier painted "d'équivoques préférences sous le masque de la Maupin," but he was afraid of the police, and Baudelaire confined his experiments to Lesbianism. Only contemporary poets have really sung "l'ère auguste des dieux et des amours bizarres," and the real symbol of the Decadence is Narcissus, with his egoistic sterility: he symbolizes a way to "se dérober au sage précepte de l'Ecriture touchant la multiplication." Laurent Tailhade in a series of poems entitled "Troisième Sexe" (August 15–November 15, 1888) described the depravities of the public parks and baths; and an *avis* in the issue of November 15, 1889, announcing the collaboration of "Mitrophane Crapoussin," invokes "les spatalocinèdes—Bathylle, Antinous, Alexis," the "Narcisses timorés des Sodomes," the "si frêles androgynes." Mitrophane will henceforth sign his own verses instead of publishing them under the names of Rimbaud, Raynaud, Tailhade, Du Plessys: "Et, tandis que Lutèce imbriaque se vautre dans son excrément... nous, les linostoles verts des futures néoménies, conglorifiant sur tels modes exténués le stérile hymen des impubères chers, nous déploirons les banderoles, fervents du seul Amour des lauriers que, pour nos tempes fait croître en ses jardins Lesbos immarcessible." As the tone suggests, the decadents were making fun of themselves; but Mitrophane's verse, for all that, is not so different from the sort of thing that the magazine had been publishing during the previous three years. Had it been written by anyone else, it would have seemed the cruellest kind of satire. I shall return to Mitrophane in my last chapter.

This depravity, as always, is mixed with sadism and mysticism. A prose-poem by Charles Evandal, "Lions," in the first number, describes a street-fair on the exterior boulevards. There is a booth of lions. The beasts are as degenerate as the audience: "tordus par le rachis, stupéfiés de morphine et annihilés par d'inavouables pratiques"[64]; their wretched state recalls, by contrast, the superior animals of the Roman arena: "O les lions des antiques décadences!... Avec quelle grâce pleine de force vous enfonciez vos griffes avides dans le sein liliale des vierges impoluées! Avec quelle avidité vous fouilliez de vos muffles hirsutes leurs chastes entrailles que vous épandiez au milieu d'un jaillissement de sang... Comme vous fixiez de votre œil allouvi les jeunes chrétiens demi-nus... dont la vue faisait tressaillir les pâles courtisanes... et allumait une flambée de désirs innommables dans les cerveaux des vieux sénateurs et dans ceux des jeunes élégants... O lions des antiques décadences! Quand nous reviendrez-vous?" Another sketch by Evandal, "Religiosité," combines this mixture of time-exoticism, sadism and perversion with Catholicism. A Lent sermon by the R. P. Gonzague, Dominican, is described: the audience consists of fashionable women and their lovers; the Latin of the Mass is "ce Latin du cinquième siècle, légèrement déliquescent"; and the preacher harangues for an hour, "avec une chasteté de termes qui n'excite que davantage l'imagination."

Contemporary poets, if they did not contribute to Le Décadent, filled their verses with the same kind of material. Jules Laforgue's Le Sanglot de la terre (written between 1878 and 1883) has the customary references to spleen and ennui; the nineteenth century is a "siècle hystérique," astronomy has destroyed the ancient faith. Like so many other decadents, Laforgue was a connoisseur of the down-at-heel Paris suburbs. "Quand j'ai le spleen," he wrote one of his friends in February 1881, "je vais dans les banlieues tristes écouter les orgues de barbarie."[65] Gustave Kahn's volume Les Palais nomades (1887) contains all the well-worn themes and epithets: "la phtisie des soirs," "les micas et les longueurs languides" of his mistress, the "névralgiques regrets" of her soul.

[64]Compare with Huysmans' description of the dancers of Edgar Degas in L'Art moderne.

[65]Correspondance (Mercure de France), 35. The barrel-organ is a reminiscence of Mallarmé's "Plainte d'automne" and Huysmans' Les Sœurs Vatard. The entire decadent movement is an extraordinary proof of the influence of literature on life. Fifty years previously, Laforgue would probably have taken his walks in the forest of Fontainebleau.

> Le palais s'est effondré sous les mousses,
> Le palais s'est désagrégé sous les efforts de partout
> Quand vinrent les musiques barbares...

we read elsewhere. Maurice Maeterlinck's *Les Serres chaudes* (1890) has poems with titles like "Serre d'ennui," "Lassitude," "Ennui," "Ronde d'ennui," "Mon âme impuissante." Some of them ("Oraison" and "Tentations") read—if the thing were possible—like parodies of Adoré Floupette. Albert Samain's volumes are full of dying harmonies, pale evening light, sexual perversions and evocations of decadent Rome. French and Roman decadence are constantly juxtaposed:

> Je n'ai plus le grand cœur des époques nubiles
> Où mon sang eût jailli, superbe, en maints combats.
> Le sang coule si rare en l'Empire si las !
> Et le fer truculent meurtrit nos yeux débiles.
>
> Trop riche du trésor des papyrus falots,
> Notre âme sous son poids de sagesse succombe...

Here is the old Rousseau bias inherited through Taine and Bourget.
"Fin d'Empire" in the same volume (*Au Jardin de l'infante*, 1893) is an imitation of Verlaine's "Langueur":

> Dans l'atrium où veille un César de porphyre,
> Arcadius, les yeux peints, les cheveux frisés,
> Par un éphèbe au corps de vierge se fait lire
> Un doux papyrus grec tout fleuri de baisers.
>
> C'est une idylle rose, où le flot bleu soupire,
> Où l'art mièvre zézaie en vers adonisés ;
> Et l'empereur, qu'un songe ambigu fait sourire,
> Respire un lis avec des gestes épuisés.
>
> Cependant d'heure en heure entrent des capitaines ;
> Ils disent la terreur des batailles lointaines ;
> Mais le maître au front ceint de roses n'entend pas.
>
> Et seul, l'aïeul de marbre au dur profil morose
> A tressailli dans l'ombre, en écoutant là-bas
> Craquer sinistrement l'Empire grandiose.

Other examples are "Soir d'Empire" and "Vision," which ends with the line "Voici, voici venir les temps de l'Androgyne"—the familiar identification of decadence with androgynism.

O. W. Milosz's volume, *Le Poème des décadences* (1899) is all its title suggests.

Nos faibles Joies n'aiment plus les rondes violentes...
Il nous faut aujourd'hui des mélodies lointaines,
Des gestes de fatigue extrême, et des couleurs dolentes.

The scene of Couture's painting, an orgy in a palace menaced by Barbarians, comes back again and again:

Le Roi ceignit l'épée antique...
— L'océan des hordes barbares, au loin,
Hurlait; les courtisans discutaient pierres précieuses.
"Seigneurs, nos murailles s'écroulent, il est temps,
Grand temps, vraiment, de se défendre, tant soit peu."
Mais la foule des patriciens répondit, sans lever les yeux :
"César, les héros font trop de gestes en mourant.
Notre ennui vaut-il la peine qu'on le défende ?...
Couchons-nous là, mourons dans des rires et dans des larmes,
Appelons, à grands cris, les Barbares libérateurs ;
Les mains des patriciens sont trop belles pour les armes...

After all this, it would seem that the decadent field had been gleaned to the stubble; but the idea held such fascination for writers of the period that repetition appears to have been the vice they feared least. They wrote and rewrote the same themes—degeneracy, now explained as neurosis, now as Romantic fatality, now as a combination of both; they used and used again the same similes, metaphors and vocabulary—decadent Rome, decadent Paris, rouged cheeks, painted lips, drugs, dance-halls, theatres, vice-haunted quays and boulevards. Jean Lorrain's work sums up this ultimate period: his life, 1855–1906, embraces it almost chronologically: his books are a sort of marsh or Cloaca Maxima (to borrow a chapter-title from *Phocas*) into which all the sewer trickles descended to fester luridly. By borrowings from previous writers and his own elaborations, Lorrain carried decadent sensibility to the point of revolt against itself. Reference has already been made to his contributions to *Le Décadent*. All the rest of his verse is of the same kind. *La Forêt bleue* (1883) continues the themes of ennui and exhaustion; *Modernités* (1885) displays the customary picture of Parisian decadence, glamorized here and there with classical references. One of the sonnets, "Décadence," is a veritable sediment of previous themes:

Saphus aux cheveux d'ambre, aux yeux de mauvais ange
Est gras, blême et malsain comme un grand nénuphar ;
Poète de Lesbos, ses vers sentent le fard,
Le cold-cream et parfois un parfum plus étrange...

Il est souple et charmeur, plein de déliquescence;
Jolie comme un éphèbe en pleine adolescence;
Comme la pourriture il est phosphorescent...

"Hérodias" transports the legend of John the Baptist from the court
of Antipas to contemporary Paris, and, doubtless to add to the effect,
turns the dancer into a pathic. The fact that he carries a woman's
head on his tray suggests that his dance represents the triumph of
pederasty. "Atavisme," dedicated to Huysmans, describes a degenerate
Russian noble who spends his days in orgies in the Paris slums;
"Anémie," dedicated to Elémir Bourges, paints a picture of decadent
heredity—Christiane in *Le Crépuscule des dieux*:

> Trop fine, trop nerveuse, exsangue et déjà lasse
> De vivre, ayant vécu le passé des aïeux...
> Elle a l'étrange attrait, la maladive grâce,
> Et la fragilité de la fin d'une race.

The next sonnet, "Prince héritier" (also dedicated to Bourges) is a
portrait of her brother Otto, "le digne enfant de ces races pourries."
The content of *Les Griseries* (1887) is very similar; that of *L'Ombre
ardente* (1897) is chiefly pederasty: there are poems on Ganymede,
Hylas, Bathylle, Athys, Antinous and Sporus (Nero's favourite, whose
castration against a background of dying gladiators and burning
Christians, is described with relish). In "Les Éphèbes," the last poem,
Lorrain claims the glory of being the first to sing of "ces êtres sans
sexe et sans nom."

His novels and short stories repeat the themes of his verse. *Très
Russe* (1887) is dedicated to Bourges apparently because (as Lorrain
admits) the heroine, Mme Litvinoff, was modelled on Julia Belcredi.
She is presented in familiar Messalina terms: she killed her husband
by "la science profonde de ses baisers"; she is a Narcissist who practises
strict chastity along with sadism. Her lover, Mauriat, is a decadent—
"nerveux," "trop compliqué," with a taste for prostitutes because "leur
perversité le charmait." *Sonyeuse* (1891) is a collection of short
stories: one deals with Lord Mordaunt, a hair-fetichist; another with
"une nymphomane à lésion cérébrale, aux appétits compliqués et
bizarres," who frequents the Bal de l'Opéra, and who is "la Messaline
éhontée, brisée mais non rassasiée, lassata, sed non satiata... la patri-
cienne féroce et délicate à qui il faut des caresses de brutes"[66]; another
with a man who marries tubercular wives so that he can watch them
die (the description of one of them in a theatre box is lifted almost

---

[66]*Sonyeuse* (Ollendorff), 192–3.

word for word from *Graindorge*[67]). In *Buveurs d'âmes* (1893), the first story "Le Verre de sang," describes Lesbianism between a woman and her step-daughter, plus blood-drinking in a slaughter-house; "Ophelius" is a case of incipient homosexuality; "Sur un Dieu mort" contains a description of a statue of Christ, "équivoque et troublante divinité d'Asie, presque androgyne... ses paupières fardées... C'était bien l'amour avec toutes ses ambiguités et ses perversions coupables"[68]; "Un soir qu'il neigeait" sketches a sadistic pervert who haunts the Place Maubert to scare the prostitutes with a razor, and so on. An analysis of the other volumes—*Sensations et souvenirs* (1895), *Un Démoniaque* (1895), *Une Femme par jour* (1896), *Ames d'automne* (1898), *Fards et poisons* (1903)—would be useless repetition. Lorrain's work is well represented by two of his novels, *Le Vice errant* and *Monsieur de Phocas*. The first, written in 1899, is a description of the corruptions and manias of the winter colony at Nice; most of it— "Coins de Byzance: Les Noronsoff"—concerns Prince Vladimir Noronsoff, a decadent in the grand manner of Des Esseintes, with neo-Romantic touches borrowed from Rachilde, Mendès and Péladan. He is a synthesis of the fatal man, the dandy, the neurotic and the half-legendary monster. Like Mendès' Count Tchercélew, he suffers from the effects of a family curse, dating from 1415. One of his ancestors raped a gipsy girl, and her lover laid an enchantment on all future Noronsoff women by means of a magic violin, whose cords were the bowels of hanged men and its bow the hair of prostitutes. All future ladies of the house will be nymphomaniacs. This is the explanation of the "hystérie héréditaire" and the "aliénation sexuelle" which afflicts the princesses of the family; and Prince Vladimir, besides inheriting it, has the blood of the Borgias through his mother, an Italian: "Nul doute que de ces deux sangs princiers, Borgia et Noronsoff, quelque redoutable fleuron n'eût jailli."[69] Here is another example of the Rougon-Macquart heredity glamorized beyond recognition: Tante Dide crossed with Lucrezia Borgia. Vladimir arrives at Nice at the age of thirty-four; his depraved debauchery has given him European notoriety and ruined his health. He is "à la fois un phtisique et un névrosé"; he looks like a decadent: "les traits étaient fins, le nez droit et le menton un peu long comme chez tous les dégénérés"; and like a true decadent he is proud of his dilapidated condition: "Il était fier de résumer en lui tant de lésions et tant de déchéances."[70] On top

67*Ibid.*, 230–1.
68*Buveurs d'âmes* (Charpentier, 1893), 169.
69*Le Vice errant* (Albin Michel), 134–5.
70*Ibid.*, 150 *et seq.* He is "un fantoche brisé de l'hystérie... débile et usé, pourri jusqu'aux moelles."

of all this is the gipsy's curse; it is insisted upon in chapter after
chapter: "Le charme abominable est revenu," says his mother, "et
l'âme affreuse des princesses de la race tourmente parfois mon
Sacha."[71] He has violent disputes with his mother, accusing her of
bringing the tainted blood of Alexander VI into the family, and above
all of having been virtuous: had she behaved like a true Noronsoff
princess and been a nymphomaniac, the curse would have fallen on
her. As it is, he must suffer from it. "J'ai une âme de fille... cette vieille
âme prostituée des princesses de la race. Je suis une victime, un
résultat d'évolution."[72] The atmosphere is still further charged with
the usual Imperial Roman reminiscences: Noronsoff is perpetually
compared to this or that degenerate Caesar, especially Nero and
Heliogabalus (pages 136, 137, 140, 141, 147, 176, 177, 204). His
manias owe much to the dandy: he gives debauched Neronian banquets, invites an actress to supper, and like Samuel Cramer, wants her
in stage costume with all her diamonds, gives another actress an
elaborate dinner and at dessert takes out his false teeth and drops
them into a glass of water, etc.; his villa at Nice has a Louis XV
drawing-room, a marble bathroom decorated with obscene frescoes,
and is filled with sycophants and hangers-on of the most suspect kind
—an orchestra of rouged gipsies, a couple of Basque sailors, the Countess
Schoboleska and her two hermaphroditic sons. The climax of Vladimir's neurosis is an attempt to bleed one of the moujiks of his guard
for a draught of young blood. He dies of apoplexy, the result of a
senile passion for a handsome Neopolitan fisherman.

Monsieur de Phocas (1901), while not Lorrain's last book, is in
many ways his most representative. The Duke de Freneuse (who goes
under the name of Phocas) shows us the decadent arrived at the point
of hating his own decadence. He is a dandy, recognizably in the line
of Baudelaire and Barbey d'Aurevilly; and like Noronsoff and so many
others has fantasies which show the connection between dandy and
sadist. He is also the last scion of an ancient race, and as such, is
haunted by neurosis and depraved tastes. His appearance is characteristic: he wears green brocade and emeralds, has "une petite tête
fine et glabre tout en méplats" and "ce frêle et blanc poignet de *fin
de race*"; his hand is "délicieusement pâle et transparente, main de
princesse et de courtisane, tel un oiseau de cire"; he takes opium,
suffers from depression, is *blasé, usé, triste*; thinks he has "une lésion

[71]*Ibid.*, 143. Also: "La vieille âme prostituée des princesses de son sang se réveillait
en lui," 191.
[72]*Ibid.*, 341–2.

du cerveau ou dépression nerveuse—la fâcheuse anémie cérébrale qui suit les grandes débauches."[73] He looks like Heliogabalus or Henri III, and rouges heavily. He has a mania for collecting green jewels, aquamarines and emeralds: it is a symptom of the "transparence glauque" which haunts him, and which he seeks vainly in the eyes of women. Frequent reference is made to this craze, and it leads to a homosexual dénouement: no woman had such eyes, but two men had, one a sailor who rowed him on the Seine, the other a peasant on his family estates. The episode recalls D'Albert's discovery of his ideal in the "chevalier" de Serannes. After meeting the sailor, Freneuse goes through a similar crisis, gasping with horror at the discovery of his own perversity. The book is full of homosexual hints, cloaked in classical references (the method had been general ever since *Maupin*): lyric passages on the Antinous of the Louvre, descriptions of dancers at the Folies Bergère, women who look like both Aphrodite and Ganymede, Astarté and Hylas. And Freneuse's sadism, like his passion for green eyes, goes back to his childhood: as a boy he liked to torture animals, and in the atmosphere of Parisian vice, this tendency develops into a psychopathic state akin to Jacques Lantier's—an overwhelming desire to throttle a woman instead of possessing her sexually. It shows clearly how decadent sensibility had reverted to a sort of neo-Romanticism; for while the situations are identical, the motivation is very different: Lantier's algolagnia was entirely patho-logical, the result of Tante Dide's neurosis and Macquart's alcoholism; the derangement from which Freneuse suffers is part of a crazy aestheticism, a species of Romantic monomania which makes it much nearer to the eccentricities of the fatal man than to authentic neurosis. His time-exoticism (like D'Albert's) is part of the same tendency. It takes the form (as we have learned to expect) of an invocation to Nero: "Oh! Néron buvant avec délices les larmes des martyrs, la volupté sinistre des Augustans jetant aux prétoriens la pudeur et l'effroi des vierges chrétiennes, les éclampsies de joie forcenée et féroce dont s'emplissaient les lieux infâmes avant les jeux sanglants du cirque, et les jeunes filles, les enfants et les femmes livrés deux fois aux bêtes, au tigre et à l'homme!"[74] Freneuse never stops com-paring modern Paris with Imperial Rome. The corruptions of the capital are described at length—the *banlieue*, low dives and theatres—and are called upon for an explanation of the duke's sadism and perversity. He has run through the whole gamut of Parisian vice,

[73]*Monsieur de Phocas* (Ollendorff, 1901), 3, 4, 14–15, 149.
[74]*Ibid.*, 363.

savouring what he calls the twentieth-century beauty" of its depravity: "La beauté du vingtième siècle, le charme d'hôpital, la grâce de cimetière... tout cet aguichant étalage de pâleur passionée, de vice savant et d'anémie exténuée et jouisseuse, tout le charme des fleurs faisandées."[75] The celebrations on the Esplanade des Invalides on July 14, 1894, make him think of the "fauves effluves d'une fête sous Néron"; and the Paris Opera, as ever, comes in for a description: the audience is an assembly of crooked bankers, corrupt publishers, prostitutes, sexual perverts: there is the inevitable Lesbian who represents the "psychique beauté du xxe siècle, beauté de fièvre et d'agonie... charme de chlorose et piment maladif," with her "mièvres élégances de fin de race": the whole place smells of corpses and is summed up in the final word: "Regardez. Nous sommes à Rome!"[76]

Freneuse's morbid tendencies reach their highest pitch under the influence of an English painter, Claudius Ethal. Ethal is another fatal man in the Romantic tradition. He lives in splendid mystery, travels widely bringing back aphrodisiacs, opium pipes, unknown orchids, strange oriental venoms, poison rings. One of these rings would do as stage property in *Lucrèce Borgia* or *Le Roi s'amuse*: it is a hollow emerald, filled with deadly poison, a copy of a jewel in the Escurial. Philip II had the original stone cut to serve as a false eye for his mistress, the Princess of Eboli, after he had torn out one of hers and *eaten* it in a fit of jealousy. Ethal, however, has none of the fatal man's emotionalism; he acts through a sort of depraved logic. In short, he is a decadent, with the decadent's cold-blooded perversity: "L'horrible l'attire, la maladie aussi; l'entorse morale et la misère physique... Il a pour le vice et les aberrations... l'espèce de vocation fervente et passionnée qu'ont pour certains cas peu connus... des tempéraments de savants et de grands médecins... C'est un collectionneur de fleurs du mal... Le fumet des déchéances l'enivre; il les comprend toutes et les aime compliquées et profondes."[77] This baroque personage sets about corrupting Freneuse, like another Vautrin with another Rastignac; he encourages his sadism, guides him through the dens of Parisian vice, encourages his homosexual tendencies, until Freneuse exclaims: "Toute une hideuse floraison a jailli d'images lubriques et de pensées honteuses. Cet Ethal! Il a tout flétri, tout souillé en moi."[78] However, considering the description he gave of himself before he met the painter, it is hard to see what there was left to corrupt. Sir Thomas Welcome, another Englishman, is supposed to represent Freneuse's

[75]*Ibid.*, 27–9.   [76]*Ibid.*, 254–61.
[77]*Ibid.*, 212–13.   [78]*Ibid.*, 279.

good genius, just as Ethal represents the evil. He also is a mysterious traveller, a "chercheur d'impossible." He undertakes to cure the duke's neurosis by preaching a return to nature; Freneuse must leave the "existences artificielles, surchauffées et nerveuses" of Paris and London: "Notre âme moderne est exténuée de lecture, de bien être et de civilisation," the only way to cure it is to go back to some sort of primitivism: "C'est la civilisation qui a déformé la vie. Chez les peuples jeunes, toute émotion est une ivresse et toute joie devient religieuse." "Ce peuple," he writes Freneuse from India, "s'use voluptueusement dans la ferveur et ne fixe que l'avenir, insouciant de goûter aux eaux croupies du passé."[79] Freneuse is secretly tempted. But just as he is on the point of leaving, Ethal tells him that Sir Thomas, for all his fine appearance, is really a scoundrel who made his fortune by prostituting himself to a millionaire, Burdhès, whom he later murdered. While this revelation lifts Sir Thomas to full *homme fatal* stature in the duke's eyes—"L'énigme de son charme était peut-être dans son crime. Une atmosphère d'épouvante et de beauté enveloppe toujours l'homme qui a tué, et les yeux des grands meurtriers dardent à travers l'histoire d'hallucinantes lueurs, dont s'auréolent leurs figures; et ce sont encore les cadavres qui piédestalisent le mieux les héros."[80] —it also shatters his last illusions on humanity. There is here a contradiction which occurs in *Les Noronsoff* also: during his entire career, Lorrain toyed with homosexuality in some form or other, his volumes of prose and poetry are full of it, he wrote lyrically of every pervert history or legend could supply, and his books abound in characters who are supposed to have practised every kind of depravity. Yet they are always represented as horrified by so much as the mention of sexual inversion. This is stretching credibility beyond all reasonable limits, and one wonders whether Lorrain was afraid of being suspected of such tendencies himself, or, like Gautier, affected horror for benefit of the censor.

In a last interview with Ethal, Freneuse kills him by smashing the poisoned emerald against his teeth; and the novel ends as he makes preparations for his departure to Egypt, exclaiming: "La ferveur! tout le secret du bonheur humain est là; aimer avec ferveur, s'intéresser passionnément aux choses, rencontrer Dieu partout et l'aimer éperdument dans chaque rencontre, désirer amoureusement toute la nature, les êtres et les choses sans s'arrêter même à la possession, s'user dans le désir effréné du monde extérieur sans même s'inquiéter si le désir

[79]*Ibid.*, 234, 221, 334, 345.
[80]*Ibid.*, 275.

est bon ou mauvais. Car toute sensation est précieuse, et la splendeur des choses ne vient que de l'ardeur que de l'ardeur que nous avons pour elles. L'importance est dans le regard et non dans la chose regardée."[81]

In some ways it is a pity that Lorrain never wrote a sequel to *Phocas*, to show what happened to Freneuse in the east. A good idea of what it might be is supplied by Octave Mirbeau's *Jardin des supplices* (1899) whose hero and heroine are another pair of decadents seeking relief from the ennui and neurosis of the Occident in a glossy variety of space-exoticism. The hero, who is never named, is a depraved boulevardier, a victim of the Poe-Baudelairean "démon de la perversité," which leads him to perform disgusting actions even when they are to his own detriment. He embarks on a voyage to India, tired of the petty corruptions of Paris, and on the boat meets Clara, a mysterious Englishwoman. She becomes his mistress and brings out his worst tendencies. Of course he cherishes her for this very reason: "Ce qui m'attachait à elle, c'étaient l'effrayante pourriture de son âme et ses crimes d'amour"; she is a sado-masochist, craving both self-abasement, "la volupté dans la pourriture," and "les horribles spectacles de douleur et de mort."[82] They go to her house in an inland Chinese city. Nearby is the public execution grounds, the Garden of Punishments; and from then on, the book is little else but a chronicle of her visits to this revolting spot. The scenes described there are incredibly atrocious; they probably outdo everything else of the kind in decadent literature; and Clara enjoys them with hysteric delight—each episode is a prolonged orgy of sadistic emotion. She reveals herself as "emportée par une force de destruction," she is "la fée des charniers, ange des décompositions et des pourritures," "une âme putréfiée" who practises her algolagnia "par un effort de sa cérébralité." Her return from the garden is always followed by a nervous crisis: "Alors, Clara commença de se débattre. Tous ses muscles se bandèrent, effroyablement soulevés et contractés... ses articulations craquèrent... De ses yeux, entre les paupières mi-fermées et battantes, on ne voyait plus qu'un mince trait blanchâtre... Un peu d'écume moussait à ses lèvres... Puis la crise, peu à peu, mollit... Elle s'affaissa, épuisée, sur le lit, les yeux pleins de larmes."[83]

---

[81]*Ibid.*, 338.   [82]*Le Jardin des supplices* (Charpentier, 1923), 141, 158.
[83]*Ibid.*, 212, 261, 275, 321–2. Clara's double nature—sadism alternating with masochism—is emphasized: "Le sang est un précieux adjuvant de la volupté, c'est le vin de l'amour," she says (200); and at the same time, "elle subissait les plus répugnantes étreintes avec une sorte de volupté pâmée" (170). On one occasion she begs her lover to kill her (276): "J'aimerais être tuée par toi, cher petit cœur!"

So the decadent makes his tour of the world and finds that all is corruption. Whether he travels in time or in space—to the empire of Nero and Heliogabalus, or the hieratic sadism of China—the results are the same: by the perverse economy of his nature he seeks and finds nothing but corruption. It is significant, and shows how his characteristics remained constant over a period of fifty years or more, that *Le Jardin des supplices*, for all its exotic allure, ends in a nervous attack identical with those of Madeleine Usher, Calixte Sombreval, Tante Dide and Des Esseintes.

"La ferveur! tout le secret du bonheur humain est là!" Freneuse's words, recall at once the "Je t'enseignerai la ferveur" and "Je veux t'apprendre la ferveur" of *Les Nourritures terrestres*. Nor is the parallel accidental. In a preface written for a new edition of the book in 1926, André Gide says that his work was so much against the taste of the period that it had little success; no critic even mentioned it. No critic, perhaps, but no less a representative of contemporary letters than Lorrain through the mouth of Freneuse. At least three quotations from *Les Nourritures* occur in *Phocas*[84]; they are the rule of life the weary duke adopts as he leaves occidental civilization for the primitivism of the East. It is not entirely certain, therefore, that *Les Nourritures* was as much out of tune with its period as Gide supposed. It was published in 1897, at a time when the decadent movement was rapidly dying: its own practitioners had made fun of it in the poems of Mitrophane Crapoussin; and Gide's own books before *Les Nourritures* contain hints of the coming change. "Quand pourrai-je," he asked in *Le Traité du Narcisse* (1892), "loin de mes moroses pensées, promener au soleil toute joie, dans l'oubli d'hier et de tant de religions inutiles, embrasser le bonheur qui viendra fortement, sans scrupule et sans crainte?"[85] It might be one of Freneuse's outbursts. *Le Voyage d'Urien* (1893) is another effort to escape from the crushing burden of civilization, an answer to the oft-expressed complaint of too much culture. "Le livre est la tentation, et nous sommes partis pour des actions glorieuses," complains Urien when he finds one of his companions reading philosophy. Marcel Schwob too, in *Le Livre de Monelle* (1895), wrote a justification of instinct and a renunciation of culture which sounds very much like *Les Nourritures*: "Brise toute coupe où tu auras bu... toute lampe ancienne est fumeuse... Nourris-

---

[84]*Monsieur de Phocas*, 317, 319, 338. It is curious to note how easily the phrases of the twentieth-century master fit into the context of Lorrain's book, and yet *Phocas* is perhaps the most characteristic work of the decadence.
[85]*Le Traité du Narcisse* (Lausanne, Mermod, 1946), 38.

toi des choses futures... Ne te retourne jamais... Ne te dirige pas vers des permanences... Ne te connais pas toi-même... Les paroles sont des paroles tandis qu'elles sont parlées. Les paroles conservées sont mortes et engendrent la pestilence. Ecoute mes paroles parlées et n'agis pas selon mes paroles écrites."[86] Words which assume added weight when we remember that they were written by a man who, in books like *Pensées* (1883–4), *Singeries* (1888) and *Vies imaginaires* (1896), dealt with characteristically decadent themes such as sterility, ennui, artificiality, depraved exoticism, etc. Gide's programme was thus traced in his own work and in the work of others; *Les Nourritures terrestres*, which he followed up and completed with *L'Immoraliste* five years later, is a calculated revolt against nearly every trait of decadent sensibility: the cult of artificiality ("J'écrivais ce livre à un moment où la littérature sentait furieusement le factice et le renfermé, où il me paraissait urgent de la faire à nouveau toucher terre et poser simplement sur le sol un pied nu"), the excessive, bookish culture of the decadence, its morbid introspection, its perverse attitudinizing, its sterility, neurosis and its studied boredom. The Gidean hero even abandons that principal characteristic of the dandy, the lust for domination: "Nathanël, à présent, jette mon livre. Emancipe-t'en. Quitte-moi... Quand ai-je dit que je te voulais pareil à moi ?"

The fact that a young writer (Gide was twenty-eight at the time), who was soon to become one of the masters of the new century, could thus demolish the basic ideas of the decadence, proved that the movement had reached its last days.

[86]*Le Livre de Monelle,* tome IV of Schwob's *Œuvres complètes* (Bernouard, 1927), 9–20. In his *Journal* (20 septembre 1931) Gide denies any mutual influence.

CHAPTER 5

THE GLAMOURS OF SYNTAX

> Le style de décadence... style ingénieux, compliqué, savant, plein de nuances et de recherches, reculant toujours les bornes de la langue, empruntant à tous les vocabulaires techniques, prenant des couleurs à toutes les palettes, des notes à tous les claviers... écoutant pour les traduire les confidences subtiles de la névrose.
>
> Gautier, "Notice," 1868

Decadent sensibility required a new style to express itself—its craving for the artificial, its passion for the abnormal, its sense of world-weariness. We can trace the beginnings of such a style in Romanticism, more especially in two reforms Victor Hugo introduced —an enlargement of the vocabulary and a tinkering with the mechanism of the classical alexandrine (*Les Contemplations*, "Réponse à un acte d'accusation"):

> Je mis un bonnet rouge au vieux dictionnaire...
> J'ai disloqué ce grand niais d'alexandrin...

The last example (*enjambement sur la césure*) became a favourite trick of decadent writing. Hugo, of course, intended nothing "decadent" by such techniques; he saw them as literary equivalents of the democratic revolution of 1789. But his reforms were directed against the classical style, and French *grand-siècle* classicism was usually identified with Augustan classicism. French critics like Nisard had long called post-Augustan Roman poets "decadent," and the temptation to do the same to the Romantics was irresistible. What in Hugo's mind was a battle of Romanticism, the new and vigorous, against Classicism, the old and outworn (more the classicism of *Zaïre* than the classicism of *Phèdre*) became a struggle of Classicism versus Decadence—the more so because of the very potentialities of the word "classical" which presented itself, and still does, as the antonym of "decadent." "Les poèmes de ce genre," wrote Benjamin Constant of

Hugo's first volumes, "sont toujours venus au moment de la décadence des littératures, lorsque les âmes n'avaient plus l'énergie nécessaire pour concevoir un plan et mettre dans les idées quelque ensemble."[1] Once again the Roman legend played a decisive role: its writers provided the nineteenth century with models, just as its wicked emperors inspired decadent sensibility; and once again too, Gautier's influence was paramount. At a very early date, his militant Romanticism led him to an interest in decadence: "Je fus assez bon élève," he says of his school-days, "mais avec des curiosités bizarres, qui ne plaisaient pas toujours aux professeurs. Je traitais les sujets de vers latins dans tous les mètres imaginables, et je me plaisais à imiter les styles qu'au collège on appelle de décadence. J'étais souvent taxé de barbarie et d'africanisme, et j'en étais charmé comme d'un compliment."[2] The remark occurs in an autobiographical sketch he wrote in 1867, and it would perhaps be a mistake to read too much into it; for if this adolescent habit had been anything comparable to his later taste for decadent literature, it is curious that he should have mentioned it so briefly—five years after his first enthusiastic discussion of the matter (his article on Baudelaire, *Les Poètes francais*, 1862) and less than a year before the "Notice" (February 1868). His schoolboy eccentricity was doubtless a Romantic trait (all the more Romantic when he saw it in retrospect), part of that desire to scandalize the classicists, the teachers, which distinguished the school of 1830. The poets imitated (*barbarie* and *africanisme* suggest Lucan, Claudian and for the vocabulary, Apuleius) were probably synonymous in his mind with Hugo, and stood in much the same anti-classical relation to the imitators of Virgil as the author of *Hernani* to the followers of Racine. Nevertheless, in view of what he later wrote about decadence, his early fascination with it is curious, and makes one think of Flaubert's remark about his own Latin classes: "Néron!... Loin des classiques leçons, je me reportais vers tes immenses voluptés, tes illuminations sanglantes, tes divertissements qui brûlent Rome."[3] We have here an amusing little picture: while the teachers expounded Caesar, Livy, Virgil or Horace, and most of their pupils dozed over the ablative absolutes of the *Commentaries* or the insipidities of "pious Aeneas,"

[1] Quoted by E. Schérer, "Décadence?" an essay written in 1887, *Etudes sur la littérature contemporaine* (Calmann-Lévy), IX, 344. Schérer links this "decadence" of Hugo with the literature of 1887; he seems to consider Hugo as the initiator of the search for stronger and stronger sensations. He makes the parallel between Roman and French decadence on page 338.

[2] "Gautier par lui-même," published 9 mars 1867, reprinted in *Souvenirs romantiques* (Garnier), 5.

[3] "Mémoires d'un fou" (1838) in *Premières Œuvres* (Librairie de France), 282.

there were a few, Gautier, Flaubert, Huysmans, for whom the ancient world was something much more lively; and they put their conjugations to unexpected use by construing Petronius and Juvenal, Tacitus, Suetonius and the Scriptores Historiae Augustae.

Gautier's most important discussion of decadence is the "Notice." But, as with his other contributions to the theory, he said little in the "Notice" that he had not said before, especially as to the content of a decadent style. In 1838, he excused the risqué tone of *Maupin* on the grounds that the nineteenth century was too sophisticated and civilized to be satisfied with the simple literature of former days: "Le monde a passé l'âge où l'on peut jouer la modestie et la pudeur... Depuis son hymen avec la civilisation la société a perdu le droit d'être ingénue et pudibonde."[4] Six years later he went a few steps further, and declared that a more complex style was necessary to express the thoughts and sensations of contemporary society: "Le monde vieillit. Toutes les idées simples, tous les magnifiques lieux communs, tous les thèmes naturels ont été employés... *L'Aurore aux doigts de rose* est une image charmante, mais un poète de notre siècle serait forcé de chercher quelque chose de moins primitif."[5] This is the idea of the "Notice"; and before Gautier developed it fully twenty-four years later, Baudelaire took it up in his second essay on Poe: "Le mot *littérature de décadence* suppose quelque chose de fatal et de providentiel... et il est tout à fait injuste de nous reprocher d'accomplir la loi mystérieuse. Tout ce que je puis comprendre dans la parole académique, c'est qu'il est honteux d'obéir à cette loi avec plaisir, et que nous sommes coupables de nous réjouir dans notre destinée... Ce à quoi les professeurs jurés n'ont pas pensé, c'est que, dans le mouvement de la vie, telle complication peut se présenter, tout à fait inattendue pour leur sagesse d'écoliers. Et alors leur langue insuffisante se trouve en défaut."[6]

The question of literary decadence preoccupied Baudelaire a good deal. In *L'Art philosophique*, an unfinished essay on which he worked during the last ten years of his life, he discusses the matter at some length, remarking that human history, like the life of the individual, is divided into childhood, virility, middle age and old age, the last corresponding to the nineteenth century.[7] He arrives at the conclusion that the literature of such an age (he calls it a decadent age) is distinguished by careful artistry, mystic tendencies, and exceptional and even morbid subjects. In his famous note to *Franciscae meae*

[4]*Mademoiselle de Maupin*, préface, 15.   [5]*Les Grotesques*, préface, ix–x.
[6]*Notes nouvelles sur Edgar Poe* (Conard), V, v–vi.
[7]*Œuvres*, II, 372.

laudes he stresses particularly the mysticism of decadent writing: "La langue de la dernière décadence latine," he says, is the "suprême soupir d'une personne robuste déjà transformée et préparée pour la vie spirituelle," an ideal instrument for expressing "la passion telle que l'a comprise et sentie le monde poétique moderne": "La mysticité est l'autre pôle de cet aimant dont Catulle et sa bande... n'ont connu que le pôle sensualité." He found the same qualities in Poe: the American's style is "extra ou suprahumaine," "extraterrestre." "Le principe de la poésie est strictement et simplement l'aspiration humaine vers une beauté supérieure... tout à fait indépendant de la passion... Car la passion est *naturelle*, trop naturelle pour ne pas introduire un ton blessant, discordant, dans le domaine de la beauté pure."[8] And this search for the ethereal does not imply a disdain for the humble details of workmanship—quite the reverse. "Autant certains écrivains affectent l'abandon, visant au chef-d'œuvre les yeux fermés... autant Edgar Poe a mis d'affectation à cacher la spontanéité, à simuler le sang-froid et la délibération." Such a method, while it may shock the disciples of inspiration ("les amateurs du délire"), is necessary to create poetry, that *objet de luxe*; and if it smacks of charlatanism (the reference to deliberation shows how Baudelaire identified the poet with the dandy), "un peu de charlatanerie est toujours permis au génie... C'est comme le fard sur les joues d'une femme naturellement belle, un assaisonnement nouveau pour l'esprit."[9] Both ideas, mysticism and artistry, thus become nearly synonymous with artificiality—passion is too natural for poetry, composition and style are condiments and rouge, poetry is an *objet de luxe*. And as a final touch, such refinements are best appreciated by an overcivilized or neurotic type of mind—the dandy with his cold self-possession and his straight-faced jokes, or the decadent, with his perverse manias. Poe was an "écrivian de nerfs" in contrast with Diderot an "auteur sanguin," and the content of his work is essentially morbid and exceptional: "les ardeurs de curiosité de la convalescence," "les temps chauds, où le vent du sud amollit et détend les nerfs," "l'hallucination," "l'hystérie," all written down "nerveusement" and "fantastiquement" and set against "des fonds violâtres et verdâtres où se révèlent la phosphorescence de la pourriture et la senteur de l'orage."[10] The decadent possibilities of this passage are not hard to see. It sketches the new sensibility with remarkable thoroughness, and some of its phrases ("la phosphorescence de la pourriture")

[8]*Notes nouvelles*, V, xx–xxi.
[9]*Ibid.*   [10]*Edgar Poe* (Conard) IV, xxviii–xxix.

can be heard detonating like fire-crackers across the rest of the century.

Thus, while mysticism and painstaking craftsmanship are not in themselves decadent (a self-evident truth), they seemed so to Baudelaire's contemporaries—partly from the poetic conventions of the time and partly from the way Baudelaire presented his ideas. Mysticism was in bad odour during the middle years of the century; the official doctrine was positivist and progressive, and seemed confirmed by the progress of science. When, as we have seen in chapter III, the psychopathologists set about investigating the human mind, they had no difficulty in deciding that mysticism was a form of degeneracy, and they were followed up by writers like the Goncourts, Zola and, until his conversion, Huysmans. In such an atmosphere, mysticism would have had to be something very austere indeed to escape criticism; and Baudelaire displayed it in such a way that it was unacceptable to even the believers. A poem like "A une Madone" begins with blasphemy (the Madonna is the poet's mistress) and ends with sadism and the Seven Deadly Sins.

The necrological articles written on Baudelaire in 1867 show what the critics of the period thought of this type of mysticism: "Un impur mélange de païenne corruption et d'austérité catholique outrée;"[11] "Obscénité, mysticisme — deux mots dont on peut marquer M. Baudelaire";[12] "Un mysticisme bêtasse et triste, où les anges avaient des ailes de chauve-souris avec des faces de catin";[13] "Un talent fait de mysticisme et d'obscénité."[14] The same strictures were repeated by later critics, like René Doumic, who defined baudelairism as "cette perversion qui consiste à mêler le catholicisme avec la débauche, et à raviver la sensualité par le ragoût de l'émotion religieuse";[15] by the Abbé Charbonnel, who called Baudelaire's work "un assemblage d'épicurienne sensualité et de christianisme ascétique, de volupté charnelle et de piété mystique, de débauche et de prière... quelle profonde perversion du sens mystique!";[16] by Paul Bourget, who wrote that "la mysticité comme le libertinage se codifie en formules dans ce cerveau qui décompose ses sensations."[17]

Franciscae meae laudes had something to do with the decadent

[11]Alphonse Duchesne, 2 mai, 1861; quoted by W. T. Bandy, *Baudelaire Judged by His Contemporaries* (New York, Columbia University Press, 1933), 50.

[12]Alcide Dusolier, 27 avril, 1864. Quoted *ibid.*, 65.

[13]Jules Vallès, 5 septembre, 1867. Quoted *ibid.*, 126.

[14]An anonymous article in *Le Nain jaune*, 5 septembre 1867; quoted by Maurice Spronck, *Les Artistes littéraires*, 87–8.

[15]*Les Jeunes* (Perrin, 1896), 248.

[16]*Les Mystiques dans la littérature présente* (Mercure de France, 1897), I, 59–63.

[17]*Essais de psychologie contemporaine*, 5.

school's interest in ecclesiastical Latin, which had the double advantage of being both mystic and decadent. "La petite pièce latine des *Fleurs du Mal* portait ses fruits," wrote Gustave Kahn in his reminiscences of the period, "de divers cotés on préparait des anthologies des pièces de basse latinité."[18] Huysmans' discussion of Christian Latin poets in *A Rebours* is one example of this; Remy de Gourmont's *Le Latin mystique* (1892) another. "Seule la littérature mystique convient à notre immense fatigue," Gourmont wrote in his preface, "nous voulons nous borner à la connaissance de nous-mêmes et des obscures rêves, divins ou sataniques, qui se donnent rendez-vous en nos âmes de jadis."[19]

As for the careful workmanship, it received much the same reception—the Romantic style demanded ebullience and inspiration, and the content of Poe's and Baudelaire's verse was at times so bizarre. "A une Madone" can be quoted as an example of this too: the sustained metaphor, the epithets, the metallic effect of the lines suggest Góngora, Marino and the early seventeenth century. The whole question of careful technique and controlled, deliberate inspiration takes us back to the cult of artificiality and the characteristics of the dandy. To let oneself go on the wings of inspiration was natural; to prepare one's effects, call upon will-power and reason to develop them, was voluntary, artificial, decadent. Such is the tone of critic after critic during the last half of the century. There is an almost universal conviction that any sort of poetic calculation implies insincerity, artificiality and corruption, and indicates an artificial and corrupt age. Taine (in 1855) called attention to "ces paradoxes de mots, ces pointes trop ingénieuses, dignes plutôt d'un Claudien ou d'un Ausone" which are to be found in Michelet's style, and which, he says, "sentent le sophiste et l'écrivain de la décadence."[20] Barbey d'Aurevilly said that Baudelaire's talent, "travaillé, ouvragé, compliqué" was "une fleur du mal venue dans les serres chaudes d'une Décadence, une poésie sinistre et violente dont rien n'approche dans les plus noirs ouvrages de ce temps qui se sent mourir."[21] Sainte-Beuve wrote that Baudelaire had produced *Les Fleurs du Mal* "en *perlant* le détail, en *pétrarquisant* sur l'horrible"[22] —the italics are in the text; and Jules Vallès, that he had tried to "*scudériser* l'ordure."[23] We find the same idea in the articles of

[18]Gustave Kahn, *Symbolistes et décadents* (Vanier, 1902), 37–8.

[19]*Le Latin mystique* (Mercure de France, 1892), 12. Huysmans wrote a preface for the volume; most of the poets chosen had already appeared in Des Esseintes' library.

[20]"Monsieur Michelet," février 1855, *Essais de critique et d'histoire*, 111.

[21]Article reprinted in the appendix of the Calmann-Lévy edition of *Les Fleurs du Mal*, 310–11.

[22]*Ibid.*, 333–4.   [23]Quoted by Bandy, *Baudelaire Judged*, 127.

Pontmartin, Schérer, Bourget, Lemaître and Pellissier: whether for or against Baudelaire, they all said approximately the same thing.

As for Gautier, he discusses Baudelaire as though he were developing his prefaces to *Maupin* and *Les Grotesques* where he had demanded a more complex, more highly coloured style to replace the simplicities and platitudes and natural themes of the past; in 1862, he found this in Baudelaire: "Il est dans chaque littérature des époques où la langue formée à pointe se prête... à l'expression limpide et facile des idées générales, des grands lieux communs... Cette période passe pour l'époque de la perfection classique... Après, selon les critiques et les rhéteurs, tout n'est que décadence... A nos yeux, ce qu'on appelle décadence est au contraire maturité complète, la civilisation extrême, le couronnement des choses. Alors un art souple, complexe... puisant des nomenclatures dans tous les dictionnaires, empruntant des couleurs à toutes les palettes, des harmonies à toutes les lyres, demandant à la science ses secrets et à la critique ses analyses, aide le poète à rendre les pensées... de son esprit. Ces pensées... sont subtiles, ténues, maniérées, persillées même de dépravation, entachées de gongorisme, bizarrement profondes, individuelles jusqu'à la monomanie... ascétiques et luxurieuses."[24] The passage may have been suggested by Baudelaire's remarks on Poe, but it elaborates the original idea. Baudelaire's essay, although it defined decadent sensibility fairly thoroughly, is both brief and general, and it was begun more as a defence than a declaration of faith. Gautier proposes something much more detailed; and in the "Notice," written six years later, he added the final touches:

Les grands maîtres du passé... avaient eu ce bonheur d'arriver dans la jeunesse du monde... Les grands lieux communs... étaient alors dans toute leur fleur, et ils suffisaient à des génies simples parlant à un peuple enfantin... Mais... la qualité du xixe siècle n'est pas précisément la naïveté, et il a besoin... d'un idiome un peu plus composite que la langue dite classique... Le couchant n'a-t-il pas sa beauté comme le matin? Ces rouges de cuivre, ces ors verts... n'offrent-ils pas autant de poésie que l'Aurore aux doigts de rose?... [Baudelaire] aimait ce qu'on appelle improprement le style de décadence, et qui n'est autre chose que l'art arrivé à ce point de maturité extrême que déterminent à leurs soleils obliques les civilisations qui vieillissent: style ingénieux, compliqué, savant, plein de nuances et de recherches, reculant toujours les bornes de la langue, empruntant à tous les vocabulaires techniques, prenant des couleurs à toutes les palettes, des notes à tous les claviers, s'efforçant à rendre la pensée dans ce qu'elle a de plus ineffable... écoutant pour les traduire les confidences subtiles de la névrose, les aveux de la passion vieillissante qui se déprave et les hallucina-

---

[24]*Les Poètes français*, IV, 595–6.

tions bizarres de l'idée fixe tournant à la folie. Ce style de décadence est le dernier mot du Verbe sommé de tout exprimer et poussé à l'extrême outrance. On peut rappeler, à propos de lui, la langue marbrée déjà des verdeurs de la décomposition et comme faisandée du bas-empire romain et les raffinements compliqués de l'école byzantine, dernière forme de l'art grec tombé en déliquescence ; mais tel est bien l'idiome nécessaire et fatal des peuples et des civilisations où la vie factice a remplacé la vie naturelle... Ce style... exprime des idées neuves avec des formes nouvelles... On pense bien que les quatorze cents mots du dialecte racinien ne suffisent pas à l'auteur qui s'est donné la rude tâche de rendre les idées et les choses modernes dans leur infinie complexité...

He concludes by noting that Baudelaire preferred, to Cicero and Virgil, Apuleius, Petronius, Juvenal, Saint Augustine and Tertullian ("dont le style a l'éclat noir de l'ébène"), and points out the ecclesiastical Latin of *Franciscae meae laudes*, of which the footnote, he adds, "explique et corrobore ce que nous venons de dire sur les idiomes de décadence."[25]

A number of points are worth noting in connection with this paragraph. It is a final version of what Gautier had written in 1838, 1844 and 1862, and shows how he applied to Baudelaire theories he had discussed long before *Les Fleurs du Mal* were even conceived: the same phrases and ideas occur at a distance of twenty-four years. It states the antinomy between classical and decadent, declaring the former outdated and inadequate: the modern is thus definitely equated with the decadent. It defines the content of the decadent style as neurotic degeneracy, and sketches its technique: the writer must seek, avoid, prune, rewrite, to escape the ideas and phraseology of the past; he must use an enlarged vocabulary and an unorthodox syntax. The rudimentary suggestions of Baudelaire's essays on Poe are developed almost out of recognition: how is it possible to take seriously Gautier's claim that the note to *Franciscae meae laudes* "explains and corroborates" what he has written of the decadent style? In short, the "Notice" gives an almost complete *ars poetica* of the decadence: themes (mental and moral disease), method, even vocabulary. The vocabulary particularly is significant: it suggests that Gautier was attempting to imitate the decadent style he attributes to Baudelaire. Terms are drawn from cosmetics, chemistry, medicine, psychology: *insomnie, impuissance, malaises, prostrations, excitations bile extravasé, blancs de chlorose, roses de phtisie, rouge, mouches, k'hol, poudre de riz, fard, céruse, burgau, gris plombé, arséniate de cuivre, bitumes, décompositions, déliquescences.* The influence of this

[25]"Notice," in Baudelaire, *Fleurs du Mal* (1868), xv–xvii.

vocabulary was profound; we find echoes of it in the work of many later writers. Gustave Kahn defined its effect when he wrote: "On se souvient de l'admirable étude de Théophile Gautier qui précède l'édition des *Fleurs du mal* et où Gautier développe la beauté particulière et chatoyante du style aux époques de décadence. Ce sont des lignes qui ne tombèrent pas dans les oreilles sourdes, et... on arriva à l'appliquer à notre époque... l'Empire, le Bas-Empire, Paris, Byzance."[26]

It is not too much to say, indeed, that the "Notice" was the matrix of all subsequent decadent writing. Novels like *La Curée*, *A Rebours* and *Le Jardin des supplices*, poems like Jean Lorrain's, parodies like those of Floupette and Crapoussin, are in many ways simply enormous elaborations of it. Had Gautier not written his essay, the nineteenth century would certainly have spent much time in morose contemplation of its own decadence, but that decadence would never have been so clearly defined, and it is very probable that there would never have been a decadent school. The very fact that the "Notice" was attached to Baudelaire (from 1868 to 1917 there was only one popular edition of *Les Fleurs du Mal*, the Lévy, and it bore the essay), that it benefited from his growing fame, explains much of its influence. It was a bell on the cat, a skilful piece of advertising. In modern terms, Gautier was Baudelaire's publicity agent, an agent of great skill, who knew how to strike the taste of the period and express his ideas in lapidary form. From 1868 on, "les verdeurs de la décomposition" was habitually coupled with Baudelaire's own "phosphorescence de la pourriture" to describe *Les Fleurs du Mal*.

Besides being a last succinct statement of Gautier's own ideas, the "Notice" was also a crystallization of much that had oft been thought but ne'er so well expressed by others. This was particularly true as regards the comprehensive nature of the decadent style and its morbid content. Ten years before (in 1858) Taine wrote that contemporary French literature "fouille toutes les plaies secrètes de l'âme et de l'histoire" and that "des quatre coins du monde, de tous les bas-fonds de la vie, de toutes les hauteurs de la philosophie et de l'art, arrivent les images, les idées, la vérité, le paradoxe."[27] A typical example of this kind of writing, he thought, was Flaubert's style—"de la littérature dégénérée" because it employed scientific terms and tried to imitate plastic art.[28] Zola wrote in the same way in the articles he composed in 1865–6. "Vous verrez en elle," he says of modern literature, "tous les

---

[26]Kahn, *Symbolistes et décadents*, 34.
[27]"Balzac," *Nouveaux Essais de critique et d'histoire*, 57–8.
[28]*Correspondance*, II, 238.

effets de la névrose qui agite notre siècle... L'humanité glisse, prise de vertige, sur la pente raide de la science; elle a mordu à la pomme, et elle veut tout savoir." The style of the Goncourts, he found, was "un mélange de crudité et de délicatesse, de mièvreries et de brutalités"; and it pleased him for those very reasons: "Mon goût, si l'on veut, est dépravé; j'aime les ragoûts littéraires fortement épicés, les œuvres de décadence où une sorte de sensibilité maladive remplace la santé plantureuse des époques classiques. Je suis de mon âge."[29] The passage suggests that he had been reading Gautier's essay of 1862 on Baude- laire; it provides an explanation for the heavy, sultry atmosphere of books like *La Curée* and *Nana*, and enables us to understand why Huysmans liked them: the disciple probably understood his master better than the master did himself.

Huysmans' conception of the decadent style is drawn almost entirely from Gautier. Comparing the Goncourts in literature with Degas in painting, he writes: "De même que pour rendre visible l'extérieur de la bête humaine... pour démonter le méchanisme de ses passions, l'abérration de ses dévoiements, la naturelle éclosion de ses vices, la plus fugitive de ses sensations, Jules et Edmond de Goncourt ont dû forger un incisif et puissant outil, créer une palette neuve de tons, un vocabulaire original, une nouvelle langue; de même... M. Degas a dû fabriquer un instrument tout à la fois ténu et large, flexible et ferme. Lui aussi a dû emprunter à tous les vocabulaires de la peinture... forger des néologismes de couleurs, briser l'ordonnance acceptée des sujets." The subjects he paints are wholly decadent: "Les anémies originelles, les déplorables lymphes des filles couchées dans les sou- pentes, éreintées par les exercices du métier, épuisées par de précoces pratiques, avant l'âge."[30] There seems to have been no check-rein on the decadent imagination. In Huysmans particularly, it became a kind of myopia; wherever he looked, he saw degeneracy, even in Degas' exquisite ballet dancers.[31] *A Rebours*, of course, contains a full discussion of the decadent style. Des Esseintes' preferences begin in a sort of adolescent anti-classicism: he compares Augustan Latin to the

[29]*Mes Haines*, 48, 55.

[30]*L'Art moderne*, 117–120, 115. And page 108, the "faisandé de peau sous les flammes du gaz" he detected in the prostitutes of one of Forain's drawings.

[31]And even in Renaissance painters like Bianchi. See his criticism of that painter's "Sacra conversazione" in the Louvre, quoted by Mario Praz, *La Carne*, 421. The whole decadent movement had a craze for reading extraordinary meanings into works of art and literature. Who nowadays, looking through one of the Goncourts' novels, finds anything like the decadence in it that Huysmans and Bourget found? Aside from their historical works, which still have a certain importance, the Goncourts' books are just dusty curiosities.

French of Louis XIV—hard, colourless, tiresome. To the monotonous classicism of Virgil and Caesar, he prefers Petronius' *Satyricon*: "écrit dans un style d'une verdeur étrange, puisant à tous les dialectes, empruntant des expressions à toutes les langues charriées dans Rome, reculant toutes les limites, toutes les entraves du soi-disant grand siècle... dépeignant... les vices d'une civilisation décrépite, d'un empire qui se fêle." The same is true of Apuleius: "La langue latine battait le plein" in his books, "roulait des limons, des eaux variées, accourues de toutes les provinces, des maniérismes, des détails nouveaux... des néologismes." Commodian used popular locutions and dislocated the classical hexameter; Tertullian employed a wide vocabulary and unorthodox syntax; Ammianus Marcelinus and Aurelius Victor had "un style blet et déjà verdi"; Claudian and Rutilius Namatianus "une langue tacheté et superbe," and Fortunatus cut his hymns in "la vieille charogne de la langue latine, épicée par les aromates de l'Eglise."[32]

Des Esseintes finds similar qualities in the "flores byzantines de cervelle" and the "déliquescences compliquées de langue" of certain modern French writers: Baudelaire, with his "idéal de maladive dépravation," his "abérrations et maladies," his "tétanos mystique, fièvre chaude de la luxure, typhoïdes et vomitos du crime, douleur, spleen, sensibilité irritée de l'âme, états morbides"; Barbey d'Aurevilly, whose style is "plein de locutions torses, de tournures inusitées, de comparaisons outrées," crammed with "faisandages, taches morbides, épidermes talés, goût blet"; Edmond de Goncourt, "un style perspicace et morbide, indispensable aux civilisations décrépites, exigeant des exceptions, des tournures, des fontes nouvelles et de phrases et de mots"; Verlaine, a nineteenth-century Commodian, distorting conventional prosody, writing verse "coupé par d'invraisemblables césures"; Corbière, "un style rocailleux, sec, hérissé de vocables inusités, de néologismes inattendus... un faisandage aux épithètes crispées, aux beautés un peu suspects"; finally Mallarmé, the most decadent of them all, a poet of "finesses byzantines": "La décadence d'une littérature, irréparablement atteinte dans son organisme affaibli par l'âge des idées, épuisée par les excès de la syntaxe, sensible seulement aux curiosités qui enfièvrent les maladies et cependant pressée de tout exprimer à son déclin, acharnée à vouloir réparer toutes les omissions de jouissance, à léguer les plus subtils souvenirs de douleur à son lit de mort,

---

[32] *A Rebours*, 36–8, 41–2, 42–3, 45, 46, 51. Des Esseintes' Latin tastes were not accepted by all writers of the decadent persuasion: Verlaine deplored his dislike of Horace and Virgil and Racine (*Le Décadent*, 15 mars 1888); Remy de Gourmont praised Catullus, Virgil, Ovid and Plautus (*Le Latin mystique*, 12).

s'était incarnée en Mallarmé... C'était l'agonie de la vieille langue qui, après s'être persillée de siècle en siècle, finissait par se désoudre, par atteindre ce deliquium de la langue latine."[33] Looking over his collection of French books, Des Esseintes smiles at the thought that in later times, some scholar will doubtless prepare a glossary of decadent French just as Du Cange compiled the terms and idioms of the later Roman Empire.

Gautier's influence was also strong on Bourget, whose essay on Baudelaire (1881) contains a definition of the decadent style as "un style où l'unité du livre se décompose pour laisser la place à l'indépendance du mot," represented by authors who "ont tendu leur machine nerveuse jusqu'à devenir hallucinés [et] dont la langue est 'marbrée déjà des verdeurs de la décomposition.'"[34] "La prose nouvelle," he writes of the Goncourts, "renverse l'ordre de la phrase, crée des vocables nouveaux, multiplie les emprunts aux dictionnaires de métiers... L'artiste s'amuse alors aux bizarreries de la syntaxe, aux curiosités du néologisme. Comme Baudelaire il se sait décadent."[35] Barbey d'Aurevilly, reviewing Rollinat's *Les Névroses* in 1883, compared him with Poe and Baudelaire. The work of all three, he says, is "la poésie du spleen, des nerfs, et du frisson, dans une vieille civilisation matérialiste et dépravée... qui est à ses derniers râles et à ses dernières pâmoisons... Poésie gâtée dans sa source, physique, maladive, empoisonnée, mauvaise, décomposée par toutes les influences morbides de la fin d'un monde qui expire."[36] By the eighties, nerves had become a distinguishing mark of decadence, a fact to which abundant reference has been made in our previous chapters; the very title of Rollinat's volume, not to mention most of its content, was borrowed partly from the literary atmosphere, partly from the medical studies of the period.

The French literature of those years, indeed, had become like a saturated solution in which a hanging string produces a crystallization; and it is scarcely surprising that books like *A Rebours*, containing as they did every aspect of the decadent idea hunted down and analysed, became like Bibles for the younger generation of writers. *A Rebours*, wrote Rodenbach, was "un hymne à la décadence" which "assimilait nos temps cosmopolites à la Rome ancienne... Alors Ausone, Pétrone, Rutilius firent succéder aux âges classiques une littérature de style

33*A Rebours*, 237, 188–91, 214–16, 242 (this appreciation of Goncourt is based on *La Faustin*), 247–250, 260.
34*Essais*, 25, 29–31.
35*Nouveaux Essais*, 182.
36*Les Œuvres et les hommes*, II, *Les Poètes* (Lemerre, 1889), 324.

décomposé, aux plaques de fard, cachant sous des poudres une langue qui s'écaille et des mots dont les lèvres sont usées," and Huysmans' book became "un programme involontaire, la loi et le code, le texte de ralliement, l'hymne des enrolés pour l'art neuf."[37] For, besides saying everything that Taine, Baudelaire, Gautier and Zola had said before, Huysmans said it more completely, incarnated it in a vivid personality, Des Esseintes, and made a serious effort to put it into practice in his own work. E. Hennequin wrote a review of A Rebours (which Huysmans approved), calling attention to the wide vocabulary of Huysmans' novels and essays; he attributed it to the author's personal experience: he was well read in Latin and French, and he frequented all types of milieux: slums, workshops, artistic circles, with the result that he was able to employ Parisianisms, provincialisms, scientific, archaic, classical and foreign locutions, thus joining "le délicat au populaire."[38] Huysmans seems to have looked on himself as a sort of modern Petronius, utilizing all the varied terms which the juxtaposition of cultures had poured into nineteenth-century Paris. Beginning with Romanticism, there was a mass invasion of new words into French; it enriched the vocabulary of the realists and Naturalists;[39] but, until Huysmans and even after him, it was employed with a certain timidity. Even Zola, for all his audacity, only uses slang in direct quotation or oratio obliqua. But Huysmans wrote slang, combining it with learned, foreign or classical words, whenever he wanted a "decadent" effect—which was quite often. To describe the reek of the female arm-pit (Croquis parisiens), for example, every sort of locution is employed: "L'arome du valérianate d'ammoniaque et de l'urine s'accentue brutalement parfois et souvent même un léger fleur d'acide prussique, une faible bouffée de pêche talée et par trop mûre passe dans le soupir des extraits de fleurs et des poudres... C'est une gamme parcourant tout le clavier de l'odorat."[40] He describes the blue-stockings of the Catholic press as "de bien lymphatiques bas-bleus et de bien dévotieuses bréhaignes"[41]; and his conversion did not decrease his verve: "C'est une pléthore de bassesse, une hémorragie de

[37]"La Poésie nouvelle: A propos des décadents et symbolistes," Revue bleu, 4 avril, 1891.

[38]"J. K. Huysmans," Revue indépendante, 4 juillet 1884.

[39]Huysmans' vocabulary has been analysed by Marcel Cressot, La Phrase et le vocabulaire de J. K. Huysmans (Droz, 1938). See pages 535 and (for the Romantic contribution) 4.

[40]"Le Gousset," Croquis parisiens, 126–7.

[41]A Rebours, 196. "Ces lymphes... écrivaient toutes comme des pensionnaires de couvent, dans une langue blanche, dans un de ces flux de la phrase qu'aucun astringent n'arrête !"

mauvais goût," he writes of the ecclesiastical art of Lourdes; "ce n'est même pas cocasse... c'est puérile et c'est ganache; ça vacarme et ça radote; [c'est] de la ratatouille de cantine et de la ripopée." From first to last, in Léon Bloy's phrase, Huysmans "traînait l'image, par les cheveux et par les pieds, dans l'escalier vermoulu de la syntaxe épouvantée."[42]

The example of such a method and such practice, when put across by a master like Huysmans, was willingly followed—even to the point of caricature. Adoré Floupette's *Déliquescences* include a definition of the decadent style borrowed from *À Rebours*: "La langue française était décidément trop pauvre... A la délicieuse corruption, au détraquement exquis de l'âme contemporaine, une suave névrose de langue devait correspondre... Une attaque de nerfs sur du papier! Voilà l'écriture moderne... Tantôt la phrase, pareille à un grand incendie, flamboyait, crépitait, rutilait, on entendit craquer ses jointures; tantôt avec le charme inconscient d'une grande dame tombée en enfance, déliquescente, un rien faisandée, elle s'abandonnait, s'effondrait, tombait par places, et rien n'était plus adorable que ces écailles de style, à demi détachées."[43] Like Floupette's verse, this passage could have been written in good faith by many contemporary authors; Rodenbach expresses himself in practically the same terms ("une langue qui s'écaille"); and most of the contents of *Le Décadent* show only a desire to be taken seriously:

A des besoins nouveaux correspondent des idées nouvelles, subtiles et nuancées à l'infini. De là la nécessité à créer des vocables inouïs, pour exprimer une telle complexité de sentiments et de sensations physiologiques... Nous vouons cette feuille aux innovations et aux audaces stupéfiantes, aux incohérences à 36 atmosphères...

Notre style doit etre rare et tourmenté, parce que la banalité est l'épouvantail de cette fin de siècle, et nous devons rajeunir des vocables tombés en désuétude ou en créer de nouveaux pour noter l'idée dans la complexité de ses nuances les plus fugaces.

La société moderne est blasée... L'homme a tout vu, il sait tout, il a éprouvé toutes les émotions... Pour l'émouvoir il faut agir directement sur ses sens... soit par d'ingénieux symboles, soit par des constructions hétéroclites... C'est la mission du Décadisme.[44]

Lorsque Rome fut énervée par le luxe, amollie par le plaisir, que devint sa littérature? Une littérature raffinée comme les mœurs, parfumée comme

---

[42]*Les Foules de Lourdes*, 101–10. Bloy's phrase is quoted with approval by Huysmans himself, *En Marge*, 60.

[43]*Les Déliquescences*, préface, xli–xlii.

[44]Articles signed by Baju, 10 avril, 16 octobre, 20 novembre 1886.

les boudoirs, délicate comme les sensations d'alors... Est-ce qu'à l'instar de Rome nous ne serions pas arrivés à une de ces phases où la fatigue anémique et la nervosité morbide de la foule exige des poètes... quelque chose de vague et d'étrange, de quintessencié et de sensationnel?... La décadence est évidente, elle appert à tout... A ce siècle mourant... usé, blasé, épuisé d'excès, ils [les décadents] veulent donner des œuvres... grasses de sucs médullaires, substantielles et savoureuses.[45]

The periodical made every effort to follow out this programme. Besides dealing in perversions (as we have seen), its contributors tried all manner of stylistic tricks. A sonnet by Martial Besson, "Poétique nouvelle" (5 juin, 1888) sums up their aims and points out the cleavage between Romanticism and Decadence:

> Le poète n'est plus le doux rêveur morose,
> L'amoureux primitif aux faciles émois,
> Qui, les cheveux au vent, par les sentes de bois,
> Jouait des airs banals sur un mirliton rose.
>
> A cette fin de siècle en proie à la névrose,
> Il faut des pleurs de sang, d'amers éclats de voix,
> Le subtil examen de nos cœurs aux abois,
> D'étranges vers, heurtés, aux allures de prose.

Certain problems, of course, had to be faced: the decadents had to deal with the old dilemma that had troubled Gautier, Baudelaire and Huysmans—a professed love of the modern and a hatred of most of its characteristic manifestations. As artists of a decadent age they wanted to write about it, and at the same time they detested its materialism and its progressivism. They tried to solve the problem by aligning themselves not only against Romanticism, but against Zola's Naturalism ("les purulences fétides issant des exutoires," as Baju defined it on January 5, 1888); they took refuge, now in an exaggerated *préciosité*, now in a careful description of the dance-hall, night-club scenery which had fascinated Baudelaire and the Goncourts. They practised, in short, what Hennequin had called both a *délicat* and a *populaire* style. Concerning the former, Verlaine wrote that *Décadisme*, while it was the literature of a decadent age, was not necessarily decadent itself: in reaction against its period, it sought "le délicat, le raffiné, l'élevé... contre les platitudes et les turpitudes ambiantes" (*Le Décadent*, 15 janvier 1888). Baju suggested a variety of symbolism: "Notre époque... est fatiguée... La littérature décadente se propose de reflèter l'image de ce monde spleenétique... Pas de descriptions... rien

[45]Charles Darantière, 4 décembre 1886.

qu'une synthèse rapide donnant l'impression des objets... Donner au
cœur la sensation des choses, soit par des constructions neuves, soit
par des symboles évoquant l'idée."[46]

The obvious symbolism of this extract raises a thorny little problem:
the connection between *décadisme* and *symbolisme*. Both groups hated
each other, yet no distinction is possible between them, and Symbolism
was always equated with Decadence by contemporaries.[47] Even George
Rodenbach, who was a Symbolist and should have seen the differences, either real or fancied, made no effort at drawing a distinction
in his article "La Poésie nouvelle: A propos des décadents et symbolistes" (*Revue Bleue*, 4 avril 1891). The essay stresses the decadent
characteristics of both groups, and contains an interesting sketch of
their literary ancestors. We have already quoted the passage on
Huysmans. "Baudelaire entraîna la poésie dans une décadence... noble
et glorieuse... Lui avait appris l'art anglais plein de mystère, où la
secrète affinité des choses devait conduire son instinct apparié." Mallarmé's poetry "marque le développement logique de l'art de décadence, inauguré par Baudelaire... c'est la décadence, la maladie équivoque, plus d'idées simples, de sentiments naturels." In Verlaine's
work, "la décadence est dans l'état d'âme du poète, sa langueur
énervée, sa satiété, sa connaissance de tout péché... La forme poétique
abdique, abandonne, son cristal se fêle... Le langage... est à la fois
très naïf et très pervers." Rimbaud's *Illuminations* (he adds) showed
how to dislocate traditional prosody; Jules Laforgue was a dreamer
who cultivated his own neuroses. And they all saved French literature
from the pernicious contagion of Zola's doctrines.

In general, perhaps, the "délicat" type of writing is more marked in
Symbolist production, while "le populaire" distinguishes the Decadents. But this is not invariably true.

An attempt at codifying the decadent and symbolist vocabulary was
made by Paul Adam in his *Glossaire pour servir à l'intelligence des*

[46]*L'Ecole décadente* (Vanier, 1887), 7, 10. Besides attacking Zola, the decadent
group was very much against Victor Hugo, who "a exercé sur notre siècle une influence néfaste." *Le Décadent*, 8 octobre 1886.

[47]Moréas, "Le Symbolisme" (*Le Figaro*, 18 septembre 1888); J. Psychari, "Les
Vers français aujourd'hui et les poètes décadents" (*Revue Bleue*, 8 juin 1891);
A. France (*Le Temps*, 30 août 1891); Prince Bibesco, *La Question du vers français
et la tentative des poètes décadents* (Lemerre, 1893), etc. Both schools had much the
same ends in view: "L'action des Symbolistes et des Décadents contre la littérature
en vogue était parallèle. Ils avaient les mêmes haines et les mêmes admirations. Ils
étaient pris du même désir d'introduire dans leurs vers plus de mystère, plus de rêve,
plus de musique... Les uns et les autres sentaient le besoin de s'affranchir de formules
surannées et de réformer la prosadie." Ernest Raynaud, *La Mêlée symboliste* (La
Renaissance du livre, 1920), I, 117.

auteurs décadents et symbolistes (Vanier, 1888); it was doubtless suggested by the passage in *A Rebours* where Des Esseintes imagines some future scholar imitating Du Cange. It is a small volume of 98 pages, with about 400 definitions; amongst the authors cited to illustrate shades of meaning are Ghil, Kahn, Laforgue, Moréas, Mallarmé, Verlaine and Rimbaud. It is scarcely a satisfactory key to the decadent style; like so many other works of the time, it gives an impression of parody. Most of its terms are neologisms of a precious kind, formed by altering the endings of common French words, usually by adding *ance* or *ure*. "*Ance*," Adam explains in the introduction, "marque particulièrement une atténuation du sens primitif, qui devient alors moins déterminé, plus vague, et se nuance d'un recul. Ex.: *lueur, luisance*. Lueur, c'est l'effet direct d'une flamme, luisance sera un reflet de flamme dans un panneau verni." Amongst other definitions we find "acaule — qui n'a pas de tige"; "adamique — pur, innocent"; "diluer — délayer"; "dômer — couvrir d'un dôme"; "dyscole — qui a mauvais caractère"; "parangonner — comparer," etc.

All this is very trifling; but it is true that traces of it occur in the writing of the time. Adam's own *Thé chez Miranda* (1886), composed in collaboration with Moréas, utilizes some of the terms — *hiémale, nacrure, luisance*. An example of how the jargon was used is the description of a man visiting a prostitute: "Dans quelque boudoir public, il ira s'annuiter et accroître, par le contact de chairs urbaines, la regrettance du rêve féminin qu'il veut oublier."[48] The volume seems to have been designed to provide examples of both the delicate and the popular styles; they alternate. Alongside the above are a number of stories written with careful and brutal detail, which recall those of Mendès and Rachilde: adultery, incest, murder. In Moréas' article on Symbolism we find expressions like "impoluées vocables," "rime illucescente," "fluidités absconces," "silhouettes obombrées"; and Lombard's *L'Agonie*, dealing with decadent Rome, had to be written in decadent style, which shows itself in perverse inversions and an abuse of anacoluthons, ablative absolutes and far-fetched detail. Ghil's *Traité* and *Méthode* bristle with such words as "vaunéant," "inharmonie," "insacrifiable," "esseulé," "inému," "plangorer," and his poetry is an extraordinary effort at being both popular and delicate. Published in 1890–5 as *Dire du mieux*, it attempts to describe modern scenes in the new style—unemployed foundry workers, factories, metallurgy, the city. The very comprehensiveness of the decadent style as Gautier defined it, borrowing terms and ideas from all sources, had a great

[48]*Le Thé chez Miranda* (Tresse et Stock 1886), 13.

danger, it made anything a subject for poetry. Amongst other abominations it resuscitated the ghost Romanticism had laid—scientific poetry, of which the eighteenth century had left some lamentable examples. Ghil did not succeed in eluding this spectre; it inspired him with lines which recall disastrously what, in the *Stuffed Owl*, is entitled "Birth of KNO_3": apostrophes to matter and gas, descriptions of a pregnancy, of a syphilitic foetus.

Most of the decadent writing which appeared in *Le Décadent* is equally atrocious. The issue of 30 octobre 1886 contains a prose-poem "Drame en forêt" by Moïse Renault: it seems to describe a gamekeeper catching a poacher. The style is a mixture of neo-Latin and archaic French terms: "Sous l'albe flambeau lunaire, luisant en le nocturne ciel et fouillant de ses hydrargyriques rayons les interstices feuillus des taillis, apparaît la sylve, argentée, monochrome et mélancolique." Another piece is entitled "Clair de lune: Fantaisie déliquescente"; it begins: "Après une journée torrescente, atmosphère languide, papillotante d'électricité. Ciel d'azur tacheté de laiteurs chlorotiques." By contrast the popular style, realistic and even naturalistic, at least as Huysmans understood naturalism, is readable, if nothing else. Amusing examples are Paul Fuchs' sonnet "Quatorzain d'été, à M. Bedaecker" (15 janvier 1889), describing a group of tourists at lunch; and Laurent Tailhade's verse, published first in *Le Décadent* and later collected in such volumes as *Au pays du mufle, A travers les grouins, Poèmes aristophanesques*. The themes are androgynism, prostitution and perversion, well-larded with boulevard slang (bobos, boxon, lopettes).[49] In such work the decadent style appears almost mathematically constructed, according to a formula which had grown stereotyped by the nineties; and the effect is, to use the vocabularly of the time, *cocasse*. Turning the pages of *Le Décadent*, one wonders, as one wonders reading Péladan, just how serious all these people were. It is perhaps an indication of their true state of mind that having exhausted every possibility of the decadent idea, they ended in a deliberate travesty of themselves, as frankly hilarious as Adoré Floupette's *Déliquescences*. It took the form of a series of poems signed "Mitrophane Crapoussin" (composed by Raynaud, Du Plessys and Tailhade), and appeared in the last numbers of the *Décadent* (février-mars 1889). They parody almost all the ideas of the movement—male prostitution ("Au café"), decadent mysticism

---

[49]Ever since Huysmans, slang had been very popular. Marcel Schwob used it in his *Singeries* (1888), partly in imitation of Villon, whom he admired. There is even a slang version of *Faust* (*Œuvres*, III, 233), and an *Etude sur l'argot français*.

("Renoncement"), neurosis ("Quatorzain pour aller à Bicêtre"). In "Recurrence," Mitrophane bids farewell to Paris which he judges insufficiently depraved:

> Les braves de l'Alma sont des piliers de ponts
> Sans que la Seine émeraudine s'en offusque ;
> Moi ! je vais retourner dans mon village étrusque
> Puisque les coqs de Gaule, aujourd'hui sont chapons.
>
> La vieille Académie est un banc de mollusques ;
> Vois-tu le bel Arthur s'affubler de crépons
> Et, certains soirs magnifiés de clartés brusques
> Ceindre la gaze arachnéenne des jupons ?
>
> Iturbide ! A nous, les molles bamboulas d'Iles !
> Les négresses puant l'huile des crocodiles
> Pour miroirs, ont ravi leur casque aux cuirassiers !
>
> Némorin a sa chambre empire où les courtines
> Citrines, qu'on prit soin d'embaumer d'églantines
> Mémorent dans leurs creux, la gloire des fessiers !

After such a skit as this, the decadent movement had nothing to do but expire, and in fact the next number of Le Décadent (avril 1889) was its last.[50]

By the end of the century, indeed, most writers had grown tired of being decadent; Jean Lorrain's misgivings in Phocas were not isolated. And it is characteristic of the antinomy between classicism and decadence that there was a return to a sort of classicism. It was rather anaemic, but it was genuine enough. Moréas gave up Baudelaire, Verlaine and Mallarmé and wrote classical tragedies—Eryphile (1894), Iphigénie (1903).[51] Raynaud's last volumes—Le Bocage, La Tour d'ivoire—are full of imitations of Catullus, Virgil, Tibullus, etc. and ornamented with Greek vignettes. Even more symptomatic of the general revolt was Jean Carrère's Les Mauvais Maîtres, a volume of essays published between 1902 and 1904 in La Revue hebdomadaire. It condemns all the great writers of Romanticism, Realism, Naturalism and the Decadence as "bad masters" (Rousseau to Zola), and was undertaken to determine which authors of the nineteenth century were responsible for the "trouble intellectuel, lassitude morale et

---

[50]A number of Le Décadent's collaborators continued to publish in La Plume, a magazine whose content was very like Baju's periodical. The number of juillet 1891 contains fragments of Fanny Bora, a novel by George Bonnamour, which is the usual mixture of vice and perversion.

[51]Esquisses et souvenirs (Mercure de France, 1908), 86, 183, 186.

inquiétude publique" which afflicted young writers of the early twentieth century. Carrère denies the decadence of contemporary society—"Partout des peuples qui naissent, des civilisations qui se préparent, des forces qui grandissent. Jamais la terre ne fut plus en mouvement"—and salutes the appearance of Moréas' *Iphigénie* as the "aube blanchissante" of a classical renaissance.[52]

The defect of this neo-classicism lay in the assumption that a profusion of Graeco-Roman garlands and a return to Hellenistic mythology sufficed to be "classical." As Valéry pointed out some years afterwards, "il ne s'agissait point de ranimer ce qui était bien mort"—the classicism of the eighteenth century and the First Empire—"mais peut-être de retrouver par d'autres voies l'esprit qui n'était plus dans ce cadavre."[53] The phrase occurs in an article on Baudelaire, in whom Valéry recognized certain classical elements; and for some years previous it had become more and more fashionable to detect the latent classicism of *Les Fleurs du Mal*.[54] This revaluation of Baudelaire, that patron saint of neurosis, gongorism, corruption and artificiality, was much more important as a reaction against decadence than Jean Moréas' rather watery ejaculations. Albert Cassagne produced a thesis in 1906 on Baudelaire's versification in which he pointed out that the poet observed most of the traditional rules, and that his vocabulary, far from being extensive and eccentric, as Gautier described it, was in reality rather poor, containing only one rare word, *calenture*.[55] Even Paul Bourget, whose 1881 essay had helped to fix the decadent label on Baudelaire, changed his tone: in *Quelques témoignages* he never stops pointing out the classical qualities of *Les Fleurs du Mal*. This re-estimation of Baudelaire did not proceed without some discredit to Gautier's famous "Notice," that corner-stone of the whole decadent edifice. It comes in for direct attack in Camille Mauclair's biography of the poet (1917) where it is described as a series of "brillantes et insuffisantes variations," which prove how little Gautier understood the work he was criticising.[56]

Like the mythical scorpion, the decadent movement killed itself with its own sting in the works of Mitrophane Crapoussin; and with

[52]*Les Mauvais Maîtres* (Plon, 1922), 7, 193, 228.
[53]"Situation de Baudelaire," written in 1924, *Variété* (Gallimard), II, 156–7.
[54]Beginning with Banville's funeral oration of 1867 (Pincebourde, 132), through Barrès ("La Folie de Charles Baudelaire", 1884), Anatole France (1887), Lanson (1894), René Doumic (*Histoire de la littérature française*, 1900), Herriot (*Précis*, 1905), Gourmont (*Promenades littéraires*, 1905), Fortunat Strowski (*Tableau*, 1912).
[55]*Versification et métrique de Charles Baudelaire* (Hachette, 1906), 23–4.
[56]*Charles Baudelaire* (Maison du Livre, 1917), 87–8.

the first years of the new century, its greatest writer was being washed clean of his decadence at the hands of the rising generation, was appearing "dépouillé de ses fards, rajeuni."[57] The decadent style is perhaps the least interesting aspect of the decadent idea. The cult of artificiality and the development of decadent sensibility look forward, however confusedly, to the future, and their influence is traceable in some of the greatest writers of the century, from Gautier to Valéry and Gide. But the decadent style, with the possible exception of Huysmans' work, produced nothing of value: at best it is amusing, at worst unreadable.

[57]Gide, "Baudelaire et M. Faguet," *Nouvelle Revue Française,* novembre 1910.

CHAPTER 6

A SUMMARY

THE READER will have noticed that the word "decadence" as it is used in the foregoing pages has a special meaning, implying not merely deterioration, but deterioration which is somehow both corrupt and alluring. This is a nineteenth-century meaning, for before the nineteenth century nobody had thought of taking a scandalous pleasure in decadence. The term signified something reprehensible, but reprehensible in a very general way, like "break down" or "collapse." Its connotations were chiefly political,[1] and Romans like Juvenal and Tacitus, if they knew the idea, lacked the word. *Decadentia* derives from *cadere*, but it is not classical Latin, and is never found in the average dictionary. The first definition occurs in Du Cange. He gives *lapsus* and *ruina* as synonyms, and a quotation from the *Chronicon Beccense* where the noun is employed no more glamorously than to describe the dilapidation of farms and mills: "Omnia maneria et molendina, quae invenit in magna decadentia, et ruina, studiose reparavit." The fact that no one would dream of calling a farm "decadent" nowadays shows how far we have travelled since Du Cange.

Just when the word assumed a new significance is not easy to say. Throughout the eighteenth century there was a slow accretion of meaning, particularly in writers like Montesquieu and Gibbon. Both studied the Romans of the later empire, and for some reason it was supposed that the inhabitants of the Eternal City spent the last three or four centuries of their power in an uninterrupted orgy. Decadence thus became identified with a period of luxurious vice and fast living. Critics found the term a convenient epithet to describe any work of which they disapproved; and by the time Romanticism flowered, they were disapproving more and more. It was criticism of this sort (Pontmartin's attack on Poe) which led Baudelaire to grasp the nettle and

[1]And still are—at least in every-day French: "Décadence: Commencement de la ruine, de la dégradation: la décadence de l'empire de Charlemagne commença aussitôt après sa mort. *Ant.* : *progrès.*" *Noveau Petit Larousse illustré* (1940).

declare that if Poe was decadent he was quite legitimately so; that what hostile criticism called a decadent style was an essentially modern style, more colourful and worthier of imitation than a classical style, since it was better suited to represent contemporary life. This was certainly the decisive step, the crystallization of the idea. Yet it merely gave a name to something which already existed. Over twenty years before, Gautier had called for just such a style (although he had not described it as "decadent"), and sketched in D'Albert the sort of personality it expressed; and Taine, contemporaneously with Baudelaire, compared Paris to the degenerate cities of Antiquity. The parallels in thought and style between Gautier, Baudelaire and Taine are often very close; so close, indeed, that it would be difficult to give credit for the definition to any one of them. And they were not alone. The 1850's saw the smoke give way to fire, a combustion hastened by the publication of *Les Fleurs du mal*. The unanimity with which critics saluted Baudelaire as decadent shows how all-pervading the idea was by 1857. It is especially interesting that several of them (notably D'Aurevilly) called him not only a decadent poet, but the poet of a decadent age. I have called attention to this fact several times; it went on with increasing frequency to the end of the century; and nobody did more towards developing it than Gautier. His essays of 1862 and 1868 express with elaborations every aspect of decadence; and as a preface to Baudelaire the second of them enjoyed a publicity it would never have had on its own. This is an essential point in the history of the idea: after 1868, the theorist of decadence and the poet of decadence were tied to each other. The association is by no means dissolved in our time—perhaps it will never be dissolved. For the "Notice," whatever its limitations, and despite all the efforts of Mauclair, Gide, Fumet, Valéry and Sartre, remains by far the most brilliant and readable of all the essays on Baudelaire—a marvelous evocation of a period and a striking analysis of personality. Who knows? Perhaps it is nearer to the "real" Baudelaire than all the mystic enthusiasm and prophetic gush we have had these past fifty years.

However, the most curious thing about all this trifling with depravity is less its manifestation in this or that writer than its general acceptance as a sort of doctrine. We might almost call it a philosophic premise. Nearly all authors of the time thought their age decadent. This was not the whim of a few eccentrics, but the settled opinion of pathologists, philosophers and critics. The fact is all the more extraordinary when we drop it back into its context. Seen from the ruins of the present, the nineteenth century looks almost unbelievably massive, an accumulation of steam, cast-iron and self-confidence, rather like one of its own international expositions. It was the century which absorbed continents and conquered the world. We are still living in its aftermath, like a dinghy in the wash of a battleship. Beside it the seventeenth century looks static, the eighteenth effete and frivolous. Why such an age, which lived a vigorous life vigorously, should have spent so much time in sullen musing on its own "decadence," real or imagined, is a strange problem to which no simple answer can be given. We have to fall back on generalizations; a few determining factors can be proposed which have some bearing on the matter.

The first was the legend of Imperial Rome. We have met it often enough; it was exploited like a convention. The nineteenth century was acutely conscious of being the culmination of an ascending process which began when Western civilization was rebuilt after the destruction of the Dark Ages. The memory of the catastrophe which overtook Rome is perhaps the central fact of the Occident's historical thought. Anyone who studies the West automatically studies decadence: the gap between ancient and modern culture is there; and while recent scholarship has tended to soften the contours, to prove that there was more a slow evolution than a brutal dislocation, the contrast between the massive splendour of Rome under the Antonines and its degradation at the hands of Alaric, Genseric, Odovacar and the rest, is too dramatic to be missed, especially when, by a little telescoping of the historical perspective, one sees Neronian fiddling as an immediate prelude to the arrival of the Barbarians. "Rien," says Flaubert, "de si terrible et de si monstrueux que les dernières heures de l'Empire"— and launches into a panegyric of Tiberius and Nero. "Regardez, nous sommes à Rome!" exclaims Lorrain of the Paris Opera in 1894. In fact, the Romans who watched Alaric plunder their city lived three centuries and a half after Nero; they were as far from him in time as the nineteenth century decadents were from Henry VIII. The material changes in civilization were perhaps less, but the spiritual and moral alterations were even greater. Fifth-century Rome bore little resemblance to the metropolis of Julio-Claudian days. It was Christian; it had abolished gladiatorial combats and pagan roistering; it certainly did not fall because of lurid sinning. That scene the decadents were so fond of—languid patricians slaughtered on their banqueting couches by furious Goths—never existed; from what documents we have, it appears that the bulk of the population sought refuge in churches. The period of riotous living—Augustus to Commodus—was precisely the period of greatest military and political vigour. And the same is true of the literature. The really depraved books—or books containing depraved detail (Petronius, Suetonius, Martial, Juvenal, Apuleius)— appeared several hundred years before the final catastrophe. The authors who actually saw the downfall, such as Claudian and Rutilius, were ardent patriots; their apostrophes to Rome are among the most eloquent in Latin; they modelled their style on Virgil's, and its qualities hardly include any "verdeurs de la décomposition." There is no more unfortunate comparison in criticism than Barbey d'Aurevilly's parallel between Claudian and Poe; it would be impossible to imagine two authors more dissimilar. The last Roman poets were only decadent because the nineteenth century wished them to be so.

The whole Roman past, indeed, was subjected to a Procrustean distortion to make it fit the contemporary scene—it is a distortion which reveals much about the nineteenth century's secret misgivings. France witnessed one lurid decline and fall in 1789, preceded by an almost model period of frivolous debauchery and painted elegance. The legendary "Après nous le déluge !" is a typically decadent phrase, too typical to be authentic.[2] The Louis XV style, mannered, exquisite, erotic, all subdued colours, curves and spasms which seem to hold immobilized in wood and bronze the memory of voluptuous attitudes and pleasures spiced with cruelty, was the very expression of a pre-catastrophic age; and when decadents such as Huysmans went back to it they knew what they were doing. The destruction of the old régime, furthermore, was something more than a change of interior decoration. Until 1789 the social machine had been controlled by a number of traditional fly-wheels, the monarchy, the church, which kept it from disintegrating through over-acceleration. Even characters like Valmont and Mme de Merteuil, so closely akin to later decadents, have a nervous solidity which is quite foreign to the nineteenth century. They never meditate dolorously on the great problems of faith and destiny; they live in the iron frame-work of an assured political and social structure. All this stability vanished with the Revolution. The result was a state of emotional anarchy, common to Romantics and decadents alike, as their pessimism, nihilism, hatred of contemporary institutions and laments for lost faith prove. Nor was 1789 the

[2]What Louis XV really said, in discussing the turbulence of the Paris parliament with Mme de Pompadour and the Duc de Gontaut, was: "Le Régent a eu bien tort de leur rendre le droit de faire des remonstrances... Ils finiront par perdre l'Etat... C'est une assemblée de républicains. En voilà au reste assez ; les choses, comme elles sont, dureront autant que moi." Mme du Hausset, *Mémoires* (Taillandier), 32. He later shook off this fatalism to the point of giving Maupeou permission to suppress the parliament.

only catastrophe. The revolutionary and Napoleonic wars ended in Waterloo. After the feverish grandeurs of the First Empire, the Restoration and the July Monarchy seemed dull and anti-climactic; *La France s'ennuyait*; the race emerged from the great adventure impoverished in blood and condemned to boredom, like a warrior who, after a career of glory, finds himself reduced to nursing his scars in a provincial garrison.[3] As if to add the last touch to this descent came the Second Empire. It was essentially a makeshift, parlously constructed from Napoleonic débris and liberal nationalism; it never commanded real respect; it was the apotheosis of a sort of raffish cosmopolitanism. Even nowadays, when its gaiety and its easy life make us look back at it with a sort of nostalgia, we give a tolerant smile. Contemporary writers, if they did not attack it directly, talked about its corruptions; and its spectacular downfall seemed like a fine example of historical logic. The decadent movement proper came into existence after the disaster of 1870; its authors lived and wrote in the memory of that fiasco which justified, or seemed to justify, the jeremiads on decadence given forth by Gautier, Baudelaire, Taine, D'Aurevilly, etc., years before the first shot was fired. From the literary point of view, the disappearance of Napoleon III was almost providential; it pointed up, by facile analogy, the "grands barbares blancs" invading the empire "à la fin de la décadence"; it provided Zola with the logical conclusion of his sermon on political corruption and degenerate heredity.

These political convulsions coincided with mighty social changes. Nineteenth-century civilization was much more complicated than what had gone before. The development of science and industry concentrated man in great cities and separated him from his traditional contacts with Nature to an unprecedented extent. Given Rousseau's ideas on the virtues of primitivism, all this seemed abnormal and pernicious. Besides which this abrupt change was accompanied, as usual in human affairs, by much squalor and suffering. Early industrial conditions were atrocious, and the swollen cities unsanitary and unaesthetic. Contemporary writers saw all this at once. At the bottom of the period's immense cultural development sits an uneasy feeling that it is all somehow perverse, in contradiction to natural law, and bound to end in well-merited chastisement. Hence the gloomy, masochistic tone of conscientious authors like Taine and Bourget, and the strident bravado of Gautier, D'Aurevilly, Huysmans and Baudelaire. Descriptions of the degenerate nineteenth-century city-dweller exist in nearly all the writers we have examined. The gambit became a platitude

[3]Louis Maigron, *Le Romantisme et les mœurs* (Champion, 1910), ch. I, *passim*.

—modern man was a creature of nervous exhaustion who compared unfavourably with the muscular Greeks and the lusty Elizabethans. Nobody seems to have understood that the progress of medicine and hygiene, by-products of industrialism, would make towns like Paris infinitely more healthy than they had been in the more "natural" past, and save more lives than occupational diseases and urban crowding lost. Modern man was living "against the grain"; he had "mordu à la pomme" (the evangelical language, particularly in such an unbeliever as Zola, is characteristic), he was further from Nature than he had ever been, and getting further every day. The phenomenon was dramatic, and writers, being writers, sought to make it more so: they looked for its most glaring aspects—they frequented slums, theatres, brothels, music halls, industry-ravaged suburbs. They forgot that Periclean Athens was plague-ridden and that Renaissance Paris, for all its picturesque varnish, was infinitely more squalid than the city of Napoleon III or the Third Republic. They spent their time describing the least attractive aspects of contemporary civilization and of course reached the conclusion that culture was just as corrupt as Rousseau said it was—a conviction which drew no small strength from the fact that it was supported by the new science of psychopathology. The age represented the greatest culmination of civilization since Rome; the lesson was obvious: a peak must be followed by a decline.

Added to these political and social circumstances was the literary factor. Romanticism degenerated very lushly and very soon; its morbid and unbalanced tendencies showed themselves immediately after the triumph of 1830, particularly in its minor writers. "Un tissu d'extravagances et d'horreurs, quand ce n'est pas un ramas d'indécences et d'obscénités," Maigron calls their works;[4] the stricture is borne out by a glance at such a book as Pétrus Borel's *Champavert*. Adultery, murder, incest, sadism, necrophilia were popular themes; it was all so atrocious that it led a magistrate of the time to write: "Pour peu qu'on fasse de ce côté encore quelques progrès et... les jours de la décadence romaine reviendront."[5] The most frequent words of the post-1830 vocabulary are already those of the decadence: *spleen, mélancolie, lassitude, ennui.*[6]

The decadent movement thus begins in Romanticism; in part it is a final development of Romanticism, but only in part. If, like Mario Praz,[7] we see in it no more than the final stage of Romantic evolution,

[4]*Ibid.*, 165.   [5]*Ibid.*, 174.   [6]*Ibid.*, 287.
[7]"La letteratura romantica (di cui il decadentismo della fine del secolo scorso non è che uno svolgimento)..." *La Carne, la morte e il diavolo nelle letteratura romantica,* terza edizione (Firenze, Sansoni, 1948), p. xi (Avvertenza alla seconda edizione).

we miss its true significance. It borrowed Romanticism's swollen emotions and spiritual exhaustion; there is something of René in all decadent characters, even in that pattern decadent, Jean des Esseintes. But it was in revolt against Romantic theory on two essential points—the cult of Nature and the cult of ideal love. Its artificiality contradicts both; it begins (in De Sade and Baudelaire) as a renunciation of Rousseau's naturism, and develops into the practice of whatever can be thought anti-natural and abnormal. Sexual perversions, as "un affranchissement de la lourde nature," are its most striking manifestation; Romanticism's *mal du siècle* becomes androgynism; and no novel with any decadent pretentions fails to include a search for depraved adventures in the Paris slums. The conceit finally reached the proportions of a mania. It is best displayed in Jean Lorrain's work: without the sexual underworld, he would have had practically nothing to say. This chase after the abnormal is linked to the main characteristic of decadent sensibility: its intellectualism, its will-power. Emotionalism and ecstasy being natural, deliberation was unnatural; and hence the dandy and the decadent, with their *sang-froid*, their perverted tastes, their carefully finished art, their passion for the city as opposed to the country. Hence also their preference for the modern to anything that had gone before—it was more artificial and therefore more corrupt. We are back at the old problem of the chicken and the egg.

Does not this very difficulty in assigning a source, a moment, to the idea, this inextricable tangle of mutual influence and confused borrowings, indicate a sort of continuity, a link between something very ancient and something which is far from extinct in our own time? There are times when, to the impartial observer, Western civilization looks like a display of mass schizophrenia, oscillating between extremes and hounded by every variety of perversion and excess. Restlessness, uneasiness, dissatisfaction, blind idolatry and sadistic iconoclasm are its hallmarks; they appear from age to age, the main themes of the great symphony. We meet them in the death-love of Greek tragedy, the grim misanthropy of the Roman historians, the animalism and mysticism of the Middle Ages, the savage theology and pagan lusts of the Renaissance. They very nearly achieve an apotheosis in the madness and depravity of the Elizabethans and the chaotic sexuality of Racine. The eighteenth century itself, Age of Reason though it was, was not exempt; in mid-course it saw in Rousseau the very essence of the anti-rational. When we come to the nineteenth century, we are struck at first by such a difference in the style of decoration, such an apparent smugness in the official creeds, that we cannot at first imagine how the old lesion could have existed there too. Yet exist it did, and even more diseased than in the past. It was "l'état nauséeux de l'âme," "la philosophie dégoûtée de l'universel néant," the craze for "la phosphorescence de la pourriture" and "les verdeurs de la décomposition." It kept right on suppurating. It no longer had a great tragic convention for its expression: its Eumenides were bill-collectors, its Até the bankruptcy court. The very complexity of civilization stifled the evil behind a massive façade of railroads and fringed table-legs and sprawling mahogany. And this confinement prevented the catharsis which, in the *Oresteia* or *Macbeth* or *Phèdre*, has periodically relieved the occidental animal from the pressure of his neuroses. The malady disappeared below the surface, became not tragic but depraved, then sent a tetter of corruption over even the finest works of the time, such as *Les Fleurs du Mal*. Nineteenth-century writers are as great as any that went before, but their works are singularly impure; they had a passion for tinsel, for false attitudes and false effects; their productions smell of the *vase clos*; they lived *à rebours*.

A sounder instinct than he knew, perhaps, prompted Huysmans to chose that adverb as title for his novel. It may be questioned whether he realized, as he traced out the manias of Jean des Esseintes, just what he was doing. The house at Fontenay, with its sealed rooms, its topsy-turvy existence, its artificial refinements, was supposed to represent man's triumph over Nature, his delight in all the fictitious charms of his civilization. But did it? The question is worth asking. For what, after all, is Des Esseintes but a photographic negative of something very well known—even odiously well known? Like the negative, he gives up his secrets when we hold him to the light—in this case the light of historical perspective. And then, along with all those other curious negatives we have been looking at, his true nature suddenly becomes apparent. The lurid city-scapes, the overstuffed boudoirs, the powder, the rouge, the learned obscenities, the tainted heredity and the nervous attacks take on their true colours: black becomes white, white black; the metamorphosis is complete. And we find ourselves looking at a familiar figure: the Noble Savage, vigorous and primitive, breathing the air of his virgin forests or fighting superbly for his tribal gods.

INDEX